D0753247

Professional Ethics Education:
Studies in Compassionate Empathy

Bruce Maxwell

Professional Ethics Education: Studies in Compassionate Empathy

 Springer

Bruce Maxwell
Westfälische
Wilhelms-Universität Münster,
Germany

ISBN: 978-1-4020-6888-1   e-ISBN: 978-1-4020-6889-8
DOI: 10.1007/ 978-1-4020-6889-8

Library of Congress Control Number: 2007942721

All Rights Reserved
© 2008 Springer Science + Business Media, B.V.
No part of this work may be reproduced, stored in a retrieval system, or transmitted in any form or by any means, electronic, mechanical, photocopying, microfilming, recording or otherwise, without written permission from the Publisher, with the exception of any material supplied specifically for the purpose of being entered and executed on a computer system, for exclusive use by the purchaser of the work.

Printed on acid-free paper

9 8 7 6 5 4 3 2 1

springer.com

For France in Germany and Roland of course

Prefatory Statement and Acknowledgements

This book is the fruit of several years' sustained reflection on conceptual questions related to the education of the personal and professional moral excellence that is commonly called "empathy." It is therefore a work of philosophy of education. More than in any other branch of practical ethics—with the possible exception of medical ethics—philosophers in education face a hard choice between remaining intellectually respectable to their peers in the mainstream of philosophy and producing work that is meaningful in the eyes of a wide and impossibly heterogeneous audience in the practice discipline. The usual warning about the likely result of trying to please everybody applies exponentially: success in the eyes of one party pretty much ipso facto guarantees failure in the eyes of the other. Not speaking from a point of view of complete impartiality and at risk of sounding *vieux jeu*, contemporary philosophy, with its comparatively high standards of rigor in conceptual analysis and argumentation and, no less importantly, its *perceptivity* to conceptual problems when they arise, belongs in the heartland of educational inquiry, not in the wild woods. The trouble is that philosophers, like British boys of a certain generation, tend also to learn that being a philosopher means being the best. This attitude does not help win many friends in other disciplines. Worse, it is positively antithetical to the kinds of relationships that are conducive to productive interdisciplinary research, those built on mutual respect and mutual curiosity. And so in this book I have tried to the best of my abilities to bring to bear only the good bits of what philosophers learn to a hunch that rumbles through the discourse in professional and applied ethics: to paraphrase Hobbes, the concern for strengthening capacities of critical ethical reflection in applied ethics teaching, like the sun to the stars, deprives certain affective moral capacities of their due treatment not by denying their influence as much as by obscuring them and hiding them with its overwhelming presence. I have written this book primarily for a broad—but philosophically curious—audience of educators working in professional and practical ethics in higher education, and if some come to the conclusion that it helps them see how professional and practical ethics education might accommodate a richer conception of moral experience, I will have achieved much of what I set out to do.

A good many parts of this book started out in life as conference papers. I am especially thankful to the Philosophy of Education Society of Great Britain, the Association of Moral Education, and the Working Group on Moral Development and Education in the Professions for providing such outward-looking, collegial, and challenging forums. When it appeared to fit the context, I have freely borrowed from these works as well as from the following previously published essay: "Naturalized compassion: a critique of Nussbaum on literature as education for compassionate citizenry" in the *Journal of Moral Education*, 35, 3 (September 2006): 335–352. The book, too, is pleasantly collaborative. Chapter 6 is based on two articles coauthored by Roland Reichenbach: "Imitation, imagination, and re-appraisal: the education of the moral emotions" in the *Journal of Moral Education*, 34, 2 (September 2005): 291–305, and "Educating moral emotions: a praxiological analysis" in *Studies in Philosophy and Education*, 26, 2 (March 2007): 147–163. Reichenbach deserves full credit and recognition as the coauthor of this chapter. Most of Section 5.4 of Chapter 5 (and few other passages here and there) have been imported from an as yet unpublished manuscript by Leonie LeSage and me titled "Are psychopaths morally sensitive? Questioning Component 1 of James Rest's four-component model of morality." Her specific contribution of knowledge of the literature on psychopathy and moral functioning greatly strengthens the argument in Chapter 5 and I regard her as its coauthor as well. I acknowledge the courtesy of the editors of Taylor & Francis for permission to reprint the relevant material.

Thanks are due as well to the Association of Moral Education and its Gift of Time Charitable Foundation for a grant that gave this project a critical push of support at the beginning. I am also grateful to the Social Sciences and Humanities Research Council of Canada for a Fellowship without which I might well have been unable to see it through to the end.

These years have also been marked by affiliations with the Institute for Educational Studies of the University of Münster, the Department of History and Philosophy of Education of the Free University of Amsterdam, and the Institute for the Ethics, History and Theory of Medicine of the University of Münster's Medical Faculty. I carry especially heavy debts of gratitude to Bettina Schöne-Seifert, Jan Steutel, and Roland Reichenbach but the grace and serious-mindedness of other members of these organizations continue to be an inspiration, and contact with them has enriched my work.

Contents

List of Figures and Tables

Chapter 1
Introduction

1.1 Practical Ethics Education at an Impasse

Why is some practical ethics training a requirement of nearly all programmes in higher education? The short answer is that it is thought to be conducive to ethical decision-making and ethical behaviour. In recent years, the received idea that competency in moral reasoning implies moral responsibility "on the ground" has been the subject of critical attention. Today, researchers in moral education widely regard moral reasoning as but one among at least four dimensions of moral development alongside moral motivation, moral character, and moral sensitivity (Rest, 1986). Reflecting these changes, educationalists in the diverse fields of medicine, education, business, and applied ethics can now be found openly questioning how to take practical ethics education beyond the development of skills in moral reasoning. Frequently topping the list of suggested improvements is to provide support for empathic capacities of response. This work gives this proposal the systematic attention that it deserves.

Contemporary applied ethics, and by extension practical and professional ethics education, can be considered an offshoot of the broad philosophical doctrine of moral realism. Moral realism takes many forms but in broad outline it is an established meta-ethical position that emerged as a seemingly attractive alternative to another family of established philosophical positions that sometimes goes under the name of "expressivism". Expressivism, again in rough terms, is the idea that ethical beliefs are mere expressions of subjective preferences, attitudes, emotions, and desires. Moral realists typically reject expressivism (as well as other forms of subjectivism in ethics) because the realist-sounding ordinary language with which moral views are debated and promoted is hard to square with the idea that moral beliefs are mere expressions of subjective preferences (cf. Darwall et al., 1992). People speak as if moral statements correspond to some real features of the world, features that exist independently of anyone's opinions or preferences. Just as the statement "The cat is on the mat" can only be regarded as true if the cat is in fact lying on the mat, a moral judgement such as "Alain is generous" is true only if it is the case that Alain actually is generous. Moral statements, like statements about the material world, seem to report facts and this suggests that there is some discernible

B. Maxwell, *Professional Ethics Education: Studies in Compassionate Empathy*,
© Springer Science + Business Media B.V. 2008

truth about moral matters. If the main claim of moral realism is the idea that the referents of moral language are fact-like, moral realism also tends to adopt, for the same reason, an internalist position on the question of moral motivation. Moral judgements, expressed seriously and in ordinary language, are not just *descriptive*. They are also *prescriptive*: when I judge, say, that it is morally preferable to eat the eggs of only free-range chickens, it implies that I, and perhaps everyone else as well, have a good reason to *actually eat* free-range eggs. That is to say, ordinary language supposes that judgements of moral rightness and wrongness come with a built-in or "internal" motivating reason to act in accordance with one's moral judgements.[1]

An educational upshot of internalism is that education in practical ethics can legitimately limit itself to promoting skills connected with moral judgement—clarity of language, attention to consistency, relevance of evidence, identification of operative moral principles, and the like[2]—because the motivational side of morality should look after itself. When people do not act in accordance with their most considered moral judgements, they are simply being practically irrational: they genuinely believe that one course of action in a set of circumstances is morally right, preferable, necessary, or required but they do not perform that action. Assuming that the competency of philosophical ethics is to address the rational grounds of moral justification and directly related questions, the problem of moral motivation may simply and quite legitimately be outsourced to psychology. In actual practical deliberation situations, moral reasons face and sometime motivationally lose out to competing non-moral reasons. Commonly, the reason why people are "morally irresponsible" in this sense is because of the intervention of some such familiar countervailing non-moral consideration as economic consequences ("I know I should expose the corruption in this company but if I do I might lose my job") or perceived special loyalties ("I know I should have told the teacher that the guys left Amos tied to the tree after recess but when you're one of the group you have to stick together"). From this perspective, the problem of moral motivation is the decidedly moral-psychological question of what motivational, affective, or cognitive dispositions and social circumstances are associated with consistency between moral judgement and moral motivation.[3] Indeed, as a review of contemporary course books confirms, a commitment to internalism is clearly discernible in contemporary practical ethics education and it comes in the form of a conspicuous insouciance with regards to moral motivation, its problems, and its circumstances as an educational problem *independent* of that of the development of skills in moral

---

[1] For a detailed discussion of internalism, various versions thereof, and its opposing counterpart externalism, see, for example, Smith (1994).

[2] See Annis (1992) for a brief but comprehensive account of the critical capacities and knowledge components that are explicitly or tacitly accepted as the cognitive aims proper to secular practical ethics education (pp. 189–191).

[3] For a statement of this view, see Habermas (1993a), who argues that the question of why some people are morally responsible and others are not is not a philosophical question but is best handled by empirical psychology.

reasoning (cf. Burkhardt & Nathaniel, 2001; Ferrell et al., 2004; Mappes, 2000; McGinn, 1992; Singer, 1993; Strike & Soltis, 1998; Hayden, 2003).

Such implicit passing of the moral-motivational buck from theoretical ethics to moral psychology would be no cause for concern if it were not for the fact that moral psychology has its own problems with the question of moral motivation. In the early years of research into cognitive moral development and in its first forays into structuring and implementing theoretically grounded interventions in moral education, the Kohlbergian cognitive-developmental programme tended to gloss over the problem of moral motivation with a theoretical assumption known as "cognitive–affective parallelism". This postulate states that greater competency in moral reasoning parallels a stronger disposition towards moral motivation (Kohlberg, 1981, 1984; Colby et al., 1987). Criticized for years on conceptual grounds by philosophers of education such as Peters (e.g., 1978) and Carr (e.g., 1996, 1991), the notion that with more differentiated capacities of moral reasoning come not just qualitatively better moral judgements (or in any case moral judgements that would presumably be considered to be more convincing from some ideal standpoint of rational moral evaluation), but also greater consistency between judgement and action has been challenged by empirical research as well. In point of fact is Augusto Blasi's notorious failure, in his widely cited 1980 review article on the relationship between moral cognition and moral action, to find a significant correlation between moral cognition and moral action. As if to add insult to injury, Colby and Damon's (1992) research on moral exemplarity has showed that moral exemplars—people who weave what most outside observers would regard as exceptionally morally good acts into the pattern of their daily lives and those who have performed at least one morally heroic act—are not always terribly sophisticated moral thinkers.[4] On the stock assumption that the central point of moral education is to promote the performance of moral actions, if one once believed that educators cannot responsibly be concerned with cognitive moral development alone because a capacity for differentiated moral reasoning is *insufficient* for the performance of moral acts, Colby and Damon's research makes it look as if it is not even *necessary*. Just what is a poor moral educator to do?

These startling and perhaps counter-intuitive findings initiated what, in Campbell's (2005) assessment, was the greatest shift in the field of empirical moral psychology since its inception in the early twentieth century. What began as the investigation of stage theories in the cognitive developmental tradition of Piaget and Dewey, today presides over a much broader range of topics and projects which include moral identity and the moral self and moral personality (cf. various texts in Lapsley & Narváez, 2004), moral exceptionality (e.g., Walker & Hennig, 2004), the reconstruction of traditional conceptions of moral character in terms of contemporary theories of

---

[4] These findings seem to mirror Arendt's (1961/1994) controversial postulate on the "banality of evil", an idea she developed while observing Eichmann's trial for war crimes. It was not, she concluded, that Eichmann had bad moral judgement. Nor was there any indication that he was motivated by hateful or diabolical ideas, as Arendt read him. He simply failed to engage in any kind of independent judgement at all (cf. esp. p. 288). For one recent discussion of this point see Todd (2007).

personality and social cognition (e.g., Narváez & Lapsley, 2005; Narváez et al., 2003), and empathy and other so-called moral emotions (e.g., Hoffman, 2000). In Nunner-Winkler's (1998) reading of the situation, a situation that has very much informed her own far-reaching research in the psychology of moral growth, moral development has not just one but "two aspects: the development of socio-cognitive understanding and the growth of moral motivation" (p. 601; cf. Nunner-Winkler, 1993, pp. 271–272).

1.2   Empathy in Practical Ethics Education?

Not always aware of current trends in the psychology of moral development, representatives from different quarters of practical and professional ethics education can be found again and again floating the idea that educators should be concerned with supporting empathic capacities of response, and this precisely as a means of expanding its purview beyond the limits of the standard judgement-focused approach to practical ethics education.

For the sake of forestalling a misconception of the present problem, however, let us right off the bat observe the distinction between empathy as an aspect of professional role morality and empathy as a more general and diffuse moral disposition (cf. Bowie, 2003). Just as certain obligations attend only to those who occupy special social functions—the most familiar example, perhaps, are parents' custodial duties to their children—certain character traits are constitutive of professional expertise. This is meant in the most normative sense that the possession of certain moral and emotional dispositions, and a sense of personal ownership of certain professional responsibilities, in some measure, is not just *necessary* to effective professional work. Rather, the idea is that it would be nothing short of *inconceivable* for a skilled professional practitioner to lack them. One can no more be an excellent writer and be bad with words than one can be a fine teacher but be little concerned for fairness.[5] Similarly, while it is certainly possible to *practise* nursing without sympathy, it is something of a conceptual truth that a *good* nurse is one who, among many other things, is disposed to feel an appropriate sense of empathic concern towards his or her patients in view of their suffering. It comes as no surprise, then, that empathy appears at the top of Beauchamp and Childress's (2001, pp. 32–33) list of the focal virtues of health professionals,[6] an assessment which is

---

[5] For a defence of the virtues at the core of professional expertise in teaching see Sockett (1993). In his reading of the situation, there are five moral excellences: honesty, courage, care, fairness, and practical wisdom.

[6] In fact, in this section of *Principles of biomedical ethics* the term they use is "compassion" but later they use the two terms synonymously (cf. 374–375). Barnbaum (2001) also treats "empathy" and "compassion" as interchangeable in reference to role morality in health care.

reflected in recent initiatives aimed at enhancing the teaching of professionalism in medical education. In this context, "empathy" comes up again and again in key policy documents as a "core competency".[7] There is, of course, much room for legitimate controversy about such problems—as how to strike the right balance in professional–client relationships between the imperative of professional distance and empathic concern—and as regards other issues connected with the fine-grained interpretation of the role-morality of empathy.[8] But in the abstract, the notion that empathy is constitutive of professional expertise in health care is at least probably not the subject of reasonable disagreement.

The same cannot, however, be said about empathy as a capacity of moral judgement or practical wisdom. Indeed, one could in all fairness regard as a chestnut the statement that the ethical theory since Kant has overlooked or generally neglected the significance of the emotions in moral life and moral thinking. As far as generalizations go, this one is in one sense particularly inaccurate. In the middle of the twentieth century, one or another version of "expressivism"— the philosophical doctrine, referred to above, according to which ethical commitments are just expressions of personal preferences—was, if anything, the default position in Anglo-Saxon meta-ethics and some of the most important work of the latter half of that century in that field was concerned with exposing the inadequacies of expressivism (cf. Darwall et al., 1992). What is true, however, is that the question of whether, and to what extent, the faculty of impartial moral judgement can or should function *in abstraction* from people's inclinations, affinities, and feelings or whether such forms of affective involvement are *presuppositions* of the proper exercise of practical wisdom has, at least since the Enlightenment, been the subject of perennial dispute. Indeed, and broadly speaking, the observation that moral judgement proceeds by *reflecting on*, rather than systematically *rejecting*, spontaneous responses of concern for others is a perennial theme in sentimentalist conceptions of ethics and is presented as key evidence of the poverty of allegedly excessively rationalistic or "Kantian" accounts of moral justification (cf. Hutcheson, 1729, 2003; Smith, 1759; Schopenhauer, 1840; Scheler, 1954; Blum, 1980; Vetlesen, 1996; Slote, 2003).

Empathy, then, conceived of as a desirable moral disposition among certain classes of professionals is one thing. Empathy conceived of as a competence, capacity, or disposition which plays a role in enabling the very faculty of moral judgement is quite another. While there is certainly no shortage of similar calls to promote empathy in professional ethics education in the former sense (e.g., Bevis & Watson, 1989; More & Milligan, 1994; Tong, 1997; Beauchamp & Childress, 2001), this study intends to focus on the distinct proposal to provide educational support for empathy regarded as a capacity which is basic to moral functioning.

---

[7] See, for example, American Association of Medical Colleges Core Curriculum Working Group (2000) and Coulehan and Williams (2003) for a discussion of this trend.

[8] For treatments of both these questions see Benbassat and Baumal (2004), Tong (1997), and various contributions to More and Milligan's (1994) edited collection, *The empathic practitioner*.

With this orientation clearly before our minds, we can find in medical ethics, for example, Self et al. (1995) asserting that doctors need strong skills in moral judgement because, whether doctors like it or not, patients often turn to them for advice and guidance on difficult moral questions. The advice they give can have a significant impact on others' well-being. Appealing to an idea they attribute to Hoffman (1991), namely that moral problems generally involve considering effects on human welfare, they suggest that empathically disposed people can be expected to come to a better initial analysis and interpretation of moral problems, and because of this they are likely to have stronger moral judgement abilities. In their words, it is for these reasons that "the moral integrity and empathic concern of the physician is of great importance in today's society" (Self et al., 1995, p. 448). In a similar vein, the thesis of David Hilfiker's 1999 keynote address to the American Society for Bioethics and Humanities was that a fundamental goal of teaching ethics in medicine should be to foster a sense of empathy (Hilfiker, 2001, p. 255). Like Self et al. (1995), he argues that the reason why ethics education needs to support empathic capacities of response is because empathizing is an important ingredient in the perception of moral problems. Hilfiker's analysis of empathy is interwoven with another agenda in the speech: to frame the lack of access to adequate health care in the United States in squarely moral terms. It nevertheless comes through clearly that empathizing, which in his evocative definition of the term is a way of seeing the world, in the manner of Rawls' (1971) prescription, "from the bottom"—from the point of view of those in society who are the most disadvantaged and excluded—can bring moral problems to light. Empathy, that is, is implicated in perceptive capacities that enable human beings to see problems they might otherwise ignore *as* moral problems. Unlike Self et al. (1995), to this observation he adds that empathy also moves people to *rectify* the moral wrongs they perceive. "If we in medicine", Hilfiker writes, "saw things from the victim's point of view, that lack of access [to healthcare for the poor] would be the primary ethical problem facing us, and each of us would feel a responsibility to participate in finding a solution" (p. 263). Empathy, that is, is morally motivating as well.[9]

In general practical ethics, similar assessments can be found among different attempts to state a set of pedagogical guidelines for the teaching of practical ethics. Both Annis (1992) and Scholz and Groarke (1996) encourage instructors to foster empathy among their students as part of a wider imperative to develop moral sensitivity and moral imagination, an idea that is traceable back to Daniel Callahan's widely cited contribution to the *Hastings centre report on ethics teaching in higher education* (1980). Indeed, the very first item on Callahan's list of "important goals in the teaching of ethics" (pp. 64–69) and preceding such accepted cognitive items as the development of analytical skills, the explication of underlying ethical principles, conceptual clarity and the like isstimulating the moral imagination.

---

[9] For a similar assessment of empathy as a faculty of moral perception from the perspective of health care see also Tong (1997).

His reasons for this prioritization are plain. Moral sensitivity is not, as a component of practical wisdom, somehow more important than moral reasoning. Rather, moral sensitivity and moral imagination are, in one sense, a presupposition of the competent exercise of moral judgement—as he puts it, "a necessary [...] condition for any serious moral discourse and reflection" (p. 65)—and, in another sense, temporally prior to the engagement of the cognitive operations characteristic of moral reasoning. With respect to the first function, Callahan suggests that it is through emotional and imaginative involvement that people come to trouble themselves about moral problems at all. Recognizing other peoples' problems and caring about them, in short, is what motivates people to do their best to solve moral problems that confront them by applying whatever competencies in moral reasoning they might have come to acquire (p. 65). But moral sensitivity is an entry point to moral reflection in a second sense as well. Rejecting a strict dichotomy between affect and cognition, Callahan states that all emotional experiences involve an appraisal of the emotion's object; the feeling of indignation, say, implies the judgement that someone has been wronged. It is from the first inchoate impressions of a situation, impressions that these, as it were, feelings of judgement[10] provide, that the basic terms of a moral problem are constructed (p. 65). Moral reasoning is then brought to bear upon the problem in order to solve it. According to Callahan:

> If one sees the moral imagination as the very source of a drive to get straight on ethics, it will continue to have a place even in the most advanced courses in ethics. A lively moral imagination is the only real corrective to the conceptual and logical analysis that is equally necessary for advanced work in ethics; it is as important at one end of the spectrum as it is at the other. Imagination without analysis is blind; analysis without imagination is sterile.

> Yet even if it is true that imagination and analysis need each other, imagination should have an initial priority in introductory courses. The emotional side of students must first be elicited or evoked—empathy, feeling, caring, sensibility. Even here, though, the cognitive must quickly enter: to discern hidden assumptions, to notice consequences of thought and behaviour, to see that pain and pleasure do not merely happen. [...]

> How should one characterize and rationally articulate a felt response of injustice, or the violation of a person's autonomy, or the nature of the anguish felt in the face of a decision about whether to keep a severely defective child alive? Part of such an attempt will require the examination of concepts, of prescriptive moral statements, and of ethical principles and moral rules. [...] If our emotional responses embody an appraisal, how are we to judge the validity of that appraisal? That is the kind of question that ought to be put to those whose moral imaginations have been stimulated. (Callahan's 1980, p. 65)

In short, Callahan's idea is that moral imagination (1) performs the informational function of attuning one to the threats to well-being that might be at stake in a situation and (2) spurs one on to solve moral problems to the best of one's abilities. That is why, for him, the stimulation of the moral imagination, and with it the encouragement of empathic responding, is a primary goal in the teaching of practical ethics.

---

[10] The term "feelings of judgement", *Urteilsgefühle*, is Meinong's (1894/1968).

In professional ethics in the field of teaching and education, Coombs (1998) has argued that ethics for educational professionals needs to expand beyond its traditional concern with developing skills in understanding, analysing, and reasoning about moral problems. He points in the direction of considering how ethics for professionals in education might contribute to the development of certain relevant virtues and something he calls moral perception and sensitivity (pp. 567–568). Coombs does not use the term "empathy" as such, but it is clear enough that he has in mind something similar to what Callahan called "moral imagination". He identifies a moral perceptive ability that helps people pick out the features of a situation which are of moral salience as a precondition of moral reflection.[11] Everyone agrees that professional ethics should strive to become better at deliberating about ethical issues but, Coombs insists, the question of how to provide educational support for the enhancement of moral perception and sensitivity is also very important because "without moral perception and sensitivity, moral reasoning cannot get started" (p. 568).

Lastly, in business ethics, Patrick Murphy puts empathy down as one of the "core virtues of international marketing" (1999, p. 113). Empathy in his conception is a disposition characterized by sensitivity to the needs and concerns of others and keenness of insight into others' perspectives and points of view (pp. 113, 116). It should be fostered in business education primarily because it is essential to good ethical and business judgement alike. For instance, in stakeholder analysis—the assessment of a business decision in terms of the impact it will have on the priorities, needs, and goals of key people who will be affected by it—because of the kind of other-directed insight that empathy affords, "managers", Murphy writes, "who are empathic likely will understand the impact more fully than those who do not practice this virtue" (p. 116). However, unlike Hilfiker, Murphy does not consider empathy to have an internal motivational dimension. Empathy involves sensitivity to others' needs and concerns but it does not necessarily imply being responsive to them. That is a different trait he calls "sympathy" and this virtue, he stresses, "should not be equated with empathy" (p. 116).

1.3   Conceptual and Psychological Questions and a Roadmap

A compelling intuition can be read off this notice of calls to encourage empathy and connected sensitivities in practical ethics education: the development of capacities of empathic response is a compelling means of addressing some of the affective and motivational deficit accrued by judgement-focused approaches, because as a moral–psychological construct it has the very interesting surface feature of being, if you will, morally protean. That is to say, empathy seems to have a hand in at least three of Rest's (1986) four dimensions of moral development

---

[11] In presenting these ideas, Coombs credits Bricker's (1993) Aristotelian perspective on ethics for professionals in education.

referred to above. It is not just implicated in capacities of moral sensitivity but empathy is *also* an aspect of moral character insofar as it is considered to be dispositional *and* it seems to be a potentially important factor in moral motivation. Although it might seem to be a small step from these observations about the moral psychology of empathy to the claim that room deserves to be made for empathic development in the already crowded agenda of practical ethics education, the above-mentioned survey also exposes some notable disagreements and raises some puzzling questions that would seem to need answering before any such curricular project can be responsibly embarked upon.

If one thing is certain, it is that the problem of how and whether support for empathic responding and empathic development among young adults in the context of higher education might be ancillary to practical ethics education's last goal of promoting ethical attitudes and behaviour is not straightforwardly empirical or susceptible to formulation as a set hypothesis ripe for experimental investigation. Even if an irrefutably demonstrated and significant positive correlation between empathic responsiveness and both moral reasoning and observable pro-social, altruistic, helping, or otherwise generally moral behaviour and moral motivation could be established, the question would still remain wide open.

One could not be faulted for interpreting the foregoing assessment as a knee-jerk aversion to inferring "oughts" from "ises" (cf. Hume, 1751/1957) or a sign of having fallen prey to the seductive mysteries of Moore's "Open Question Argument" (Moore, 1903). It is not. There is one very simple reason why the question's cause will not be furthered using empirical methods alone—and why, incidentally, it seems that it is the kind of question that can only be addressed adequately if one is inclined to disciplinary *promiscuity* and firmly opposed to disciplinary *xenophobia*— and that is because it requires answers to both prior empirical question and prior philosophical questions. And this is the same reason why, of course, a philosophical approach which deploys philosophy's techniques of conceptual and linguistic analysis and draws on the relevant insights of the philosophical literature but which is uninformed about relevant empirical research is no less apt than a strict empirical approach to stray far afield indeed.

Consider, to begin with, the set of highly relevant and purely *conceptual* and *definitional* questions. First and foremost, what is empathy? Is it, as Murphy (1999) suggests, just the faculty of other-directed insight and thus a synonym for the well-worked concept referred to in social psychology as "social perspective taking" (Selman, 1980) and "role-taking" in ethics (Mead, 1934; Habermas, 1984, 1987)? Or, as per Hilfiker (2001) and Callahan (1980), does empathy have internal moral and motivational content, bringing moral problems to light and urging a response to them? But if this is the case, is empathy distinct from compassion and sympathy? Getting clear about these differences is not pedantry. For if empathy is just the means by which human beings gather information about others' inner states, it can be rallied indiscriminately for the sake of morally bad or good ends. If this is true, one might reasonably question whether its development, unqualified, is a worthy goal of practical ethics education. Hucksters, torturers, and psychopaths would presumably score very high on measures of empathy in this sense but their characteristic traits are the very antithesis of those one hopes practical ethics education fosters. At the very least, this situation calls for a sensitive delineation of empathy with an eye to identifying its connections with such apparently related concepts as compassion, sympathy, role-taking, sensitivity, perspective-taking, and caring.

But in addition to these conceptual problems there is as well a range of clearly *psychological* questions that would need to be addressed if one wishes to take the suggestion to support empathy in practical ethics education in due seriousness. Hilfiker (2001) claims that empathy is motivating. Surely, most people would unhesitatingly concede that feelings of involvement in another's adversity commonly motivate helping acts, but what evidence is there in the psychological literature that this is anything other than a bit of folk psychology? Questions may be raised as well about the role of the imagination in empathizing, an issue that was prominent in Callahan's (1980) account of moral perception. The answer one gives to this question has significant curricular implications. If empathizing is richly imaginative and involves a process of vicariously placing oneself in another's position, educators would likely want to favour curricular means which encourage and develop imaginative abilities such as reading literature and engaging in other activities that exercise role-taking skills. If, on the other hand, there are a variety of psychological routes to empathy and, in particular, if empathizing does not necessarily require the cognitively demanding exercise of the imagination, a more varied curricular response might be in order. Film, plays, service learning, and possibly even music would in this case pose a serious threat to the pedagogical hegemony of the written word.

Finally, none of the authors petitioned above raise the question of how empathic responding *develops*. It is all well and good to claim that empathy should be elicited and evoked in practical ethics education but what if empathy is such that its developmental achievements occur in early childhood? In that case, practical ethics educators would be faced with a situation of educational saturation: by the time people reach early adulthood they are simply beyond the reach of any further educational intervention in empathic development. If so, initiatives to support empathic development in higher education will be neither here nor there. No matter what they experience in the classroom or lecture hall, those who are highly empathically sensitive will remain so, as will those who have experienced developmental stagnation. Here, again, familiarity with relevant current knowledge in developmental psychology would undoubtedly prove illuminating.

The next chapter—and the first substantive one—Chapter 2, surveys empathy's diverse significations in social psychology, moral philosophy, psychotherapy, and aesthetics, the field where the term was first used. "Empathy", it is shown, designates two separate psychological phenomena: first, the faculty of forming beliefs about other people's inner states and, second, the way that emotional responses sometimes come to match or mirror perceptions of others' inner states, especially distressing, painful, and aversive states. It also observes that the term has numerous synonyms and that this is a source of confusion about its meaning. The chapter concludes that the emotion assumed in the diverse suggestions to promote empathy in practical ethics education sketched above is in ordinary language typically referred to as "compassion" or "sympathy" rather than "empathy". In full cognisance of the fact that "empathy" is a beguiling term and one that has too often been abused in order to lend airs of psychological erudition to a perfectly pedestrian emotion, it is argued that it remains the best term for this work's central construct on the grounds that "empathy", more than "sympathy" and "compassion", connotes not just *reactive* distress at another's aversive state but considered, justified, and hence *rational* distress.

Chapter 3 assembles a conceptual and empirical impression of compassionate empathy. Drawing on Lawrence Blum's pioneering work on this theme, it defends an account of the objects, judgements, knowledge conditions, and affective attitudes that characterize compassionate empathy. Compassionate empathy is a state of involvement in another's suffering as something to be alleviated, a conception that is consistent with the empirical evidence from social psychology that there is a strong link between empathy and motivation to help. Undoubtedly, it is a positive social emotion but is compassionate empathy a *moral* emotion as well?

Chapter 4 analyses what I describe as the paradox of the moral worth of compassionate empathy. Because of its affinities with a moral outlook, compassionate empathy seems to have inherent moral worth. But because it can also motivate morally questionable or even squarely morally wrong acts, it appears to have only contingent moral value. I argue that this paradox largely dissolves when one differentiates between three senses in which emotions are ordinarily held to have moral significance: (1) as judgement-distorting passions; (2) as particular "moral emotions" that are conducive to moral behaviour; and (3) as components of moral virtue. Compassionate empathy is *both* the moral emotion par excellence *and*, like most emotions, can become passionate—that is, it can interfere with one's ability to view a moral problem *dis*passionately.

A brief review of the evidence accumulated in social psychology on empathic bias shows that its incompatibility with the ideal of impartial moral judgement is striking. On the other hand, critics of ethical rationalism have long argued that compassionate empathy or "sympathy" is a precondition of the exercise of the faculty of moral judgement. The following chapter, Chapter 5, wades into the vexed debate over whether emotions are on the whole detrimental to impartial moral judgement or enable it. The approach adopted attempts to identify grounds for accepting or rejecting the claim that a failing in empathic capacities entails a deficiency in the exercise of moral judgement. It is argued that while it seems clear that the ability to construct moral problems presupposes the mastery of certain moral concepts connected with human well-being and interest, the question remains open as to whether the mastery of these categories implies active affective engagement as well. Knowledge in clinical psychology about psychopathy, a condition of full cognitive integrity accompanied by extreme emotional shallowness, seems to shed some light on this issue. Evidence indicates that psychopaths are no less competent in moral reasoning than the emotionally normal. Psychopaths' contrasting lack of interest either in acting morally or exercising practical judgement in concrete situations, however, suggests that concern for others is a vital ingredient in bothering about morality: acting according to one's best moral judgements and being driven to get moral problems right.

Chapter 6 and the final chapter (Chapter 7) lay bare the conception of the basic problem of educating for compassionate empathy in the context of practical ethics implied by the work's findings. Practical ethics educators should view support for empathic capacities of response as dovetailing with practical ethics education's pre-existing goal of assisting in the *perfection* of students' abilities to exercise mature moral judgement, abilities which should and can reasonably be viewed as being already well grounded prior to any exposure to practical ethics in higher education. The challenge, I argue, is how to encourage the appropriate extension of natural concern for those with whom one identifies to the strangers with whom one shares the broader social world. To this end, I make three substantive pedagogical suggestions. First, I argue that a discussion of consideration for others as a dimension of moral experience should be included in the theoretical introduction to courses in practical ethics on the grounds that doing so would appear to support a disposition towards moral motivation. The second suggestion is to consider "décalage"—crudely stated, the phenomenon where people's propensity for appropriate empathic response can vary dramatically, depending on the degree to which they identify with the object of compassionate involvement—by selecting cases and dilemma problems in which as wide a range of moral domains and moral objects as possible is represented. Finally, I suggest adopting a varied curricular response to teaching practical ethics in order to use the multifacetedness of empathic responding as an educational resource—because compassionate empathizing is mediated by psychological mechanisms ranging from the cognitively simple to the cognitively demanding. A strong case can be made in favour of using visual media and certain types of face-to-face experience learning and imaginative role-playing exercises in addition to standard text-based material.

From a methodological standpoint, because of its focus on the *interplay* between behavioural, cognitive, and affective dimensions of moral experience—rather than on just one of these dimensions—this study is seated within the virtue ethics research agenda in moral education as characterized by Carr and Steutel (1999, p. 252). Furthermore, by attempting to marry moral philosophy with empirical and theoretical studies in psychology, it is clearly "naturalist". Naturalism, a more or less well-established approach to practical and theoretical problems in ethics which strives for sensitivity to relevant and existing empirical knowledge in the human sciences, is contested. And so, being aware that this is not the place to attempt to give full coverage to the perplexing questions ethical naturalism raises about the relation between facts and norms and the proper intercourse between moral philosophy and moral psychology, at least a few words in defence of the adoption of ethical naturalism in the present work are in order.

1.4 Methodological Excursus on Ethical Naturalism

Perhaps the most familiar variety of ethical naturalism holds that normative prescriptions and, in particular, prescriptions about the traits of character, which are morally good to cultivate and possess, are not fully comprehensible when abstracted from the facts and natural circumstances of human experience[12] or from a conception of what it means to "flourish" or "do well" in respect of the essential needs, aspirations, and behaviours typical of human beings as a natural kind.[13] Gary Larson's portrayal of the sex lives of one-celled organisms in his *Far side* series of cartoons frequently suggests the first of these distinct claims: the very meaning of human sexual virtues and vices are bound up intimately (as it were) with the fact that human beings are organisms that reproduce sexually. To get a taste of the idea of grounding virtues in human ethology or some conception of natural human dispositions, behaviour, and needs, it would be hard to imagine, say, compassion being *recommendable* as a virtue if it were not for the fact that human beings are capable of suffering, because the avoidance and alleviation of suffering frequently depend on involvement on the part of others and that care and concern can play an important role in motivating such cooperation. When distinguished from other forms of ethical naturalism, this latter form of ethical naturalism is sometimes referred to as "neo-Aristotelian ethical naturalism" (cf. Lenman, 2006) and it is easy to see the source of its Aristotelian credentials. In line with the fundamental assumptions of Aristotle's ethics, neo-Aristotelian ethical naturalism seems committed to something like the idea that all living creatures have an internal and biologically guaranteed nature and this nature specifies what it means to do well or flourish for them; even if it is not immediately clear what the "good of man" consists in, man has a good, it can be rationally investigated, and it is the specific purpose of the field of ethics or "politics" to investigate it (Aristotle, 4th century B.C.E./1955, 1094a22–b12).

A second variety of ethical naturalism, which holds that the standards of judgement, action, and character a theory of normative ethics prescribes must be realistically attainable by human beings of ordinary cognitive and affective ability, can be instructively referred to as "naturalized normative ethics". Williams's (1976) well-known "one-thought-too-many" argument is naturalized in this sense. Williams's argument is intended as a case against modern moral philosophy's prioritization of the principle of universality. Its point is that the demand for strict impartiality in moral deliberation (usually insinuated by those with a penchant for act consequentialism in the form of slightly bizarre thought experiments where one is to imagine, for instance, a situation where one is forced to make an excruciating choice between saving a figure of some social importance or one's own sister, wife, or mother from death by fire, drowning, or firing squad) potentially requires one to renounce much of what makes life meaningful and fulfilling: one's closest attachments and relationships. This cannot be expected of any normal person.[14] More recently, Owen Flanagan has articulated this criterion for the adequacy of a theory of normative

---

[12] Anscombe (1958), Geach (1956), and more recently Thomson (2001) provide elaborations of this view.

[13] For statement of this conception of ethical naturalism see Hursthouse (1999), Foot (2001), and most recently McKinnon (2005).

[14] See Cottingham (1983) and Nagel (1986) for comparable deployments of the naturalist strategy against the ideal of impartiality in normative ethics.

ethics in the form of the "principle of minimal psychological realism" (PMPR) which reads as follows: "Make sure when constructing a moral theory or projecting a moral ideal that the character, decision processing, and behaviour prescribed are possible, or are perceived to be possible, for creatures like us" (1991, p. 35).

Unlike naturalized normative ethics and neo-Aristotelian ethical naturalism, which raise many complex and contestable issues in contemporary ethics, the third discernible variety of ethical naturalism, "evidential ethical naturalism" to coin a phrase, is relatively plain and free of controversy (Table 1.1). The leading idea of evidential ethical naturalism is that, apart from meta-ethics presumably, it is simply not possible to get very far in moral philosophy without, in Doris and Stich's (2003) folksy expression, "stubbing one's toe on empirical claims" (p. 115). The idea can be conveniently illustrated by reference to Flanagan's (1996) distinction between ethics' "normative" component, on one hand, and its "descriptive–genealogical–nomological" component, on the other (cf. pp. 117–119). The study of human moral deliberation, functioning, and agency is concerned with *prescribing* ethical standards—advancing and defending claims, essentially about how from a moral perspective people should act, respond to each other, and think about moral problems. But it is also concerned with the *description* and *explanation* of certain faculties, capacities, and inclinations which humans possess and which are relevant to functioning in the moral domain (Flanagan, 1996, p. 118ff.).

Table 1.1 Varieties of naturalism in contemporary ethics

	Leading idea	References
1. Neo-Aristotelian ethical naturalism	Moral prescriptions and especially concepts of virtue and vice cannot be comprehended in abstraction from human ethology or the natural circumstances of human experience	Geach (1956), Anscombe (1958), Hursthouse (1999), Thomson (2001), Foot (2001), McKinnon (2005)
2. Naturalized normative ethics	The standards of judgement, action, and character prescribed by a theory of normative ethics are acceptable insofar as they are realistically attainable by human beings of ordinary cognitive and affective ability	Williams (1976), Cottingham (1983), Nagel (1991), Flanagan (1986)
3. Evidential ethical naturalism	Inquiry in the fields of normative and practical ethics should be informed about, and take into consideration, relevant and existing knowledge from the human sciences and especially from moral psychology	Darwall et al. (1997), Doris and Stich (2003)

In spite of Flanagan's own potentially misleading presentation of the matter, ethics' bipolarity, if you will, is not a feature that is unique to "naturalized ethics" under his or any other interpretation of this idea. Historically, moral philosophers have tended to assume answers to the descriptive–genealogical–nomological questions of ethics and, not infrequently, to haggle over empirical claims as if they could be decided on conceptual grounds. This tendency is in large part attributable to an historical absence of research in the human sciences. Prior to, say, the mid-twentieth century, since little or no such research had been conducted, moral philosophers, in Darwall et al.'s, (1997) words, had no choice but to "invent their psychology and anthropology from scratch" (pp. 34–35; quoted in Doris & Stich, 2003, p. 114). Armchair psychology in ethics is no longer defensible, and even if, as will necessarily often be the case, the relevant research is unavailable, inexistent, or insusceptible to straightforward use for philosophical purposes, self-imposed scientific benightedness would seem to be intellectually irresponsible at best and, at worst, philistine.[15]

It would perhaps at this point be sufficient to observe that of the three varieties of ethical naturalism just petitioned, the one with which this study explicitly associates itself is neither naturalized normative ethics nor neo-Aristotelian ethical naturalism but the comparatively uncontroversial evidential ethical naturalism, and proceed to other matters. But there persists in certain quarters of the field of moral philosophy a decidedly "anti-naturalist" bent which invites recognition and some response, however brief.

Ostensibly motivated by lingering worries about Hume's (1751/1957) stern warning against deducing prescriptive claims from descriptive claims, anti-naturalism in ethics is highly suspicious of empirical claims in moral arguments and is thus wary of having any truck or trade with research findings in empirical moral psychology and the human sciences more generally. Fortunately there is no need to risk getting tangled up in the intricacies of the contested is/ought fallacy and its confusing relation to Moore's (1903) "naturalistic fallacy" to see that even wholesale endorsement of the idea that any inference from, say, a claim about the way human beings are (e.g., human beings are mostly motivated by narrow self-interest) to an evaluative claim about how human beings should be (e.g., human beings should be mostly motivated by narrow self-interest) is strictly invalid (which, in the case of the present example, seems obvious enough) does not license the conclusion

---

[15] See Doris and Stich (2003) for a recent review of ways in which relevant and available empirical evidence, when in the hands of moral philosophers, has been put to use in order to suggest new directions vis-à-vis such intractable philosophical problems as the indeterminacy of moral character, the problem of moral motivation, and the possibility of convergence of opinion among fully rational moral agents. The conclusions reached in the examples of well-conducted empirically informed philosophical research they survey might not in every case be convincing but their case studies leave no doubt of the potential heuristic value for ethics of engagement with relevant empirical literature and forcefully make their point that, as these authors state it, "ethical theorizing should be an (in part) a posteriori inquiry richly informed by relevant empirical considerations" (p. 115).

that the empirical findings of the human sciences are categorically irrelevant to normative inquiry. Indeed, the suggestion that it does, if anyone has ever made it, is indicative of such an intricate knot of confusion that one scarcely knows how to begin to unravel it. For starters, it profoundly misunderstands the significance of the is/ought fallacy in practical ethics. At least as Hume seemed to see it, the basic problem is that giving descriptive moral assessment of acts, characters, and intentions with which ordinary English abounds—for example, "Katia is vindictive"; "Speaking to me like that is wrong!"; "Charity is a virtue"—does not *logically* commit one to believing that anyone should act in ways that are consistent with such judgements, much less act in such ways oneself. So, an action does not accord with a moral belief as a requirement of practical reason, as is so commonly held. Rather, the will conforms to a moral commitment only insofar as there happens to be present an essentially distinct *desire* to conform the will to a moral commitment. Incidentally, it was on the basis of such observations that Hume memorably stated, "reason is [...] the slave of the passions, and can never pretend to any other office than to serve and obey them".[16] In sum, Hume's point was that descriptive-sounding moral judgements ("is" statements) do not in and of themselves contain rational prescriptive or motivational force (the are and can only in vain aspire to being "ought" statements), and emphatically not that empirical or factual claims are somehow irrelevant to the *justification* of moral claims. Neither was this Moore's (1903) point when he formulated the alleged naturalistic fallacy. Moore's idea was rather that the property of something being "good" cannot, and this contrary to the pretensions of his utilitarian contemporaries who as he saw it equated "goodness" with "conduciveness to happiness", coherently be analysed in terms of the describable features in virtue of which it is supposed to be good. The "open question argument", as it came to be known, posited that no matter what naturally occurring property one considers to be the source of value or "goodness", that property can never exhaust the meaning of goodness as a moral predicate since the possibility always remains open for something to both possess the property yet not to be good. A certain reductivist approach to moral justification was Moore's target and, again, not that observable reality is across the board irrelevant to the full range of problems in normative and practical ethics.

I would venture that it would have crossed neither Hume's nor Moore's mind to deny that empirical claims are relevant to the construction of theories of normative ethics and *a fortiori* moral deliberation in particular cases. Flanagan's (1996) list of testable hypotheses that have recurred in moral philosophy is illustrative: Are the virtues unitary? Does moral behaviour depend on extrinsic constraints? Do conditions of material abundance favour beneficence? (p. 118). For an example of the relevance of facts in applied ethics, we can conveniently turn to the recent controversy in biomedical ethics over the case of Ashley, where a medical team, acting on the express request of parents, used hormone treatment to attenuate the growth and sexual development of their severely disabled child. As the consulting physicians take pains

---

[16] For an in-depth discussion of this key point of Humean moral psychology see Smith (1994, p. 92ff).

to point out in a public defence of their choice to medically treat Ashley as her parents wished, the ethics of the intervention turns on *at least* these two rather cut-and-dry empirical matters: (1) whether the parents or other primary caregivers ask for the treatment and (2) whether there is evidence that the treatment entails significant counter-indicating medical risks (cf. Gunther & Diekema, 2006).

How then can anti-naturalism in ethics be accounted for? One possible explanation might point to the combined effects of disciplinary inertia and a lack of acquaintance with the field of psychology. For most of the twentieth century, moral philosophy was concerned almost exclusively with meta-ethics (cf. Darwall et al., 1992) and here the relevance of empirical issues is much more obscure. The other dominant theme not just in moral philosophy but in philosophy of the twentieth century writ large was conceptual and linguistic analysis which, when joined with a creeping fear of the possibility that there might not be anything else philosophers can call their own area of genuine expertise, can lead to a defensive sense of disciplinary superiority. Hence, it is not infrequent that moral philosophers, usually informally and without checking, can be heard claiming that social scientists must be terribly confused about their use of terms. Add to this assumption a legitimate worry in the humanities generally that quantification in the human sciences cannot but simplify complex and historically rooted social phenomena and human behaviour beyond recognition and we have a rich anti-naturalistic cocktail indeed. Without for a moment wishing to play the role of the human sciences' public defender on these points, I can nevertheless confirm—and this is merely an anecdotal assessment made by a disciplinary outsider with a comparatively passing acquaintance with the field of social and cognitive psychology—that reports of conceptual confusion in psychology are grossly exaggerated. As for quantification, some of the force of the standard objection against it is attenuated once one appreciates the stipulative nature of the basic methodological technique of "operationalization" (i.e., assigning a numerical value to a concept, variable, or condition for the sake of studying it, roughly speaking) and that, far from being some conspiracy of positivism, many psychologists are themselves well aware of its limits.

1.5 What is Practical Ethics Education and is Improving Moral Behaviour one of its Legitimate Aims?

Before taking the first steps to address directly the question of the prospects of educationally promoting empathy in practical ethics education, it would be amiss not to attend, if only briefly, to two interrelated issues. The first issue amounts to facing an objection to what has been taken so far as an unquestioned premise: that promoting moral attitudes and behaviour is a legitimate aim of practical ethics education. Secondly, I would like to underline, in case it is not already obvious enough, that this work adopts an institutional conception of practical and professional ethics and, in doing so, presents the widely accepted goals of practical and professional ethics in higher education and sketches the typical teaching methods used to teach it.

To address the second point first, it would respect both one way the word "education" is ordinarily used in English and the standard division of education into formal education or "schooling" and informal education or "socialization" (cf. Dewey, 1916/1944) not to restrict practical and professional ethics education to a subject taught at universities. In saying, for example, that gaining first-hand acquaintance with the life conditions and personal history of a family seeking political asylum was "a real moral education", one does not imply an experience mediated by books, instructors, and learning schedules. Keeping with this usage, one might think of the whole loose ensemble of socialization processes and educational and professional experiences that could reasonably be regarded as playing a role in improving a person's ability to handle and respond to moral problems in life as constituting one's "practical ethics education". By contrast, "practical and professional ethics education"—or even more generically "ethics teaching"—as it is considered here is instead meant to bring to mind two distinct but overlapping *formal* educational activities. One is instruction in ethical theory (or moral philosophy). This is an area of academic study which is itself divisible into *normative ethics*, first-order questioning into the reasons why some acts are morally better than others (because they are conducive to more overall good, cohere with fundamental moral principles, or instantiate virtuous conduct?), and *meta-ethics*, the second-order investigation into a clutch of highly abstract questions regarding the fundamental nature of moral experience and moral justification (What is moral goodness? How do we know the difference between right and wrong? Are there objective moral truths? What is the origin of moral value? Why be moral?). The other is instruction in practical ethics, also commonly referred to as "applied ethics". Practical ethics pertains to the ground-floor moral questions which are the stock and trade of ethicists and which preoccupy almost everyone from time to time. Among these problems are, of course, the contemporary moral issues widely debated in the mass media—abortion, capital punishment, physician-assisted suicide, the treatment of animals, and so on—but practical ethics encompasses professional ethics as well and touches on issues of a more personal nature such as the value of friendship, honesty, marital fidelity, political participation, and even particular leisure activities.

While contemporary moral philosophy aspires to the status of a purely theoretical enterprise, practical ethics is, by contrast, commonly regarded as contributing to pragmatic ends. Annis's (1992) summary of the goals of an ethics course is taken as representative. Ethics teaching should (1) introduce the standard theories of normative ethics (i.e., duty theory, consequentialism, and virtue theory) and the basic concepts and principles involved in practical reasoning; (2) illustrate how these theories and concepts apply to particular moral problems; (3) promote clear thinking and communication about ethics and ethical problems; (4) encourage students to be self-critical as regards their own moral values and commitments and to become more open-minded, tolerant, and differentiated in their responses to ethical controversies; and (5) stimulate moral sensitivity and moral imagination by engaging students with moral problems in non-intellectual ways. *Professional* ethics teaching embraces all these goals but should additionally (6) raise awareness of the profession's established ethical norms (as expressed, for instance, in a code of ethics) and expose the conceptual connections between these norms and the profession's social purpose and the realities and requirements of professional practice and judgement.

Although the methods used to teach ethics tend to be flexible and subject to considerable variation from instructor to instructor, it is nevertheless possible to identify three principal pedagogical approaches: the academic method, the plug-and-play method, and the casebook method.

The academic method analyses and critiques moral arguments as they appear in published philosophical essays authored by ethicists.[17] A course's base texts are typically grouped according to themes such as biomedical ethics, environmental ethics, or information technology ethics, or they offer a representative sampling of rival perspectives on one specific moral problem (e.g., informed consent, pornography, or peer-to-peer file sharing). This approach to teaching ethics is sometimes referred to as "theory-based teaching" because it focuses on moral problems understood in relatively abstract and general terms. The theory-based teaching of the academic method contrasts with so-called case-based teaching, which focuses instead on cases: more or less detailed narrative descriptions of a moral agent faced with a concrete moral problem in a particular set of circumstances.[18] The plug-and-play method and the casebook method are case-based in this sense.

The plug-and-play method[19] studies cases by *applying* to them the standard theories of normative ethics. So, for instance, in approaching a case where a terminally ill patient requests assisted suicide, one would encourage students to begin by either attempting to identify the applicable higher-order moral principles (in the manner of duty theory), estimate the good and bad consequences for all those affected by the act (as in consequentialism), or question which virtues would be instantiated in the adoption of one action alternative or another (virtue theory). The educational value of this approach is that it illustrates the utility of philosophical theories in solving a moral problem, strengthens students' comprehension of the theories themselves, and gives them hands-on practice using them as a justificatory framework. The plug-and-play method is also sometimes recruited to serve theoretical ends because it can be used to draw attention to the practical limitations of the theories of normative ethics (as when their application to a particular case shows they can justify egregiously immoral acts) and to suggest their incommensurability as justificatory procedures (as when the application of two different theories justifies incompatible actions).

The casebook method studies cases by *deriving* moral principles from one's intuitive responses to the case. Here, students are encouraged to, first, articulate moral principles that could justify their beliefs regarding the correct solution to the

---

[17] The term is derived from a similar usage in Schläfli et al. (1985).

[18] On the distinction between case-based and theory-based teaching, see, for example, Jonsen and Toulmin (1988).

[19] The term is Barnbaum's (2001).

moral problem the case presents and, second, to test these moral principles for adequacy either by attempting to apply them in other situations, by verifying their consistency with other more fundamental moral principles, or by some other means. The aim of such exercises is for students to achieve "reflective equilibrium" (Rawls, 1971) or a state where commitments to basic moral principles come to cohere with particular moral judgements through a process of deliberation and reasoned adjustment. This method of teaching ethics is closely akin to the well-known casebook method of teaching law where students learn legal principles by deriving them from judges' rulings in legal cases, hence the name.

As this brief rehearsal of the standard methods of practical ethics teaching is something to go on, the objectives of contemporary practical ethics education seem to be manifestly *academic* in the pejorative sense of the term: concerned with intellectual inquiry for its own sake and utterly unpractical. In light of this curricular orientation it is not surprising, perhaps, that according to one prevalent conception it is indeed a serious misconstrual of practical ethics education to think of it as being implicated in promoting moral attitudes or improving students' moral behaviour. Callahan (1980), we saw, placed the stimulation of the moral imagination at the top of his list of the important goals in the teaching of ethics. Later in the same text, he presents a corresponding list of "doubtful" goals in the teaching of ethics and the first item on *that* list is "to influence conduct" (p. 69). The weightiest reason Callahan volunteers to justify his position is that since ethical questions are highly complex and difficult, and are the subject of disagreement between reasonable people, the point of an ethics course cannot simply be that of encouraging good behaviour. One cannot teach others to behave well unless first one knows oneself what it is to behave well. But to hold such a belief would be presumptuous. "No teacher of ethics", Callahan says, "can assume that he or she has such a solid grasp on the nature of morality as to pretend to know what finally counts as good moral conduct" (1980. p. 71). Ethics teaching that begins with a "pre-established blueprint of what will count as acceptable moral behaviour" cannot but be disingenuous (p. 70). Instead, the proper point of an ethics course is "critical inquiry": not encouraging good behaviour as such but rather "inquiring into what should count as good behaviour" (pp. 69–70). The same point about the essentially contested nature of ethical problems has been put more recently and with particular force by Carr (2001), who has gone so far as to advance that a sure sign that a practical problem is in fact not a moral problem at all is that it is susceptible to a straightforward and uncontroversial solution. "The beginnings of wisdom concerning the nature of moral life, inquiry and reflection", Carr writes, "lie in recognizing that disagreement and controversy are of its very *essence*: in this light, one might reasonably suspect that any practical question that turned out to be resolvable by statistical or other quasi-empirical methods would *not* be a genuine moral problem" (2001, pp. 71–72).

Neither Carr nor Callahan derive subjectivist conclusions from the thought that moral problems might not be susceptible to definitive solutions. There exist criteria to distinguish better from worse answers to moral problems, as they both forthrightly affirm; scepticism towards the possibility of authoritative judgements in ethics does not entail that morality is a matter of mere personal preference (cf. Callahan, 1980, p. 71; Carr, 2001, p. 72). Notwithstanding, they both do seem to suggest that to establish behavioural outcomes in advance of moral education is to be at significant risk of confusing education with social control, if not tantamount to conflating them. However, Callahan (unlike Carr I believe[20]) considers that social control has its time and place. It is the proper business of the *moral education of children*—and emphatically not that of practical ethics education—to set out to improve moral conduct, promote moral responsibility, and encourage the formation of what are held to be morally desirable dispositions (1980, p. 71). By contrast, it is a basic supposition of not just ethics in higher education but indeed higher education writ large, Callahan (1980) says, that "students are at an age where they have to begin coming to their own conclusions and shaping their own view of the world. It is the time and place to teach them intellectual independence, and to instil in them a spirit of critical inquiry" (p. 71). Thus, in his reading of the situation, the only kind of behaviour that education in practical ethics can justifiably try to change is "verbal behaviour", by which he means the clarity of expression, consistency, and coherence indicative of strong skills in moral reasoning (p. 70).

I suspect that many would find misguided Callahan's idea itself that teachers of ethics are misguided if they understand themselves as being implicated in attempting to encourage morally good and to discourage morally bad behaviour. After all, and as Scholz and Groarke (1996) remind us, the reason why almost all business and professional programmes make success in ethics courses degree requirements nowadays is not, perhaps unfortunately, "because they want to promote moral philosophy but because they want to promote (and be seen as promoting) ethical attitudes and behaviour" (p. 338). A case in point, arguably, is the delayed arrival of professional ethics in teaching as a field of research in its own right and as an independent subject of study in professional training programmes. While professional ethics in medicine, law, and business has been well established for decades, professional ethics in *education* has emerged only in the last 10 or 15 years, and one can plausibly speculate that one reason for this is because scandals and cases of gross malpractice in teaching are, thankfully, comparatively rare occurrences.[21] In short, it might very well be that the ubiquitous ethics requirement would not exist were it not that curriculum planners and the public believe that studying ethics, if not conducive to ethical behaviour, is at least a prophylactic against unethical conduct. Of course, whether this is in fact the case is another question entirely.

My intention in raising professional ethics education is not in order to object to Callahan's claim that there are no definite and uncontroversial moral dos and don'ts in life, the claim which underlies, as we have seen, his belief that promoting morally good behaviour is a dubious aim of practical ethics education. That said, I suppose professional conduct is one arena where identifying specific morally sanctionable acts might not seem especially unproblematic—codes of ethics are

---

[20] Cf. especially Carr (2000, pp. 186ff).

[21] For a similar assessment see the discussion of this point in Strike and Ternasky (1993).

certainly not shy about listing specific prohibited acts—and, with a little effort, this suggestion could be worked into full-blown objection to Callahan's point. My point in the first instance is rather to draw attention to the fact that in professional ethics education, which as we observed above often blurs with practical ethics education, there seems to be considerable room for something the kind of formative and constraining objectives Callahan associates with moral education. Furthermore, the educational pursuit of such objective would seem to be perfectly legitimate, if not necessary, for the survival of the profession. Insofar as accounts of the dispositions and excellences and statements of the specific conduct that are held to be constitutive of professional expertise are arrived at by way of an open, reasonable, and honest process, it is almost certainly to the good of professionalism in any field for accreditation bodies and educators to have such ideals clearly before their minds; such considerations are the very heart of professional role morality (cf. Bowie, 2003). For better or for worse, it is a longstanding standard practice in Anglo-American medical schools to use candidacy interviews in order to assess whether applicants demonstrate a potential to acquire desirable professional dispositions, and those who do not convince the panel of their potential in this regard can be turned away.[22] Traditionally, however, the formation of professional values and dispositions was, to varying degrees of awareness on the part of educators themselves, taken for granted as part of the socialization process which occurs naturally in any programme of professional preparation. This is the material of the so-called hidden curriculum. More recently, however, specific professional ethics courses appear to be increasingly seen as the appropriate forum in which to *explicitly* introduce trainees to the values, virtues, duties, and responsibilities of their prospective professions. This new vocation for practical ethics contrasts sharply with the traditional fare of courses in ethics for professionals. The instruction of these courses, sometimes labelled disparagingly "bolt-on" ethics courses, is commonly outsourced to a teacher affiliated with a philosophy department or taught by a specially trained ethicist in the home field. Certainly, one purpose of such courses is to raise awareness of the field as a site of ethical controversy and to expose students to some of the substance of those controversies. But, above all, their putative primary *raison d'être* is to raise students' levels of moral reasoning. Moral reasoning, in this context, is understood as a general rather than a profession-specific competence—a "soft skill"—but it is nevertheless regarded as being highly relevant to professional practice. Experienced professionals in all fields will readily confirm that professional life is replete with moral problems. Indeed, to echo Carr's statement about the nature of moral problems cited above, one might reasonably doubt whether any occupation wherein practitioners do not at least sometimes face difficult moral problems deserves to be considered a genuine profession at all.

---

[22] In medicine as well explicit descriptions of the social, emotional, and moral competencies of professional expertise also seem to be becoming a standard feature of policy documents used in the accreditation process. See, for example, American Association of Medical Colleges Core Curriculum Working Group (2000). See Coulehan and Williams (2003) for a discussion of this trend.

For the sake of not mixing them up, let us now depart slightly from our earlier characterization of the relationship between professional and practical ethics education and refer to the first of these educational imperatives, that of promoting moral aspects of professionalism, as "professional ethics education" and to the second, the imperative of promoting skills in moral reasoning, as "practical ethics education". The temptation might seem great to see an easy settlement of the question of whether teaching ethics in higher education aims to influence conduct by claiming that it depends on what you mean by "teaching ethics in higher education". Professional ethics education does and practical ethics education does not. But on closer inspection, this proposal founders on both counts.

Professional ethics education may merely serve as a notice board of professional rights and wrongs. Taught in a more richly educational spirit, however, professional ethics will almost certainly be centrally concerned with exposing the conceptual relationships between established professional norms and virtues, and the profession's social purpose and characteristic aims. For example, one reason commonly given to explain why sleeping with a student or client is unethical is because professional competency depends on a certain degree of impartiality and distance in the client–professional relationship. Similarly, using professional knowledge for the sake of commercial exploitation is regarded as unethical, when it is, because commercial interest is highly susceptible to conflicting with the interest of the basic welfare rights, which it is the specific purpose of professions to provide—protection from disease, injustice, ignorance, and the like.[23] In professional ethics education conducted in this spirit of inquiry, the question of whether substantive sanctionable behaviours are acceptable must be presented as an open one—open, more precisely, to free and rational assent or indeed the free and rational *rejection* on the part of professional trainees.

As for practical ethics education, to derive the conclusion, following Callahan (1980), that practical ethics education is not legitimately concerned with changing behaviour from the rather unquestionable assumption that one can never be certain in advance of a delicate moral situation what the right response to it will be seems to be nothing more or less than the refusal of ethics as a *practical*, as opposed to an exclusively *theoretical*, domain. Music, like ethics, is a practical subject with a theoretical component. Excellence in both music and ethics is a complex matter and significantly open-ended. Despite this, music tutors teach their students music theory, give them fingering exercises and scales to practice, and have them listen to excellent performances because, as any music teacher will gladly explain, doing these things helps musicians play better music. So too, one hopes, the skills, insight, and judgement that practical ethics courses are supposed to support would help students make better moral decisions than they would have if they had never had the experience of studying ethics. Indeed, a failure to have any influence on conduct in this sense would *ipso facto* seem to be a very good reason to suspect that students are actually being taught the wrong things.

---

[23] For a development of this conception of professional ethics see Carr (2000 p. 149ff).

Setting out to teach practical ethics with the aim of improving moral behaviour and with the understanding that what this means is that there are certain skills and dispositions which it is the proper business of practical ethics to teach, and that these skills and dispositions help people tell between better and worse moral decisions is not at all the same thing as embarking on practical ethics to teach right and wrong. But it is setting out to improve moral conduct all the same. I hazard to advance an error theory: only mind under the grip of a certain inflexibility of thought borne of the bad linguistic habit of expressing moral judgements in terms of dichotomies could fail to see the fallacy involved in inferring from the virtual certainty that genuine moral problems are essentially contestable to the claim that the point of practical and professional ethics education cannot be to promote morally good behaviour. If the language of ethics is the language of ambiguity, incommensurability, and complexity, the importance of exclusive moral alternatives like "good" and "bad", "right" and "wrong", "ought" and "ought not" is at most secondary.

In the foregoing stipulative senses of "practical ethics education" and "professional ethics education", the study that follows is concerned with practical ethics education understood as but one dimension of professional ethics education, namely the dimension which is concerned with analysing and responding appropriately to moral problems that arise in the course of professional life. Hill (2000) says that Kant saw the fundamental ethical question as "What should I do?" asked seriously from the first-person deliberative perspective in the face of a moral problem. The idea that this question might be derivative of the more fundamental question of "Who should I be?" has been the subject of serious philosophical debate in recent years.[24] Pending an answer from meta-ethics on whether or not Kant hit the mark on this point, I propose to err on the side of tradition and assume that he did and, correspondingly, that practical ethics education should try to prepare people to answer this question the best that they can. From this perspective, if it turns out that Callahan is right and that the constellation of dispositions comprising moral imagination, empathy, and concern for others is the very source of the drive to get ethical problems straight, educators have every reason to believe that it belongs at the top of the list of important goals in the teaching of ethics.

---

[24]On this point see various contributions in Darwall (2002), Crisp (1998), and Crisp and Slote (1997).

Chapter 2
The Disambiguation of "Empathy": Affective and Cognitive Conceptions

2.1 Introduction

The question of the desirability, status, and, perhaps, the practicability of empathic responsiveness as a skill to be developed in the context of professional ethics education turns on what the words "empathy" and its derivatives mean in one's mouth. In everyday English, "empathy" connotes imaginative involvement in another person's experience of some form of suffering. Being touched or affected by it is also typically implied. That much is clear. Already departing from this usage, however, Murphy (1999), as we have seen, regarded empathy as merely perspicacity in understanding another person's perspective. While the ability to gain insight into others' feelings, beliefs, values, and desires is certainly a morally *relevant* competence insofar as facts about others' inner states are almost invariably relevant to moral problems, this skill is quite a different animal from the one Callahan (1980), Hilfiker (2001), and Coombs (1998) had in mind. These authors understood the psychological phenomenon in question less as a skill than as some kind of *faculty* that enables people to perceive morally salient features of a situation and to understand that moral problems demand attention and a judicious response. If Murphy is right, empathy is a non-moral merit which one could put to use indiscriminately for good or bad ends. If Callahan, Hilfiker, and Coombs' perceptive conception of empathy is on the right track, empathy appears to be a moral merit which, like justice, mercy, and benevolence, is oriented with apparent conceptual necessity, if at times imperfectly in practice, towards the realization of morally good ends. What, then, does "empathy" actually mean? This study aims to pursue this question but with an eye to answering another one which goes directly to the point of the broader purposes of this work: namely, is empathy a suitable label for that singular capacity to become mindful, through an imaginative act, of others' needs, feelings, desires, and threats to their weal and woe? It was this capacity, or something like it, that seemed quite plausibly basic to moral functioning and *ipso facto* crucial not to overlook in thinking about how to responsibly teach practical and professional ethics (cf. §1.2). The study will confirm, by way of an overview of the principal uses of the word in the philosophical and psychological literature, that "empathy" is a term badly in need of disambiguation; it is multifaceted,

B. Maxwell, *Professional Ethics Education: Studies in Compassionate Empathy*,
© Springer Science + Business Media B.V. 2008

ambiguous, and therefore beguiling and, accordingly, there is no plain satisfactory answer to the question, "what is empathy?". As for the second question, it will be argued that despite this confusing overlay of meaning, "empathy" carries imaginative, reflective, and intentional connotations which make the term attractive for our purposes but only on the condition that it carries the modifier "compassionate" as a bit of insurance against equivocation.

With another word, it might have been sufficient to save oneself the trouble of such a review and to content oneself to follow the time-honoured philosophical tradition to seek conceptual clarity through straightforward linguistic analysis of everyday use. Where a word has multiple discrete senses linguistic analysis can of course guard against equivocation. However, words whose use in ordinary language is erratic resist uncontroversial analyses. In these cases, linguistic analysis faces something of a paradox: it is either faithful to the word's use and then falls short of achieving the purpose of analysis because it fails to yield clear distinctions, or if it does establish clear distinctions, it can only do so by stipulating them and then it is no longer linguistic *analysis* (cf. Wittgenstein, 1953/1992). "Empathy" is unquestionably a term that falls into the latter category. Neologisms are linguistic labels affixed to a concept with no prior name and they tend to be chosen because they seem, for whatever reason, to be an appropriate fit for the referent. This in itself is, of course, no necessary source of confusion; when a person says "I'm going to go check something on the web", the risk of misunderstanding that he means to go investigate the cobwebs in the attic is minimal. The particular difficulty with "empathy", however, is that it has been judged to be an appropriate neologism by some who had quite different ideas in mind. For the sake of keeping things straight, the following discussion will be framed following Sherman's (1998) instructive distinction between two broad and to some degree overlapping notions of empathy. The first considers empathy principally as an affective psychological state. It includes "*Einfühlung*" (empathy) as it was used in nineteenth-century German aesthetics as well as empathy as it is understood in contemporary research in social and developmental psychology on pro-social behaviour, a conception of empathy that, as we will see, invites close comparison with the notion of sympathy in classical moral sense theory. The second class of empathy conceptions privileges cognition over affect and views empathy as an innate human faculty which enables one to be aware of others' inner states. Therapeutic conceptions of empathy, particularly those developed by Heinz Kohut and Carl Rogers, clearly mirror this conception, as does the broad research programme in social cognition theory directed towards examining perspective-taking. Even though the term "empathy" as such is not used in Mead's, Rawls', and Habermas' formulations of the moral point of view, it becomes clear that competency in the exercise of the faculty of vicarious introspection— empathy in the cognitive sense—is, on their views, a precondition of differentiated moral reasoning.

Before proceeding, a caveat. The use of the terms "affective" and "cognitive" to distinguish between the two broad forms of empathy considered here is not entirely felicitous. "Cognitive" classically refers to representational or predicative thinking and is held to stand in contrast with mental states that are "affective" or consisting in emotions or feelings (and, additionally, with "conative" or mental states of desire) (cf., e.g., Dunlop, 1984). The tendency to view cognitive and affective states as somehow strictly dichotomous and mutually opposed rather than being merely analytic categories or, even worse, to assign qualitative priority to either type of mental states as "ways of knowing" (cf., e.g., Alcoff & Potter, 1993; Code, 1991; Jaggar, 1996; Longino, 1991) risks being projected onto the difference between the two forms of empathy to which the cognitive–affective empathy distinction draws attention. This would be an unfortunate misunderstanding. At the very least, empathy understood as affect or feeling as well as emotions generally have a cognitive dimension in virtue of being *intentional*—that is to say, they have object (e.g., a person) who has a certain property or properties (e.g., suffering) understood to be a component of the affective experience (e.g., empathy) (cf., e.g., de Sousa, 1987; van Dam & Steutel, 1996). Hence, empathy understood as an affective response to another person's situation, far from precluding those cognitive processes recruited in order to gain insight into another person's inner states or being a distinct mode of knowing different from cognitive perception, in fact presupposes them. In sum, the contrast between affective and cognitive conceptions of empathy does not point to rival conceptions vying for analytic or normative superiority but intends rather to draw attention to which dimension of a conception of empathy, the affective or the cognitive, seems to be predominant.

2.2   Affective Conceptions of Empathy

2.2.1   *"Einfühlung" in Nineteenth-Century German Aesthetics*

It is generally agreed that the psychology pioneer Edward Titchener introduced the word "empathy" into English (cf. Sherman, 1998; Verducci, 2000; Wispé, 1987). In the course of one of his renowned lectures, published as a compilation in 1909 titled *Experimental psychology in the thought processes*, Titchener refers to the work of the nineteenth-century German psychologist Theodor Lipps, rendering Lipps' term *Einfühlung* (literally "feeling in") as "empathy". Titchener's coinage of "empathy", as Sherman (1998, p. 83) and Wispé (1987, p. 21) note, drew on his knowledge of ancient Greek; Aristotle, for instance, used the term *empatheia* in the *Rhetoric* (1991) to suggest the feeling of being profoundly moved or touched.

   Lipps himself did not coin the term *"Einfühlung"* but rather had purchased it second hand from one of his contemporaries in the field of aesthetics, specifically from the somewhat mystical writings of Robert Vischer on aesthetic experience. Starting from the observation that a typical aesthetic experience somehow involves an artistic medium *expressing* some familiar emotion or feeling—a "joyful" piece of music, a "sombre" painting, the coo of dove as "mournful", and so on—Vischer proposed that aesthetic experience involved the projection of the viewer's emotions onto or into the work of art. Today, this idea might seem platitudinous but the suggestion that aesthetic experience was not purely perceptive but involved a kind of dialectic between perception and projection (and thus a certain blurring of the distinction between the perceiving subject and its object) was at that time groundbreaking (cf. Verducci, 2000, pp. 67–68). This "symbolic interjection of emotions into objective forms" (quoted in Verducci, 2000, p. 67) Vischer labelled "*Einfühlung*". As plausible as Vischer's obviously Kant-inspired basic insight might seem, he still had to explain the fact that it is generally regarded as being pleasant and worth seeking out, since there does not seem to be any *prima facie* reason to suppose that the projection of an emotion into an aesthetic object would be enjoyable in itself. In short, he found the solution to this problem in Romantic metaphysics. Vischer claimed that both the mechanism and the pleasure of aesthetic experience could be accounted for in terms of human beings' innate impulse towards unity and harmony with nature or, in their words, in "nothing other than the pantheistic urge for union with the world" (quoted in Verducci, 2000, p. 68).

Lipps' work on aesthetics appropriated Vischer's idea of a sort of aesthetic unity between the object and subject; like Vischer, Lipps held that the aesthetic object stirs certain feelings in the viewing subject, which are in turn projected back on the object such that they come to be perceived as properties of it (Lipps, 1903/1960; cf. Verducci, 2000, p. 68). However, Lipps rejected Vischer's pantheistic explanation of aesthetic pleasure and spontaneity in favour of the psychoanalytic idea of the ego. Aesthetic projection, he seems to have held, is an unconscious process whereby the imagination enlivens the aesthetic object with its own senses of striving, freedom, and power. Accordingly, aesthetic pleasure is the ego's enjoyment of its self expression. As Lipps put it, the cause of aesthetic enjoyment is "objectified enjoyment of the self" (Lipps, 1903/1960).

Whatever we wish to make of Lipps' now rather quaint-sounding hypothesis concerning the mechanism behind aesthetic enjoyment, the important thing is that "*Einfühlung*" was Lipps' and Vischer's neologism for the unmistakeably modern idea that the meaning of aesthetic objects stems in large part from the imaginative involvement of the subject's feelings with the object, an idea that Lipps quickly extended to the comprehension of the consciousness and experiences of other persons.

2.2.2 Pro-social Behaviour Research: Empathy as Affective Matching

For over 30 years, a research programme exploring connections between empathy and what is broadly labelled positive social behaviour has been apparent in social and developmental psychology. Its leading researchers include Nancy Eisenberg, Daniel Batson, Martin Hoffman, and Mark Davis. A central concern of these psychologist has been to accumulate empirical evidence in support of the claim that empathy amplifies motivation to perform pro-social and altruistic acts (see Eisenberg & Miller, 1987b; Batson, 1991; and Hoffman, 1981, 2000 for reviews) and related issues of whether empathic responding is innate or learned (e.g., Hoffman, 1981,

2000) and which circumstantial factors strengthen correlations between empathy and helping behaviours (e.g., Batson & Coke, 1981).

As Wispé (1986) argues, the term "empathy" in this context is something of a misnomer and the term is in fact used to refer to a constellation of emotional responses to another person's distress that is commonly referred to as "sympathy". Wispé argues that "empathy" should be reserved for a psychological process "whereby one person tries to understand accurately the subjectivity of another person, without prejudice" (1986, p. 320)—in other words, a faculty that will be discussed in §2.3 under the heading of "epistemological conceptions of empathy". By contrast, contemporary social psychology tends to admit a nominal distinction between empathy, sympathy, and possibly other affective states such as compassion and tenderness (cf. Batson et al., 1995) but then treat them all as just variations of the broad affective phenomenon they wish to consider. This constellation of empathic phenomena is then referred to in shorthand as "empathy". For example, in Eisenberg and Miller's 1987 review of empirical research on the association between empathy and helping the authors state that, while both empathy and sympathy are emotional responses somehow causally connected with the perception of another person's emotional state, empathy is characterized by a degree of *affective match* between the observer and the observed. Sympathy, they say, is instead characterized by a certain *congruence* between the feeling of the observer and the observed but without affective match as such. Understood in this sense, empathy is most commonly an experience associated with the enjoyment of narrative arts (cf., e.g., Sherman, 1989, p. 87). We see that circumstances have caused a character to feel frightened, anxious, or joyous and, vicariously placing ourselves in the character's position, we feel those emotions too. This conception of empathy as affective matching is evocatively captured in Titchener's 1915 definition:

> We have a natural tendency to feel ourselves into what we perceive or imagine. As we read about the forest, we may, as it were, become the explorer; we feel for ourselves the gloom, the silence, the humidity, the oppression, the sense of lurking danger; everything is strange, but it is to us that strange experience has come. [...] This tendency to feel oneself into a situation is called EMPATHY. (Quoted in Wispé, 1987, p. 22)

In opposition to this kind of affective matching experienced by an empathizer—feeling roughly *the same way* that the object of empathy feels—a sympathizer, for his or her part, characteristically has emotions that are quite different from the emotional state of the observed. A case, say, where one reacts with indignation or sadness on hearing from a despondent friend that she has been unfairly dismissed from her job is according to this distinction an instance of sympathy not empathy because of the lack of affective matching: you feel indignant but your friend feels despondent (cf. Eisenberg & Strayer, 1987; Sober & Wilson, 1998). Because of the centrality of affective matching in empathy on Eisenberg and Miller's definition, the range of feelings of the empathizer may have has no limits; one may with as much coherence empathize with another's feelings of pride at another person's success or grief at another's loss. Sympathy, even in ordinary language, refers more narrowly to, in Eisenberg and Miller's words, "feelings of sorrow or concern for another's welfare" (1987a, p. 92; cf. Wispé, 1986; Nagel, 1970).

Despite this distinction in principle between empathy and sympathy, owing to the fact that the kind of helping behaviour that empathy research is interested in studying typically involves the relief of discomfort, danger, and other forms of distress, sympathy and negative empathy are treated as a single phenomenon. In order to allow for this conceptual range, Hoffman in more technical moments refers to "empathic distress", which he defines broadly as "the involvement of psychological processes that make a person have feelings that are more congruent with another's situation than with his own situation" connected with perceptions of others in states of "discomfort, pain, danger, or some other type of distress" (Hoffman, 2000, p. 30). But most frequently Hoffman, like his colleagues, refers to this constellation of feelings simply as "empathy".

When systematic inquiries, in psychology or elsewhere, borrow words from ordinary language in order to label key concepts, these words almost invariably take on ostensive definitions. Such shifts in meaning, as is well known, are typically a response to the need for clarity around the research question's central construct and in order to minimize variables for the sake of a study's manageability. The restricted coverage of "empathy" to feelings related to another's distress is less a limitation of the empirical study of positive social behaviour than it is a function of it.[1] And nor, it seems, is the fact that "empathy" is defined in helping behaviour research without reference to connation. Intuitively, of course, empathy understood as sympathy in the non-technical sense is not simply affective distress at another person's predicament; such distress seems analytically inseparable from a wish or desire to relieve it. Sympathy, in Wispé's (1986) words, seems best understood as not just awareness of another person's distress, but it is a kind of affective involvement "in the suffering of another person as *something to be relieved*" (p. 318, emphasis added). Nagel (1970) reached similar conclusions about sympathy and this feature of empathy is what Code (1994) has aptly referred to as empathy's "project directedness" (p. 83). Clearly, if pro-social and helping behaviour research were to adopt a definition of empathy, according to which it supposes a conative element, it would make a little point in their research, for the central question of whether empathy amplifies desire to help those in need would clearly be begged.

2.2.3 Empathy in Moral Sense Theory: "Changing Places in Fancy with the Sufferer"

The notion that sympathy plays a central role in motivating altruistic or moral acts is an important undercurrent of the school of moral sense theory which goes back, in the Anglo-Saxon philosophical tradition, to at least Shaftesbury

---

[1] Olinck (1984) offers less generous but possibly more accurate assessment of this situation, claiming that "empathy" is merely a buzz word that psychologists prefer over "sympathy" and "compassion" for its perceived air of erudition.

(1711/1999). And so at this juncture a comparison between the notion of empathy as conceived by contemporary empathy research in psychology and its analogue in the philosophical tradition of moral sense theory would seem both inevitable and illuminating.

There is little doubt that particularly in the hands of Adam Smith, widely considered to have developed one of the most elaborate expressions of moral sense theory in his 1759 *Theory of moral sentiments*, "sympathy" has all the hallmarks of "empathy" as conceived of in empathy research in contemporary psychology. In both cases, the phenomenon is identified as a spontaneous affective or emotional disturbance which (1) may or may not involve affective matching, (2) is caused, typically but not exclusively, by the direct perception of another person in distress, and (3) issues in feelings of solidarity or as Smith put it "fellow-feelings". He writes,

> The word sympathy, in its most proper and primitive signification, denotes our fellow-feeling with the suffering and not that with the enjoyments of others (43). ... That this is the source of our fellow-feeling for the misery of others, that is by changing places in fancy with the sufferer, that we come either to conceive or to be affected by what he feels, may be demonstrated by many obvious observations, if it should not be thought sufficiently evident of itself (10). ... [But] neither is it those circumstances only, which create pain or sorrow, that call forth our fellow-feeling. Whatever is the passion which arises from any object in the person principally concerned, an analogous emotion springs up, at the thought of the situation, in the breast of every attentive spectator (10).

Unlike the broad swathe of contemporary empathy research, however, Smith's interest in empathy was thoroughgoingly critical. Smith's critical starting point, a starting point shared by all moral sense theorists—Smith's contemporaries Hutcheson (1729/2003), Shaftesbury (1711/1999), and Hume (1751/1957) as well as the more recent avatars Scheler (1954), Blum (1980a), Vetlesen (1994), and arguably Hoffman (2000)—was the general suspicion that rationalist moral theory is severely limited in its ability to explain the normative validity of moral rules or principles, or what is sometimes referred to as their "bindingness" (cf. Darwall, 1995). Of course, scepticism regarding rationalism in ethics is not unique to moral sense theory; the position in Anglo-Saxon meta-ethics known as "externalism", the communitarian orientation in contemporary social and political theory as well as the current movement in normative ethics known as virtue ethics can all be considered as having similar critical underpinning.[2] What seems to be unique to moral sense theory is the proposal that such moral concepts arise from a universal human capacity for sympathy. The opening lines of the Smith's *Theory of moral sentiments* read, "How selfish soever man may be supposed, there are evidently some principles in his nature, which interest him in the fortune of others, and render their happiness necessary to him, though he derives nothing from it, except the pleasure of seeing it. ... The greatest ruffian, the most hardened violator of the laws of society, is not altogether without it" (p. 9). And Smith goes on in the same work to build an elaborate defence of sympathetic foundationalism in ethics. Anticipating Smith,

---

[2] For similar assessments, see Smith (1994) on externalism, O'Neill (1996) on communitarianism, and Crisp and Slote (1997) on virtue ethics.

Hume came around to the position, really only suggested at the end of his *Treatise of human nature* (1751/1957), that sympathy seemed to be a precondition of a human being's ability to recognize what he labelled the "artificial virtues" (pp. 574–578) and stated boldly if sketchily that "we have no extensive concern for society but from sympathy" (p. 579).

As Smith's statement that even the "greatest ruffian" is not without sympathy makes plain the contingent fact that sometimes some people have feelings of solidarity in sympathy with others, and act on those feelings, is hardly stable ground for moral theory. What Smith meant by "sympathy" of course was *also* that people have a capacity for or a faculty of sympathy—a "moral sense" analogous to sight or hearing—that, when functioning correctly, issues in the moral sentiments associated with sympathy understood in the *other* sense as an affective perception. For Smith, the principal mechanism of this largely involuntary and cognitive faculty is the vicarious consideration of another's perspective, what is now usually referred to as the process of role-taking and what Smith refers to in the passage quoted above as the imaginative act of "changing places in fancy with the sufferer". The postulation of such a moral sense allows Smith (and moral sense theory more generally) to close the gap between the contingency of moral sentiments and the normativity of moral judgement—that is, the idea that moral judgements are applicable and are binding independently of any affective attachments a moral agent might have with regards to the object of a particular moral judgement or the action it prescribes. Very roughly, if the proper exercise of the faculty of sympathy and the feelings associated with it have intrinsic moral worth, a point Smith took pains to support, it can legitimately claimed that anyone failing to have such feelings morally *should* do (cf. Raphael, 1976; Sherman 1998).

Returning now to contemporary psychology, unlike moral sense theory, empathy research has, with again the exception of Hoffman, little direct interest in the conceptual grounds of morality and at most a secondary interest even in morality in a strict sense as such. Adopting a sociobiological framework that is not always made explicit (cf. Hoffman, esp. 1981, 1994; Batson, 1991), empathy research submits to empirical scrutiny the observation that the range of feelings and thoughts referred to as "empathy" seems to correlate positively with self-sacrificing, cooperative, and helpful behaviours, the kinds of behaviours that are thought important for or even a sine qua non of collective enterprise (and hence of the recognized productive efficiency and material advantage associated with efficient cooperation) and of harmonious interpersonal relations (and hence of strong interpersonal cohesiveness). Seen from this angle, the system of behaviours, feelings, and beliefs corresponding to "morality" would seem to be best considered an interesting subset or possibly special case of the broader class of helping behaviours. Eisenberg and Miller (1987a), for instance, distinguish between pro-social behaviour, which in their definition is "voluntary, intentional behaviour that results in benefits for another; the motive is unspecified and may be positive, negative or both" and "altruistic behaviour", "a subtype of pro-social behaviour—as voluntary behaviour intended to benefit another, which is not performed with the expectation of receiving external rewards or avoiding externally produced aversive stimuli or punishments"

(p. 92). They mention morality only in connection with the remark that, unlike philosophers, psychologists tend to be concerned with the role of empathy in such behaviours and tend to disregard the particular moral status of such behaviours either generically or on a case-by-case basis.

And why shouldn't they? Given the complexity of practical judgement, any attempt to frame a category of "moral behaviours" for the purposes of empirical study seems bound to be endlessly controversial. Still, and as an aside, it would seem to be a mistake to conclude on the grounds that empathy research in social psychology is not directly concerned with the moral domain that it is not relevant to the normative dimension of ethics. For one thing, from the point of view of so-called internalist views of moral judgement that tend to consider a lack of moral motivation as being principally a failure of practical rationality (cf. Smith, 1994), confirmation of the received idea that empathy indeed does contribute to helping behaviours raises very concretely the possibility that empathic feelings contribute to consistency between an agent's moral judgements and his or her actions (cf. discussion in Doris & Stich, 2003). Further, given the close conceptual relation between altruism as defined in empathy research (cf. Eisenberg & Miller's 1987a definition above) and the idea that a moral intention is, among other things, an intention that is necessarily focused on others, rather than self-directed, from the point of view of moral socialization and education, it is not at all beside the point to know something about whether empathic responding is innate or learned (e.g., Hoffman, 1981, 2000) and which circumstantial factors strengthen correlations between empathy and helping behaviours (e.g., Batson & Coke, 1981). Indeed, one can with confidence speculate that it is precisely because empathy research seems to have implications for conceptions of morality and moral education that psychologists are drawn to the empirical study of empathy in the first place.

2.3 Cognitive Conceptions of Empathy

2.3.1 Social Cognition Theory: Perspective-Taking, Social Referencing, and Empathic Accuracy

To call forth a concept, as Wispé reminds us in the subtitle of his 1986 paper, a word is needed and in light of the state of confusion pertaining in regards to "sympathy" and "empathy" in psychology—a state of affairs that he ably exposes—he argues that a great deal of this confusion would be cleared up should "sympathy" be reserved to refer to the phenomenon of responding to another's suffering with feelings of compassion and a desire to help. His delineation of "empathy" by contrast captures the introspective, objective, and often effortful process of attempting to understand other people's thoughts and emotions. In these terms, sympathy is relational and affective; it is an experience of openness "to the immediate reality of another's subjective experience" (Wispé, 1986, p. 318). Empathy is rather a vehicle for understanding or knowing what others think. As such, its "most important problem", as Wispé puts it, is "empathic accuracy" (p. 318): the problem of whether one's judgements about another's inner experiences are correct. Though unquestionably attractive, his plea that future research be oriented in relation to the distinction between empathy and sympathy, as he sees it, strikes one as being something of a solution in search of a problem, a situation that demonstrates the persisting validity of his own thesis that there is, to say the least, little consistency in the use of the word "empathy" in psychology (as elsewhere). As we have already seen, contemporary empathy research indeed studies *exactly* questions surrounding what he terms "sympathy". For its part, questions concerning Wispé's "empathy" have, for over 30 years, been studied as a branch of contemporary psychology known as social cognition theory.

In contemporary psychology "social cognition" seems to be an umbrella term for research interest in the cognitive processes involved in social interaction, how people understand themselves and others, and interactions with others in social contexts broadly construed; using the tools and based on the assumptions of cognitive psychology, it currently dominates as the approach and model in social psychology (cf. Sternberg, 1994). Naturally, one particular issue in social cognition theory is that of how people come to accurately (and inaccurately) infer other people's feelings, intentions, and thoughts. This problem, process, faculty, or competence has gone under the name of "perspective-taking" or "role-taking" (see, e.g., Schantz, 1975; Selman, 1980; Flavell, 1992) and, its latest avatars, "mental simulation" (Gordon, 1996) and "empathic accuracy" (Ickes, 1997). The latter term, despite the fact that it refers to the *aim* of the process under study rather than the process itself, is the most, if you will, accurate of the three on the grounds that the others could be interpreted as begging the question of the psychological mechanisms by which people acquire information about others' internal states—that is, by "taking their perspective" in one's imagination.

For it is far from being obvious that comprehension of other people's thoughts and feelings is primarily mediated by imagining oneself in another's position. Indeed, cases of believing simply *that* a person is having a certain thought or feeling are quite obviously not. The judgement, for instance, that "Maria thinks she will win the match" is surely better understood as being inferred from visual and contextual cues rather than from imagining oneself in Maria's situation. That said, *understanding* Maria's thought of winning the match and *sharing* some of the feelings that often supervene in such circumstances are far more plausible candidates for psychological events mediated by some kind of vicarious involvement. The pervasive view in social psychology that individuals seek knowledge about others' inner states by imagining themselves into the other's place is, according to Higgins (1981) and Davis (1994), a bias that is traceable back to Piaget's foundational work in developmental psychology on visual perspective-taking (e.g., Piaget, 1955; cf. Eisenberg et al., 1997, p. 75). Be that as it may, there is no doubt that cognitive and affective perspective-taking have received overwhelmingly more systematic attention in social psychological research than have other pathways to other-directed introspection.

According to Flavell's (1992) analysis, the ability to comprehend others' emotions or mental representations presupposes four knowledge components or competencies: (1) that mental states *exist* (what he calls "existence"); (2) that some situations *call for* knowledge of other's mental states ("need"); (3) the competency to *obtain* such knowledge ("inference"); and, (4) the competency to appropriately *use* inference skills ("application") (cf. Eisenberg et al., 1997, p. 74). The bulk of research in social cognition focuses on the existence and inference components even though, as Eisenberg et al. (1997) point out, the others are by no means of secondary interest (p. 74). Most important, however, is the observation that in addition to perspective-taking, the inference and application components of empathic accuracy may involve other processes such as those that would seem to fall under Higgins' (1981) idea of "social reference". As Higgins (1981) contends, a judger's beliefs about the motives, attitudes, and responses of a "target person" are sometimes generated by way of a process in which the judger first places the target person into either a known category of persons or compares the target person with a person she knows well (i.e., a parent or friend)— what Higgins (1981) calls a "salient individual"—and then assumes that the target person's motives, attitudes, and responses and so on will be the same or very similar to the known social group or individual (see Higgins, 1981, esp. pp. 139–141). Another process discussed by Karniol (1982, 1995) involves a parallel process wherein only the central reference is made to familiar and, hence, predictable narrative patterns or social scripts rather than to specific social categories or salient others.

An interesting corollary of this "mixed economy" view of empathic accuracy is that we might expect, as Higgins (1981) implies, that part of the application component is to decide which of these various inference strategies—perspective-taking, social referencing, or some other process—is called for or is best adapted to particular situations. For instance, comprehending a friend's thoughts and feelings while in the throes of romantic love might best be achieved by drawing on memories of one's own past experience of being in the throes of romantic love oneself rather than attempting to imaginatively adopt the friend's perspective. Comprehending the feelings of a person in completely unfamiliar or unlikely situations—being the last person alive on Earth or winning at Wimbledon will stand as examples—would seem far more likely to demand the prioritization of imagination rather than memory retrieval. In any case, if one accepts that mental simulation is just one of a range of cognitive processes that aims to achieve empathic accuracy, social cognition research can be credited with providing a conception of empathy (understood as a type of social cognition of others' inner states) according to which it is possible to experience empathy without "empathizing" (understood as a process of *vicarious* introspection): a conception, in other words, of the a cognitive process by which people come to have information about others' inner states that does not necessarily entail imagining themselves in another's place.

2.3.2 Formalist Ethics and Empathy: Mead, Rawls, and Habermas, and the Moral Point of View

As noted above, moral sense theory characteristically assigns empathy *in the affective sense* a central place in moral life and moral deliberation: feelings of empathy, understood as being underwritten by a natural sense of concern for others and the ability to perceive threats to others' weal and woe, help to explain both the validity of moral principles in terms of rules or norms that promote human well-being and also why people are motivated to act in accordance with moral principles—namely, to promote others' well-being and avoid harm. Because such feelings presuppose a capacity for insight into others' inner states, it should come as no surprise that empathy in the perceptive sense is a staple of traditional thinking about moral justification. The so-called Golden Rule's exhortation to consider whether one would accept to be treated in the same way that one proposes to treat another is nothing other than a test of the moral validity of particular acts that centralizes perspective-taking. In the same vein, what the formalist ethics of Mead, Rawls, and Habermas all have in common is that they provide a principle of justification—that is, one that is meant to discriminate between legitimate and illegitimate norms in terms of their impartiality or fairness—that explicitly (albeit at times in subtle ways) invokes perspective-taking (cf. Habermas, 1990c, pp. 197–198). According to Mead's notion of ideal role-taking (cf. 1943) norms or plans of action are justified from a moral point of view only if they can pass the test of being accepted by all those affected; the moral judgement, therefore, is principally concerned with vicariously putting oneself in the position of those affected by an action proposal (cf. Joas, 1985, p. 121ff.). Similarly, Rawls proposes that valid social policies are those that would survive assessment from the "original position": an abstract and idealized judgement situation in which the rational judge is ignorant of how he or she would stand to benefit or loose out if the policy were adopted (i.e., of her "social position") (cf. Rawls, 1971, pp. 118–192). For its part, Habermas' combined principles of discourse (D) and universalization (U) provide a similar test for the validity of norms. Taken together, they state roughly that only those norms are morally valid that could be met with approval in an ideal discourse situation involving the fair participation of all those potentially affected by the norm being accepted (Habermas, 1984, 1987, 1990a, 1990b, 1993b). Both Rawls and Habermas state explicitly that their conceptualizations of the moral point of view are consistent with Kohlberg's (cf., e.g., 1978) empirically grounded analysis that development towards the highest levels of moral reasoning coincide with improved competency in perspective-taking (cf. Rawls, 1971, pp. 461–462; Habermas, 1990b, pp. 119–133). According to Kohlberg's schema, the progress from the pre-moral through to the conventional and the post-conventional levels of cognitive moral development is underlain by a progressive shift from an egocentric or first-person perspective (punishment and reward, approval and disapproval) to one which is able to coordinate and assess the validity of diverse perspectives, a process labelled "de-centration" in good piagetan tradition.

2.3.3 Kohut, Rogers, and Psychotherapy: Empathy as Vicarious Introspection

The conception of empathy assumed by contemporary empathy research and moral sense theory captures one important dimension of ordinary intuitions about empathy: people seem universally endowed with a capacity to engage in a processes of vicarious identification with others and that when such imaginative attention is directed towards the suffering of others it typically and spontaneously gives rise to feelings of sympathy, solidarity, and a desire to help. From this perspective, empathy's potential worth as a moral motivator, if not somehow as a precondition of moral judgement itself, seems obvious if complex (cf. Maxwell & Reichenbach, 2007). However, this conceptualization of empathy fails to capture another important normative dimension of empathy, namely, empathy viewed as a moral excellence related to caring or responding to others. In Sherman's (1998, p. 86) words:

> To be a good listener, to be caring, to communicate not just through action but also through affect are part of our contemporary culture. We expect political candidates to be not just policy wonks but to be caring; doctors to know medicine, but also to express an interest in their patients and understand something of their patients' fears and anxieties in facing illness; good parenting to involve the transmission of values and skills, but as importantly, to show a concrete engagement in a child's interests and feelings. Empathy seems part of our new age sensitivity.

One may disagree with Sherman's assessment that empathy as a component of caring is anything particularly new. Indeed, it is hard to imagine a world in which something akin to empathic responsiveness as she characterizes it is not desirable in caregiving. As Sherman points out herself (1998, p. 91), Smith (1759/1976), hardly classifiable as a new-age thinker, seemed to have had an appreciation for this dimension of empathy. Further, a stance of mutual empathy for the sake of promoting self-understanding and awareness is central to Aristotle's (4th Century B.C.E./1995) conception of mature friendship (cf. Books 8 and 9).

What does seem attractive in Sherman's analysis, though, is her claim that the popular contemporary conception that empathy is a social or moral excellence is strongly informed by the psychoanalytic intellectual tradition of the twentieth century. The new normative grounding that psychoanalysis provided for the capacity to understand and be compassionate with others as an aspect of caring, she suggests, is connected with the assumption that there exists some kind of basic universal human need to be understood and to be recognized by others—a need, in other words, to be *empathized with*. If empathy is inherently therapeutic both clinically as well as in an informal social sense it is because it fills this need. Sherman (1998) tells us that Freud's (1953–1975) mention of Lipps' (1903/1960) notion of *Einfühlung* is limited to a few scattered remarks about group psychology and humour but that his followers Theodore Reik (1948/1983) and Robert Fliess (see Sharma, 1992) elaborated further on the idea and anticipated a larger role for empathy in the therapeutic process (cf. Verducci, 2000, p. 71–73). It was not, however, until Heinz Kohut, founder of "self-psychology", and Carl Rogers, founder of "client-centred therapy", did empathy come to be seen as *the* central competency of the effective psychotherapist. Interest in "talking cures" has lost ground in recent years to pharmaceutical intervention in emotional disturbances, but the influence of psychoanalysis over the popular psychological discourse among the educated classes was for decades during the twentieth century more than considerable; arguably it was through the influence of these two towering figures of psychotherapy that the importance of empathy as a dimension of human relationships found new support in an interpretation of empathy as being an integral support to personal psychological well-being and health.

From the point of view of psychoanalytic theory and practice, Kohut's major contribution was to strongly challenge the earlier Freudian orthodoxy that the Oedipal conflict is central to human motivation and psychological pathology (Wolf, 2000). Working clinically early in his career with a particular subgroup of patients diagnosed as "narcissistically vulnerable", or as having a fragile or disturbed sense of self, Kohut developed the hypothesis that such disturbances were connected with insufficiency of relationships with others that provide experiences necessary for the development, achievement, and maintenance of a strong and cohesive self, what Kohut called "selfobject experiences" (Lang, 1994; Wolf, 2000). Further study of the idea, which grew out of, and was initially intended to complement, classical Freudian theory, led to its extension; Kohut and many like-minded psychoanalysts came to view Kohutian psychoanalysis as superseding classical formulations (Lang, 1994). On a more popular level, Kohut is known as challenging the early psychoanalytic view of the cold and aloof therapist (Sherman, 1998), a reputation which was based on his identification of empathy as the psychoanalyst's definitive faculty, skill, and tool (Lang, 1994). By engaging in a process that he referred to variously as "vicarious introspection", "thinking oneself into another's place" and imagining the experience of another "as if it were our own" (Kohut, 1959; cf. Wispé, 1987), Kohut believed that experiences, feelings, and memories otherwise left obscured using traditional methods became available to the therapist for analysis and interpretation (cf. Lang, 1994, pp. 102–103). In this sense, empathy was for Kohut, the "mode of cognition specifically attuned to the perception of complex psychological configurations" (cf. Kohut, 1971, p. 300, 1980, p. 485; quoted in Wispé, 1987, p. 30) that are the object of clinical analysis (cf. Lang, 1994).

In order to avoid an easy misconception of Kohut's understanding of empathy it is important to underscore, as Kohut did himself repeatedly in his writings, that there is nothing inherently therapeutic about empathy. Similarly, while empathy may be at most a precondition of sympathy and compassion, it is by no means their equivalent. Like the moral sense theorists, Kohut viewed empathy as common human faculty of perception on par with the senses. But unlike the senses which are designed for "extro-spection", experiencing the outer world, empathy is "intro-spective" in that it is directed towards others' inner worlds. Except for its introspective orientation, empathy is for all intents and purposes much the same as the five recognized senses: "the empathic understanding of the experience of other human beings", Kohut wrote, "is as basic an endowment as his vision, hearing, touch, taste and smell" (Kohut, 1977, p. 144; quoted in Wispé, 1987, p. 30). Because of the intangibility of its object, empathy, far more so than the extro-spective faculties, is fallible and empathic competency profits from training, practice, and exercise. Finally, because empathy is simply the faculty that enables human beings to find out about the inner experiences, it is quite a glaring mistake to suppose that empathy would necessarily give rise to feelings of solidarity, compassion, or sympathy. To illustrate the point, Kohut referred more than once in his œuvre to the use of howling sirens during air raids on civilian populations during the Second World War, an example which illustrates how planners' accurate use of empathy enabled them to find a way to add further terror to the experience of being bombed (cf. Wispé, 1986, p. 319). More mundane examples are those of are charming sociopaths, certain used-car salesmen, and other con men who, on perceiving others' suffering, far from having feelings of solidarity and sympathy well up inside them, use their perspicacity to others' disadvantage (cf. Lang, 1994). In sum, according to Kohut, empathy is first and foremost an "information-gathering activity". He writes:

> Empathy is a value-neutral mode of observation; a mode of observation attuned to the inner life of man, just as extro-spection is a mode of observation attuned to the external world, [...] a mental activity, whether employed in every day life, or in scientific pursuits. [...] As an information-gathering activity, empathy, as I have stressed many times [...], can be right or wrong, in the service of compassion or hostility, pursued slowly and ploddingly or "intuitively", that is, at great speed. In this sense empathy is never by itself supportive or therapeutic. It is, however, a precondition to being successfully supportive and therapeutic. (Kohut, 1984, pp. 84–85; quoted in Lang, 1994, p. 103)

Despite Kohut's insistence on the objectivity of empathy, there was apparently a certain tension with regards to the therapeutic value of empathy built into his system. As Lang (1994) notes, critics and followers alike pointed out that one dimension of healthy "selfobject experiences" seemed to be support and empathy. Under pressure he eventually came to the reluctant admission that "empathy per se, the mere presence of empathy, has also a beneficial, in a broad sense, therapeutic effect—both in the clinical setting and in human life, in general" (Kohut, 1984, p. 85; quoted in Lang, 1994, p. 104). But Kohut never went as far as Rogers in claiming that it is the therapist's empathy that can provide the reparative support needed to heal the damaged self.

The approach to therapy known as "client-centered" and founded by Carl Rogers beginning in the 1950s can arguably be seen as being framed by two core assumptions. First, human beings have a natural propensity towards "self-actualization", a condition that can be understood for present purposes as equivalent to psychological well-being or health. Second, the natural process of growth or development towards this state is thwarted by involvement in social relations, especially in childhood, that encourage feelings of self-depreciation or self-devaluation (cf. Shaffer, 1978). The role of Rogerian therapy, in essence, is to provide an atmosphere which enables the client to himself or herself remove the obstacles to the process of growth towards self-actualization (Rogers, 1977). This "growth-promoting climate" is characterized by three dispositions or attitudes on the part of the therapist: (1) congruence or genuineness; (2) unconditional positive regard for the client or "always being on the client's side"; and (3) empathy (Rogers, 1959, 1961).

Rogers described empathy as "one of the most potent factors" in the therapeutic situation (Rogers, 1975, p. 3; quoted in Wispé, 1987, p. 28). His 1975 description of it is deservedly oft cited. Empathy, Rogers said, means

> entering the private perceptual world of the other and becoming thoroughly at home in it. It involves being sensitive [...] to the changing felt meanings which flow in this other person. [...] It means temporarily living in his/her life, moving about in it delicately without

making judgement, sensing meanings of which he/she is scarcely aware. [...] It includes communicating your sensings of his/her world as you look with fresh and unfrightened eyes at elements of which the individual is fearful. It means frequently checking with him/her as to the accuracy of your sensings, and being guided by the responses you receive. [...] To be with another in this way means that for the time being you lay aside the views and values you hold for yourself in order to enter another world without prejudice. (Rogers, 1975, p. 4; quoted in Sherman, 1998, p. 92; Wispé, 1987, p. 28; Verducci, 2000, p. 76)

Taken as a *definition* of "empathy", this could be taken as a textbook example of the irrational technique of persuasion known in critical thinking circles as "persuasive redefinition" (cf., e.g., Hughes, 2000, pp. 276–278). However, it is not a *description* of empathy as much it is a rather impressionistic *prescription* aimed at clinicians and with regards to what it means to adopt an attitude of empathy in the process of therapy. Understood as simply "a term to convey that particular attitude of non-judgementally entering into another's perceptual world [...] regarded as important in psychotherapy" (p. 29), "empathy" is an apt choice, as Wispé (1987) indeed observes. In this sense it is very closely related to Titchener's early 1915 definition, cited above, in which empathy is conceived as "feeling oneself into a situation". In another respect, however, Rogers' conception of empathy departs from both Titchener's definition and the definition supposed by empathy research in social psychology. Empathic engagement, Rogers insists, implies that the therapist under-stands the client's emotions. But the therapist should not for all that *experience* those emotions himself or herself. "The counsellor", Rogers writes, "is perceiving the hates and hopes and fears of the client through immersion in an empathic process, but without himself, as counsellor, experiencing those hates and hopes and fears" (Rogers, 1951, p. 29; quoted in Sherman, p. 93). To use the term from contemporary pro-social behaviour research, in client-centred therapy empathy not only falls short of involving affective matching but therapists are advised to avoid emotional identification with their clients' feelings as well. Rogerian empathy departs quite dramatically from Kohutian empathy too in the sense that it is less the therapist's tool of observation than it is a particular therapeutic style or mode of communication. Empathy informs the attitudinal tenor of the therapist's remarks. Most importantly, perhaps, an empathic stance frames role in the therapeutic process of "mirroring" wherein the therapist, attuned to what the client is "ready to hear", relays the clients' thoughts and feelings back to him or her in his or her own language and elicits feedback from the client vis-à-vis the accuracy of the therapist's interpretation (cf. Rogers, 1951; Ogden, 1996; Dunn, 1995; and Sherman, 1998).

Rogers' influence not just on counselling and psychology but education and the social sciences more generally, though subtle and today often forgotten, was phenom-enal in both senses of the word. His work seemed at once to articulate, reflect, and provide a language for the Romantic revival of the second half of the twentieth century. Rogers' ideas about empathy have undoubtedly filtered down into popular conscious-ness (cf. Sherman, 1998). But whether or not Rogers' influence had anything to do with it, what is certain is that it is now scarcely possible, barring the most stipulative of definitions, to describe a person's use of insight into another's inner life for harmful, deceitful, or otherwise malicious ends as "empathic". This, surely, is what makes

Kohut's conception of empathy as a "value-neutral" mode of introspection so vulnerable to misunderstanding, and accounts for Lang's (1994) reports of hostile reaction to her attempts to defend a Kohutian conception of empathy as the most useful one in the context of clinical ethics in medicine. It also helps to explain why Wispé's (1986) otherwise sensible proposal that the research programme in pro-social and helping behaviour in social psychology use "empathy" to refer exclusively to the predominantly cognitive faculty of other-directed insight and "compassion" or "sympathy" to refer exclusively to distressed responses to insight into another's aversive state had to fail. In ordinary language the notion of an "empathic knave" *is* a contradiction in terms because empathy even understood as a faculty of introspection is aimed at understanding and comprehension for the sake of providing support and expressing solidarity. One could call skill in gathering information about other people's inner states "insight", "acumen", or even "perspicacity" but "empathy" rings false.

2.4   Summary and Discussion

The term "empathy" emerged as a term of art in the field of aesthetics in the late nineteenth century and analogous concepts—primarily sympathy, perspective-taking, and role-taking—which make reference to empathy's core idea of vicariously sharing another's experience have recurrently been considered important in understanding moral appraisal and moral judgement. The treatment of empathy as an explicit theoretical construct, however, is almost exclusive to psychology and in particular social, developmental, and counselling psychology. But even here, the basic divide between empathy conceived of in predominantly affective terms, as opposed to the view of empathy as being predominantly a cognitive phenomenon, is clearly perceptible. In contemporary research on pro-social and helping behaviour in social and developmental psychology, "empathy" is meant to capture distressing *feelings* in response to other people's suffering. In social cognition theory, by contrast, "empathy" refers to a grab bag of psychological processes, faculties, and competencies which have in common only that they are instrumental in the way that people gain *insight into* others' thoughts, feelings, and beliefs. Similarly, in Rogerian and Kohutian conceptions of counselling therapy, empathy is singled out as the psychotherapist's core competency precisely because it is through empathy that the therapist becomes acquainted with the intricate workings of his client's inner world. The distinction between cognitive and affective conceptions of empathy, however, should not distract one from the fact that affective empathy and cognitive empathy are not wholly discrete. The operation of the latter is a precondition of experiencing the former in that one can hardly have aversive feelings *about* other people's suffering unless one is first aware that they *are* suffering. This conceptual overlap occurring, as it does, in an aggravating linguistic environment where empathy in both its cognitive and the affective senses have multiple synonyms, helps to explain why this basic distinction is only occasionally explicitly recognized even in specialist literatures. Involvement in another person's suffering as something to be alleviated is referred to in both ordinary language and in the philosophical literature as "sympathy" and "compassion". Most empirical research on pro-social and helping behaviour and altruism refers to their focal construct as "empathy" but Hoffman often employs the term "empathic distress". For its part, insight into other's states without an affective component—Kohut's "other-directed introspection"—is referred to variously as "mental simulation", "empathic accuracy", "social perspective-taking", or simply "perspective-taking" as well as "role-taking". When it comes to "empathy", the waters of terminological confusion run deep indeed (see Fig. 2.1).

These observations about the meaning of "empathy" would seem to suggest strongly that, if it is clarity that one is after, the use of "empathy" calls for careful stipulation. The formulation is over-used but we have here one case where it truly fits: what "empathy" means depends on what one means by "empathy". In this light, and returning to this study's original question of whether "empathy" is an appropriate term to capture the idea of imaginative sensitivity to others' well-being regarded as being integral to moral functioning, it might seem to go without saying that the adoption of an alternative might be well advised, should a suitable candidate be available. Indeed, as luck would have it, and as a moment spent with any dictionary will confirm, English is comfortably furnished with not one but two words, "sympathy" and "compassion", both of which express much of what is intended. Why, then, not use one of them instead? The decision calls for delicate semantic judgement but there are good reasons to believe that neither term would be preferable to "empathy", at least in the present context and without modification.

The disadvantages of "empathy" have already been suggested and will not be belaboured. The sort of moral responsiveness to others' well-being in question falls under the rubric of affective conceptions of empathy but "empathy" *tout court* is at permanent risk of being conflated with "empathy" in the cognitive sense. To make matters worse, some commentators, as we have seen, refuse even to acknowledge the affective

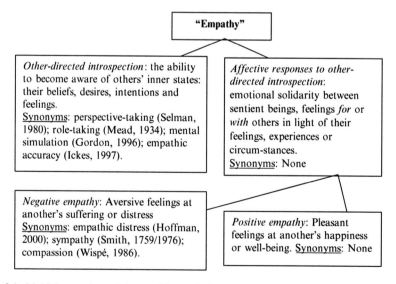

Fig. 2.1 Multiple meanings of the word "empathy"

sense of empathy and suggest that it is nothing other than a *misnomer* to regard "empathy" as synonymous with "sympathy" and "compassion" (cf. Wispé, 1986; Cole, 1994; Kohut, 1959). "Empathy", however, has decisive advantage of carrying highly pertinent connotations that both "sympathy" and "compassion" lack. Well aware that this argument takes us out onto the thin ice of subtle linguistic associations, which are susceptible to variance from person to person, "empathy", first, *clearly* connotes imaginative involvement. It is, of course, *possible* for imaginative involvement to mediate feelings of sympathy or compassion but it seems more typical to refer to reactive and unreflective responses to situations whose injurious features require no great psychological acumen to appreciate—a poor wretch on the gallows, a young woman dying of disease, a victim of crushing poverty or gross physical injury, and the like—as instances of compassion and sympathy. The word "empathy", however, seems to suggest a response to situations whose aversive features are more subtle, imperceptible, ambiguous, complex, and therefore requiring skills of discernment and possibly imaginative dwelling in order to perceive and appreciate—precisely the sorts of harms and injustices that are, of course, typically at stake in moral *problems*. Perhaps it is this difference between sympathy and compassion, on one hand, and empathy, on the other—the difference being that empathy is a *skilled* response while compassion and sympathy are *reactive* responses—which accounts for why the idea of developing, educating, or cultivating empathy makes a fair bit of intuitive sense, whereas the idea of developing, educating, or cultivating sympathy and compassion has a comparatively odd ring to it. As Wispé (1986) put it—correctly I think—in connection with becoming sympathetic, compassionate, or empathic, the problem for sympathy is "how does one open oneself to the immediate reality of another's subjective experiences?" (p. 318). The problem for empathy (by which he means cognitive empathy in no uncertain terms) is how to correctly appraise another's situation, of "empathic accuracy" in his wording (Wispé, 1986, p. 318). But, it seems, the capacities of moral sensitivity which are of present concern involve *both* "opening oneself" to others' subjective experiences *and getting judgements about other's subjective experiences right.* A term of art, then, is proposed: "compassionate empathy"—"empathy" in order to capitalize on the word's reflective and imaginative connotations. The modifier "compassionate" has a double advantage in that its use minimizes the risk of confusing the construct with the perceptive faculty of other-directed introspection and makes the fact that we are concerned with empathy in the "negative" sense (i.e., feeling distress in solidarity with or for a person in a situation of adversity) but not empathy in its "positive" sense (i.e., pleasant feelings with or for another's happiness or well-being) unmistakeable.[3]

---

[3] One may raise the point that two viable alternatives have been overlooked: "moral perception" and "moral sensitivity". Both these terms are unattractive in the present context. "Moral perception" simply lacks the required affective connotations. In another world, "moral sensitivity" might be the ideal choice but unfortunately it is already widely used in moral psychology and has there a narrow technical definition: the place-holder for the first dimension of Rest's (1986) four dimension model of morality. Even if it turns out that "compassionate empathy" is for all intents and purposes coextensive with Rest's idea of "moral sensitivity" it would seem advisable to adopt a more expansive term so as not to beg questions about the meaning and significance of the concept for moral functioning.

Chapter 3
A Conceptual and Empirical Sketch of Compassionate Empathy

3.1 Introduction

Taken in one sense, the question of whether encouraging compassionate empathic responding is a legitimate aim of a higher education in ethics is at best trivial and at worst inane. For better or for worse, there is a long if now routed tradition, strongest in the United States but apparent in the structure of British universities as well, that the final stage of the long process of personal, social, and moral development stretching from the earliest years of childhood and into the primary and secondary school years was college, understood as an opportunity for the refinement of one's moral character through sophisticated cultural initiation and personal development. In this connection, it is not insignificant to observe that during most of the nineteenth century the keystone of the college curriculum in United States was moral philosophy. The course was required of all students and usually taught by the college president himself.[1] One can reasonably assume that, before this flower of renaissance humanism began to fade, *not* to provide a college environment supportive of compassionate empathy, along side other such character traits as honesty, courage, fairmindedness, and integrity, would be inconsistent with the college system's own *raison d'être* and constitute, therefore, an educational failure through neglect. From this perspective, even to *entertain* the question of whether it might or might not be a good thing for young people to be initiated into sympathy and compassion, in practical ethics education as elsewhere in higher education, might be accused of being, in Williams' (1981) evocative phrase, one thought too many.

Be that as it may, beyond vague and abstract generalities about compassion as a positive social emotion, serious questions emerge concerning the promotion of empathic capacities of response as a moral educational goal. First, it is apposite to distinguish, with Kant (1789/1974), sympathy understood as "sensitivity" or "delicate feeling", emotions which work in conjunction with obligations to alleviate suffering, from "maudlin sentimentality", mere passive lamentation over another's

---

[1] For discussions on higher education's former vocation as a site for the perfection of moral character, see Sloan (1980), Annis (1992), McNeel (1994), Gutek (1995), and Sandin (1989).

plight (Kant, 1789/1974, p. 104, 1992, pp. 97–98) and to be sensitive of the point at which one becomes the other. Second, even varieties of sensitivity to others which seem in the abstract and in general terms to be genuine moral traits are nevertheless susceptible to personal predilection; it is well known, for instance, that people tend to have more sympathy towards those with whom they identify. These considerations raise the distinct possibility that rather than being a moral virtue on par with justice, morally good in itself, sympathy is a mere social virtue comparable to loyalty and politeness in that it has moral worth only insofar as it operates under the wise tutelage of sound moral judgement. Furthermore, if one suspects, as it seems entirely reasonable to do, that particular experiences of compassion or sympathy are not always based on considered reflection but are mediated by spontaneous and involuntary emotional responses, the possibility arises that one's empathic responses are not as amenable to educational intervention as they might at appear to be at first blush. This situation seems to call for, at the very least, greater clarity around what kind of emotion compassionate empathy is and how and in what circumstances it is experienced. It is the aim of this chapter to provide just such a sketch. First, and by way of a critical development of Blum's (1980b) account of compassion, the characteristic judgements which underlie experiences of compassionate empathy are presented (§3.2.1) and its apparent knowledge-conditions are discussed (§3.2.3). The following section (§3.3) treats Blum's suggestion that the characteristic emotional attitude of compassionate empathy is one of caring and that this orientation implies a conative interest in the alleviation of suffering and involves an experience of shared humanity. Section 3.4 considers the implications of a body of psychological literature, in particular works by Hoffman's (2000), Davis (1994), and Eisenberg et al., (1991), which together provide an empirically based catalogue of various psychological processes associated with experiences of compassionate empathy. The fact that these "modes of empathic arousal" represent a range of cognitive sophistication, it is claimed, belies a philosophical bias or pre-psychological folk belief according to which compassionate empathy necessarily implicates the imaginative engagement. The chapter concludes that while the internal relation between feelings of compassionate empathy and desire to alleviate the suffering that is the object of the emotion leaves little doubt concerning its values as a positive social motivation, the account of the psychological processes associated with compassionate empathy confirms as well that its arousal in particular circumstances depends largely on the vagaries of socialization and past personal experiences, a situation that raises difficult questions about compassionate empathy's status as a moral emotion and about what it might mean to make it the subject of educational intervention.

3.2 Judgements of Compassionate Empathy

As regards compassionate empathy understood as an emotional attitude or state of concern for another's well-being and despite the increased interest among professional philosophers in the theme of the emotions over the last decade or so,[2] Lawrence Blum's *Friendship, altruism and morality* (1980a) and the connected essay "Compassion" (1980b) remain invaluable resources. For anyone familiar with this work, this assessment might sound odd since "empathy" does not appear on his list of the particular "altruistic" or "other-regarding" emotions he identifies as being characterized as having as their objects "others in virtue of their suffering, misery, pain or travail" (p. 12)—namely, sympathy, compassion, and concern. Rather than being of substance, this discrepancy is one of style, or more specifically of word choice. The article titled "Compassion" (1980b) and the way the term is used in the larger work leaves little doubt that the concept of compassion of which he endeavours to give an account is a close analogue of the concept of compassionate empathy, as I have labelled that morally enabling affective perceptive disposition. "Compassion", as Blum (1980b) has it, encompasses those affective responses to another person's suffering that presuppose some comprehension of another's perspective and which, in his estimation, are apparently only hypothetically separable from a desire to alleviate that suffering.

3.2.1   Objects of Judgements of Compassionate Empathy

Blum (1980b) deliberates over the question of what it means to view someone with compassion (p. 507), and finds that experiences of compassionate empathy have at least three major components. First, compassion presupposes judging a person to be in a condition that is of consequence to general well-being. The idea of viewing someone compassionately implies not just judging him or her to be in some unenvious or, as it is often put "negative" or "aversive" state (cf. Blum, 1980b; Wispé, 1986, 1987; Nagel, 1970); the difficulty that a person as an object of compassion faces is not minor or trivial but must touch on his most central interests as a person. For this reason, to use Blum's (1980b) example, the inconvenience of having to take a detour because of roadwork or, one might add, one's disappointment at not winning the lottery, are not "compassion-grounding conditions" (p. 508). They are the stuff of complaints. Being diagnosed with a debilitating chronic disease or experiencing a marital breakdown, by contrast, clearly are. As Blum (1980b) puts it, "the negative condition must be relatively central to a person's life and well-being, describable as pain, misery, hardship, suffering, affliction and the like" (p. 508).

The second feature of compassionate empathy Blum (1980b) identifies is that compassion is person- not condition-focused. While compassion entails a judgement that a person is in a particular condition that is inconsistent with her well-being,

---

[2] A sampling of major philosophical analyses of emotion would include Gordon (1987), de Sousa (1987), Ben Ze'ev (2000), Solomon (1984), and Nussbaum (2001). For works focusing more specifically on emotions and ethics, see Stocker (1996) Tappolet (2000), Oakley (1992), and Gibbard (1990).

the condition itself is not the object of compassion but rather a particular person (or possibly set of persons) *in* a particular condition. One feels indignation, say, or sorrow or perhaps anger at chronic hunger but one does not feel compassion at it; one feels compassion for an individual or groups of individual human beings who *suffer from* chronic hunger (cf. Blum, 1980b, p. 508). Snow (2000) makes the same point in her discussion of the emotion she calls "sympathy". Sympathy, in her view, is characterized not by "feeling *with*" another person but "feeling *for*" that person (p. 66). What she means by this is that when one sympathizes with another person, one does not experience aversive emotions about the same event or circumstances causing the person to suffer but rather *because* the person suffers. The person, not the suffering-causing event or condition, is sympathy's "focus" (p. 66).

The third principal aspect of Blum's (1980b) conception of compassionate empathy is that compassion is not necessarily connected with *somme tout* judgements of a person's well-being. As Blum (1980b) observes, there is no inconsistency in viewing someone compassionately with regards to a particular condition and judging that, all things considered, they as persons are not the proper object of compassionate feelings. Blum's (1980b) example is that of a blind person whose life is generally happy despite his blindness. He suggests that there is no inconsistency in, on one hand, viewing a certain blind person with compassion in virtue of his blindness while at the same time viewing him with pleasure and admiration at his success in overcoming his disability. That said, there seems to be no doubt that judgements connected with compassion *may* regard a person's overall state, as in the case of the natural sympathy one might feel for a single mother parenting young children on her own and in cases where a person is perceived to have ruined himself through some defect of character. In this regard, compassion differs from love and hate for persons and from despair, all of which seem to be necessarily connected with *somme-tout* assessments of another person's or, in the case of despair, oneself.

It is noteworthy that the other-regardingness of compassion, the fact that it is an emotional attitude involving distress *at* or *about* or *for* others in virtue of their being faced with significant suffering, sets compassionate empathy apart from another closely related affective phenomenon. The assessment that another is in a particular state of serious distress, rather than evoking concern for the other's well-being, may evoke thoughts and feelings connected to one's own well-being. This phenomenon is documented in the psychological literature. Batson, for instance, has discussed it under the heading of "personal distress" (see, e.g., Batson, 1991; Batson & Coke, 1981), and Hoffman (2000) labels it "egoistic drift" (p. 59; pp. 205–206), and considers it a form of empathic over-arousal and an example of empathy's broader tendency towards evaluative bias (p. 59; pp. 205–206).[3] As an example, take a young woman witnessing an emotional account of another woman's story of being stalked by a stranger. The thoughts and feelings focusing on concern for the victim in this case would seem to be classed as compassionate, but any thoughts and feelings

---

[3] For a brief general discussion of "personal distress" as distinct from "empathy", see Eisenberg and Strayer (1987, pp. 7–8).

connected to the observer's concern for her own security or possibly disturbing memories of a similar experience, as comprehensible and even natural as such worries might be, is not compassion as such on grounds of being self- rather than other-directed.

3.2.2   Knowledge Conditions of Judgements of Compassionate Empathy

Should a person viewed with compassion know or be aware of his or her suffering? To what degree, if any, must the person viewing with compassion be *right* in his or her assessments of the other's suffering? These considerations raise the question of the knowledge conditions of compassionate empathy.

The answer to the first question might seem obvious. After all, if compassionate empathy is an affective response to a person viewed as being in a condition posing a serious threat to his or her well-being it is hard to imagine someone being in such a state yet not knowing about it. There appear, however, to be at least two categories of cases in which it is clearly possible. Blum (1980a) makes reference to the first when he sets down the condition that, "it is not necessary that the object of compassion be aware of his condition; he might be deceiving himself with regard to it" (p. 508). This seems to be correct. These are cases of false consciousness in which a person fails, one might say, to perceive his situation as it really is. Typical of this sort of case is Dickens' character Ebenezer Scrooge who seems not to be unhappy in his miserliness. Indeed, what seems to characterize such states of false consciousness is the fact of being in a state that an impartial observer would regard as a serious threat to one's well-being while not judging oneself to be suffering at all (except possibly in occasional moments of lucidity). The second case in which one may rightly be viewed with compassion but not be aware of the condition responsible for it is that of simple ignorance of the facts of one's circumstances as, for instance, when one is incognisant of a philandering spouse or the fact that one's job is soon to be cut (cf. Sober & Wilson, 1998, pp. 234; Snow, 2000). An extreme example in this category is that of the proverbial Good Samaritan who sympathizes with someone who is apparently not aware of anything about his or her circumstances at all—namely, a man lying unconscious at the side of the road (cf. Sober & Wilson, 1998, p. 352, n. 10). Note, however, that in the latter case the problem is not, as it is in the first, that the object of compassion is regarded as suffering but just not knowing about it. The person is not in fact suffering at all. Despite this, such people still seem to be legitimate objects of compassionate empathy. Why might this be so? This seems to be a special case where compassionate empathy is felt in virtue not of present suffering but suffering which has occurred in the past or which is expected to occur in the future. One feels compassionate empathy for a colleague who is due to receive a proverbial pink slip because one knows that he will soon be devastated at the loss of his job. Similarly, it seems correct to say that one feels compassionate empathy for, say, a parent who lost a child in an accident even decades ago but who today is at peace with this sad event. Here, the compassionate empathy felt is for the person's suffering in the past. Bearing this special case in mind, a fourth generalization about judgements of compassionate empathy seems safe: a person need not be aware of his suffering in order to be the object of compassion.

Although the object of compassion need not be aware of his or her grave situation in order to be the proper object of compassionate feelings, the person viewing with compassion necessarily believes the object of their compassion is in some aversive situation. But do the judgements of suffering underlying the viewpoint of compassion have to be empathically accurate? On this point, according to Sober and Wilson (1998), empathy differs from sympathy. These authors follow the definition of empathy standardly stipulated in empathy research in social psychology (but as we saw earlier in §2.2.2 generally unadhered to) as involving "affective matching". That is, strictly speaking, one experiences empathy for a person only if the perception that that person is having some emotion and triggers roughly the same emotional response in the observer; Bob empathizes with Barbara if, when perceiving Barbara's joy at her success feels joy with her (Sober & Wison, pp. 233–234). Thus defined, empathy entails an accuracy condition on the part of the observer. Now imagine that Bob perceives Barbara's tears of joy at her success yet interprets them as tears of sadness at the loss of her father and feels grief. Sober and Wilson claim that, correctly speaking, in this case Bob does *not* empathize with Barbara exactly because Bob is *wrong* about how she feels. No such accuracy condition seems to hold in the case of sympathy. Whatever compassion Bob might feel towards Barbara in connection with his mistaken perception of her being grieved is no less compassion for being based on an erroneous belief about Barbara's inner state. To be sure, mistaken, misplaced, or even irrational compassion (irrational in the sense of being based on a false or otherwise mistaken belief) is qualitatively different from accurate compassion but, unlike empathy, a failure of empathic accuracy does not *ipso facto* disqualify it as compassion. Accordingly, Sober and Wilson (1998) consider empathic accuracy as an "if and only if" condition of empathy whereas in their conception of sympathy it is sufficient for the sympathizer merely to "believe that something bad has happened" to the object of sympathy (p. 235). In light of these considerations, it would seem safe to add a fifth and final generalization about judgements of compassionate empathy: judgements of compassionate empathy need not be empathically accurate in order to be the basis of genuine or rightly so-called experiences of compassionate empathy. One should not assume that the fact that an experience of compassionate empathy *may* be based on a false belief somehow confuses compassionate empathy's status as a moral merit. Viewed from the first-person perspective an experience of compassionate empathy is no less an experience of compassionate empathy for being based on a false belief any more than a false judgement is less a judgement for being false. Viewed from the perspective of a skill or moral merit, however, compassionate empathy strives for empathic accuracy just as the faculty of judgement can be said to strive for epistemological accuracy. Here again the two analytically distinct dimensions of compassionate empathy are brought into focus: a perceptive dimension consisting in sensitivity to harm to others and an affective dimension involving a response of concern to perceived harms. It is to an examination of the latter dimension and the relation between the two dimensions that we now turn.

3.3 Compassionate Empathy as an Attitude of Caring

This sketch of compassionate empathy has so far focused on compassion's cognitive profile—that is to say, the characteristic prepositional beliefs involved in viewing a person with compassion. Without some specification of what might be called its affective tenor it would be incomplete; as Blum (1980b) observes, attitudes of intellectual curiosity, total disinterest, or even *Shadenfreude* are all compatible with the kinds of judgements characteristic of compassionate empathy as they have been characterized so far (p. 509). In order to round out the account, then, Blum (1980b) advances that compassionate empathy must additionally involve a certain characteristic type of *emotional attitude* and he argues that this characteristic attitude of compassionate empathy has four discernable aspects. These are that compassionate empathy (1) necessarily involves the imaginative reconstruction of the other's compassion-evoking condition, (2) is an attitude of concern or regard for the sufferer's good, (3) involves "a sense of shared humanity", and (4) has a certain prerequisite degree of affective strength and duration.

Point (2) is the centrepiece of Blum's schema; indeed, the idea that notion of "concern" about a person suffering it seems to go most of the distance towards characterizing the emotional attitude of compassionate empathy. Clearly, in experiencing compassionate empathy one does not merely mentally record or believe that a person is in a situation seriously threatening his or her well-being. One must also, in Blum's (1980b) wording, "care about that suffering and desire its alleviation" (p. 511). In opting for this two-part conception which views compassionate empathy as comprising both an affective dimension (i.e., care for or concern with a person's suffering) *and* a conative dimension (i.e., a desire that the suffering be removed) Blum follows a general tendency in the analysis of compassion or sympathy (cf., e.g., Wispé, 1986; Mercer, 1972; Nagel, 1970; Olinck, 1984), an analysis which is misleading if the relationship between these two dimensions are not clarified.

A case in point is Wispé's (1986) discussion of the issue of the relation in empathy between the perception of suffering and the desire to relieve it. Wispé (1986) does not rule out the possibility that the desiderative dimension of compassionate empathy is merely an incidental accompaniment to the attitude of care or concern rather than being internally connected. If so, it would be conceivable for a person to have a heightened sense of awareness of another's suffering (in the characteristically compassionate sense intended) yet utterly devoid of any desire to relieve it. Because this is not at all obvious, Wispé (1986) takes it upon himself to come up with evidence that that compassionate empathy has this particular necessary conative aspect. Indeed, Wispé (1986) argues for the point counterfactually as follows: if compassionate empathy did not involve a desire to alleviate the object's suffering, it should be coherent to talk about sympathizing with another person's happiness. But this is absurd. No one could reasonably desire to terminate another person's happiness (p. 318, n. 1). Apart from not being a particularly good argument (it is not at all obvious that happiness is in all cases or in every sense inherently a state to be sustained as there are evidently circumstances in which suffering is on the contrary preferable or even morally required[4]), it seems unnecessary to resort to such argumentative gymnastics. All that is required is a clear-sighted grasp of the meaning of concern as a dimension of the particular emotional attitude of compassionate empathy.

"Concern" refers generally to a state of involvement or interest. As such, it can take many forms and have many objects; a person can legitimately be as much concerned with her financial investments, with bicycles, or with her flower beds as with another human being. Concern in this general sense even when directed towards a vulnerable person need not be tied up with a desire to relieve that vulnerability. There does not seem to be anything incoherent, for instance, about describing a man's keen interest in the declining health of his great aunt—for whom he cares nothing and from whom he stands to inherit a fortune once she dies—as genuine concern. The particular kind of concern characteristic of the emotional attitude of compassionate empathy must be more specific. The term that captures best the notion of concern for another's well-being or flourishing seems to be "care" in the positive sense in which it is said that nurses care for their patients, parents care for their children, and that a person cares for his garden. In this sense, caring just means to have an interest in—by *desiring*—the well-being or flourishing of the object of care. Thus, it is because the characteristic affective attitude of compassionate empathy is *caring* that it is an alloy, if you will, of both awareness and sensitivity to another's well-being and a desire for it. Put another way, it is the attitude of caring that seems to define and single out compassionate empathy. States of concern with another's well-being which lack an attitude of care are of course possible but they are just not compassionate empathy but some other emotion, such as *Schadenfreude*, malice, or, perhaps, indifference. It is in this sense, it seems, that compassionate empathy, as Blum (1980b) put it, "involves an active and objective interest in another person's welfare" (p. 516; cf. pp. 12–14).

It is one thing, it might be objected, to conclude on the basis of a conceptual analysis that there is an internal relationship between compassionate empathy and desire to help and quite another to claim that people who experience compassionate empathy are in fact disposed towards having benevolent motivations. The link has been empirically investigated and it is strongly corroborated by the research. Hoffman (1981, 2000), for instance, identifies a collection of studies which, as he

---

[4] For instance, the smug satisfaction or comfort people sometimes take in the misfortune of others, an emotion on which the tabloid press capitalizes lavishly, is a form of happiness one might judge worthy of removal. Similarly, the exercise of the so-called virtues of will power, self-control, and deliberation, characteristically involve choosing self-denial, a form of suffering, with an eye to achieving some future goal (cf. Steutel, 1999).

argues, can be interpreted as providing evidence for this connection. Two widely cited reviews of the vast number of empirical investigations into a correlation between empathy (variously construed and measured) and helping behaviours (also variously construed and measured) by Batson (1991) and Eisenberg and Miller (1987b) leave little doubt that feelings of empathy for a person in need increase the likelihood of responding by helping to relieve that need, although the strength of this correlation varied to a noteworthy degree depending on the empathy-arousing situation (e.g., picture/story showed a weaker match than other empathic induction procedures) and age group (i.e., children's behaviour response was weaker than that of adults) (cf. Eisenberg & Miller, 1987b). As both Batson (1991) and Hoffman (1981, 2000) concede, however, the conclusion that there is such a relationship between empathy and helping behaviour is not in and of itself evidence that the feelings of empathy are motivationally responsible for helping. A study, such as Penner et al.'s, (1995) which shows that college students who score high on a standard measure of empathy are more likely to engage in volunteer activities, does not rule out a common cause responsible for both high empathy and pro-social behaviours. That, in Hoffman's (1981, 2000) apparently reasonable assessment, would require evidence that what he calls "empathic distress" both *precedes* and *contributes to* helping behaviour, a hypothesis for which he finds support most notably in a classic study by Gaertner and Dovidio (1977).[5] Briefly, these researchers showed that, in a situation where research subjects were easily able to assist a confederate in (fictitious) danger, research subjects who scored higher on an objective measure of empathy (i.e., rate of increase of heart-rate acceleration) systematically rose more quickly from their chairs to help on realizing the dangerous situation. Hoffman suggest that further support that empathic feelings contribute to helping would be gained by evidence that empathic distress becomes less intense when one helps but persist when one does not help (cf. 1981, p. 131; 2000, pp. 32–33). What this criterion is supposed to capture is the counterfactual causal intuition that if distress did not diminish after helping, the distress could not possibly be the cause of the helping behaviour. This formulation, however, seems to be somewhat off the mark. If, as all sides tacitly agree, one's empathic distress is aroused by the realization of another's distress (cf. Batson, 1991, pp. 93–94), one should not expect attempts at helping in and of themselves to reduced empathic distress, as Hoffman's wording of it implies, but rather *either* empathic distress diminishes only if one's help succeeds in reducing the distress-causing situation (and persist where attempts are ineffectual) *or* when the victim is out of danger irrespective of any help provided by the observer. Indeed, two studies headed by Batson in the context of his long-standing research programme on altruistic behaviour (cf. Batson, 1991) conclude that the sheer act of helping does not alleviate empathic distress but that empathic distress continues when, in spite of failed attempts, victims' distress is not relieved (Batson & Weeks, 1996; Batson & Shaw, 1991).

---

[5] For a review of other similar studies, see Hoffman (1978).

Of course, even if there is such an internal connection between compassionate empathy and motivation to help, it does not imply that compassion always leads to helping in practice; countervailing egoistic motives such as a distaste for incurring the various sorts of personal cost and phenomena such as that which Darley and Latane (1968) labelled "responsibility diffusion", the assumption that someone else has already reacted to the crisis or is responsible for reacting to such situations, commonly intervene as countervailing motivations (cf. Hoffmann, 2000, pp. 33–35). Nor should it be mistaken for the claim that desires to alleviate another person's suffering is somehow analytically distinct from caring. Blum (1980b) reminds us that "a genuine interest in relieving someone's suffering can stem from meeting an intellectual or professional challenge rather than from compassion" (p. 509). Indeed, without denying that doctors and nurses as a class are generally highly caring people, it is likely that no hospital is without a contingent of medical staff who, despite being clinicians highly skilled in relieving people's suffering, are not compassionate precisely because they lack care or concern for their patients. The main point is the conceptual one that compassion is not just perceiving someone's suffering or desiring to relieve someone's suffering but *caring about* their suffering, viewing it, as Nagel (1970) put it, as *something to be relieved* (p. 80, n. 1) or, in Blum's (1980b) formulation, compassionate empathy is an expression of concern for another's plight; it is not merely "tacked on" as an independent component (p. 511).

Component (3) of Blum's conception of the emotional attitude of compassion, that it involves a sense of shared humanity, seems best regarded as an implication of component (2), that compassionate empathy is an attitude of concern or regard for a sufferer's good. Nevertheless, it deserves a separate treatment in this discussion because, as Blum suggests, it lends to compassionate empathy a distinctly moral dimension. The idea is an elusive one, but it does seem plausible to interpret the viewpoint of caring for another person's well-being as involving *identification* with that person as a human being or, put another way, *recognition* of the other person as a human being like oneself. Blum's (1980b) way of filling this out is by saying that caring for another person's suffering involves seeing their suffering as "the kind of thing that could happen to anyone, including oneself insofar as one is a human being" (p. 511). For another formulation one could with as much right, it seems, draw on a Kantian concept and say that compassionate empathy seems to suppose viewing another person suffering as a "person"—that is, as a human being, like oneself, endowed with "dignity" which Kant (1797/1996) defines as the "absolute inner worth" of persons which makes demands on others (p. 186). Either way, the intuition seems to be that what the attitude of compassionate empathy and the deliberative viewpoint of morality have in common is that they both presuppose a recognition that other human beings (or in the case of compassionate empathy, the particular sufferer) are fundamentally similar to oneself in they have the same *need for* and are *deserving of* the kinds of consideration, attention, and respect that one has for oneself. This, or something like it, is what Blum (1980a) describes as the "moral force of compassion" (p. 512). Convincingly, Blum (1980a) argues that it is precisely with regards to this experience of equality that pity differs from compassionate empathy. Both compassionate empathy and pity involve a regard of solicitude but in pitying, rather than viewing the person's affliction as a source of identification and fundamental sameness, it is viewed as a source of fundamental *difference*. In this sense, says Blum (1908b), pity is condescending and hence of lesser moral worth than compassionate empathy (p. 512).

Do experiences of care for another person's suffering have to reach a certain strength and duration to count as genuine experiences of compassionate empathy? Blum thinks that they do: "Though there are degrees of compassion, the threshold of emotional strength required from compassion (in contrast with other altruistic attitudes) is relatively high and enduring" (pp. 512–513) and "there is a threshold of the strength of [the desire for another person's good] below which an emotion cannot go and still be compassion, concern, sympathy" (1980b, p. 19). If, as it seems to be, the claim being made is that when an attitude of caring towards another person's suffering reaches a certain degree of weakness that it ceases to be caring, I cannot agree. To be sure, there are emotions that involve the same objects and attitudes but which carry different names depending on their strength. For example, embarrassment seems to be mild shame (and shame strong embarrassment), guilt mild remorse (and remorse strong guilt), and the emotions labelled "malice", "spite", and "rancour" all sit somewhere along a spectrum running from more to less intense feelings of ill will or hatred (cf. Maxwell & Reichenbach, 2005) Compassionate empathy just does not seem to be one of these emotions which is susceptible to degrees of variation in quite the same way. It might be better if compassionate empathy were strong and enduring emotions—perceiving that someone's well-being is seriously threatened perhaps *should* inspire strong reactions—but the fact seems to be that weak compassionate empathy is no less compassionate empathy for it.

For these reasons, and for whatever it is worth, quasi-quantitative concepts such as "strength" and "duration" certainly do not have heuristic in the case of every emotion and possibly only in quite rare exceptions.[6] With the exception of very visceral emotions, and possibly only fear, the degree of felt experience of emotions is intangible to the extreme. A more helpful approach seems to be to adopt some version of Heller's (1979) general definition of emotions as "involvement" (p. 7) and then to characterize individual emotions in terms of the object and orientation of this involvement. The question of strength and duration then becomes one of the degree of involvement or how important the engagement with the object of the emotion is.

This section's sketch of the characteristic attitude of compassionate empathy as a necessary addendum to the discussion of its cognitive profile has focused on three aspects of Blum's (1980b) four-aspect analysis. We saw that compassionate empathy is an attitude of caring towards another's suffering—this was Blum's point (2)—and that it involves an identification of a certain basic sameness between the empathizer and the object of compassionate empathy—Blum's point (3). Finally, a few words were said about the question of its strength and duration—Blum's point (4). His first point, that compassionate empathy necessarily involves the imaginative

---

[6] For a contrary view, see Ben Ze'ev (2000).

reconstruction of the other's compassion-evoking condition, has so far been avoided because it seems to be plain wrong: there is strong evidence that, contrary to Blum (1980b), perspective-taking, far from being a characteristic aspect of the emotional attitude of compassionate empathy, is just one in a rich array of psychological processes of varying degrees of cognitive and imaginative sophistication which are capable of generating and sustaining experiences of compassionate empathy. The next section (§3.4) presents this evidence in the form of a catalogue of relevant psychological processes which, taken together, demonstrate that compassionate empathy is not always and by no means necessarily an imaginative or even a cognitively complex affair.

3.4 Psychological Processes Involved in the Arousal of Compassionate Empathy

Paralleling the bias in social psychology, traceable perhaps to Piaget's influence, towards the supposition that social perspective-taking is mediated by imaginative identification (see §2.3.1) is a bias in philosophical treatments of compassionate empathy to view it similarly as characteristically involving what Blum (1980a) calls "imaginative dwelling on the condition of the other person" (p. 509) and the "imaginative reconstruction" of the object of compassionate empathy's situation (p. 510). We already saw the role of imagination in Smith (1759/1976) who went so far as to build this process into the very definition of sympathy, conceiving it as "changing places in fancy with the sufferer" (see §2.2.3). According to Smith's analysis, the role that perspective-taking appears to play in the mediation of sympathy is that of enabling insight into another's internal state of suffering; whether and to what extent one responds to that insight with compassion depends on a discrete evaluation of the cause of a person's suffering. In particular, it depends on whether or not and to what extent the sufferer *deserves* to be in their current aversive state. In regards to the question of the psychological process governing the faculty of other-directed introspection, Smith (1759/1976) is unequivocal: "as we have no immediate experience of what other men feel, we can form no idea of the manner in which they are affected, but by conceiving what we ourselves should feel in the like situation" (quoted in Gordon, 1996, p. 178). A similar account, as recorded earlier (cf. §2.2.3), can be found in Hume (1751/1957).

Jumping ahead two centuries, another example of the apparent philosophical bias that perspective-taking is a *sine qua non* of compassionate empathy is Robert Gordon's essay "Sympathy, simulation and the impartial spectator" (1996). His case is of particular interest, and worth pausing to consider briefly, because despite the fact that Gordon has made something of a personal cottage industry of arguing that the role of perspective-taking—he calls it "mental simulation"—is generally overestimated in accounts of social psychological processes (cf. 1986, 1995, 1996) when he turns his attention to moral functioning his reasoning seems strongly influenced by the bias in question.

Gordon's (1996) account starts out promisingly enough. His stated aim is to "show how [Hume's account of sympathy] needs to be updated and corrected in the light of recent empirical research" (p. 165) and goes on to document numerous psychological mechanisms varying in their degrees of cognitive sophistication which may intervene in the exercise of the faculty of other-directed introspection. These include what he calls "lower forms of empathy" such as non-inferential cognition of another's emotional state and motor mimicry and "higher forms of empathy", most notably "simulation", Gordon's label for perspective-taking as I have already said. This faculty, that Hume refers to infelicitously (if not downright misleadingly) as "sympathy", is not compassion in either Smith's or Blum's sense but what was referred to earlier as the empathy in the cognitive sense (cf. esp. §2.4 and Fig. 2.1). Although Gordon argues that a number of psychological processes beyond perspective-taking or imaginatively "putting oneself in the other's place" may be rallied in the formation of cognitions about other's emotional states, when it comes to empathy in the context of *ethical* judgement, Gordon implies, with Smith, Hume, and Blum, that the perspective-taking is necessarily implicated (p. 177).[7]

Gordon makes two main points in this connection. First, he states that perspective-taking "appears essential to the application of reciprocity principles such as the golden rule" (1996, p. 8). The golden rule is a crude principle of ethical justification according to which only those acts of which one could accept oneself to be the object are acceptable from the moral point of view.[8] So, for instance, according to the golden rule, I am under a moral obligation to assist an elderly person who has collapsed in the street if I concede that I myself would want to be assisted if I were in the same vulnerable position. Under such a construal, moral judgements so justified appear to presuppose a process of vicarious identification. Second, in appreciating the surface feature of moral judgement that moral judgement sometimes seems to require one to withhold or at least to regulate one's feelings of sympathy, Gordon (1996) states his preference for Smith's account of sympathy over Hume's. The weakness of Hume's account, he says, is that it pictures sympathy as being merely reactive: one responds with pleasure to the perception of another's pleasure and to suffering with suffering. Smith introduces the "impartial spectator" in order to explain what would otherwise be discrepancies such as—this is Smith's example—feeling pity for a condemned man (presumably known to be rightly convicted) being brought to the scaffold (cf., e.g., 1759/1976, ch. III). Smith connects appropriate sympathy with the causes of another's emotions and the possibility of desert (or what he refers to as "propriety"; cf. Smith, 1759/1976, part II, ch. II). One simple example to illustrate sympathy as the basis of moral judgement in this sense

---

[7] Gordon does not make explicit reference to compassion but his albeit brief account of the role of vicarious identification in ethical judgement suggests that he has in mind an analogous emotion.

[8] Crude because, for one thing, it does not allow room for moral obligations to oneself. Cf. Kant (1797/1996, pp. 17–175), *Metaphysics of morals*.

is that of feeling sorrow at another's injuries. One considers the injury, its causes and if, by placing ourselves in the position of the injured, we judge that we too would feel sorrow in his place, we share his sorrow. If, through perspective-taking, one concludes instead that one would not feel the same sorrow, one's response is not to have shared feelings or "empathy" but to judge rather, perhaps, that he was making a bit of a meal out of his situation. What is never called into doubt in either Smith's or Gordon's account, however, is that we might not need to have recourse to imaginative simulation to explain such judgements.

But a moment's reflection reveals that this claim, if it is not obviously false, it is at least not obviously true. For example, it appears plausible that in order to accept the results of the application of the golden rule to the case of the injured person above one would merely have to concede that being so debilitated is distressing and being in such a situation of distress is, for myself as well as for anyone else, not a situation one would wish to be in. Neither of these beliefs are inconceivable in the absence of perspective-taking unless one presupposes that the only or the character- istic means by which one comes to conclude that some state or other is distressing for human beings like myself to be in is by way of a process of imaginatively placing oneself in that situation. One possible alternative source of such inferences might be referencing to social scripts, bits of stereotyped knowledge about how people react in certain very specific circumstances: with grief when a loved one dies, with jeal- ousy when an intimate shows special preference for another person, with gratitude, approval, or, where appropriate in the context, indignation when witnessing justice being served. Finally, it is surely even quite difficult to say with certainty whether, for instance, the pang of compassion one might feel on glimpsing a grossly obese stranger struggling to get out of her car involves "dwelling in one's imagination" on that person's distressful condition or vicariously experiencing how the other person feels "given his character, beliefs, and values" (Blum, 1980b, p. 510).

It would not be too much of a stretch, then, to speak of a perspective-taking/compas- sionate empathy hypothesis—that is, the more or less unquestioned assumption that perspective-taking is *the* genetic psychological process behind experiences of compas- sionate empathy—and consider that it is not just a folk belief—a *false* folk belief at that.[9] This is not to say, of course, that compassionate empathy *never* involves imagina- tive reconstruction. However, making it a *requirement* seems to set the bar too high.

This situation would seem to call for a more nuanced sketch of the psychological processes associated with compassionate empathy. To this end, we turn to the psy- chological literature on social and emotional development and, drawing primarily

---

[9] I would hazard to advance that the perspective-taking/compassion folk belief is endemic to philo- sophical discussion from at least the time of Adam Smith to the present. This suggestion, that one would be hard-pressed to find a published philosophical discussion of compassion that neither presupposes nor argues explicitly that perspective-taking is indispensable to the experience of compassion, is admittedly a presumptuous claim and I do not pretend to have done it anything like justice. However, for further partial confirmation, which the reader may pursue at his or her lei- sure and inclination, see discussions of compassion and analogues and the role centrality of imagi- native dwelling therein in Nussbaum (2001), Scheler (1954), and Mercer (1972).

on reviews of the cognitive processes involved in empathy and sympathy (i.e., those found in Hoffmann (2000), Eisenberg et al. (1991) and Davis (1994), elucidate at least seven interrelated processes: conditioning, mimicry, direct association, language-mediated association, cognitive networking, labelling, and finally perspective-taking. These processes are analysable in terms of two broad categories according to whether the experience of compassionate empathy evoked is best understood as a response or reaction to some particular feature, element, or characteristic of the object of compassionate empathy or his circumstances or whether they are based on the empathizer's beliefs about the object of compassionate empathy's internal states—that is, his or her feeling, thoughts, perceptions, etc. For this reason, I label the first category "reactive processes" and the latter "introspective processes". This distinction frames the presentation that follows.

3.4.1   Reactive Processes

One relatively elementary way that human beings may come to have feelings of compassionate empathy is via conditioning. In cases where a person's own distress in the past has become linked with certain stimuli—for instance, the sight of blood, a frowning face, or the sound of weeping—these cues can elicit distressing feelings (cf., e.g., Afronreed, 1968; Lanzetta & Orr, 1986). Hoffman (2000) suggests that the pairing of feelings of distress with certain facial and vocal expressions of distress—worried looks, furrowed eyebrows, frowns, sighs, moans, etc.—may occur in infancy in the course of close day-to-day physical contact between the child and primary caregiver. He describes the process this way:

> When a mother feels anxiety or tension, her body may stiffen and the stiffening may transmit her distress to the infant she is holding. This infant is now distressed; and the stiffening of the mother's body was the direct cause—the unconditioned stimulus. The mother's accompanying facial and verbal expressions then become conditioned stimuli, which can subsequently evoke distress in the child even in the absence of physical contact. (pp. 45–46)

In support for this claim, he adduces an old study by a Escalona (1945) who, in research on a programme enabling incarcerated women to continue to care for their children, found that "the infants were most upset when their mothers were waiting to appear before a parole board" (p. 46), presumably owing to the presence of the conditioned stimuli—namely, the mothers' anxious expressions. Such conditioning, Hoffman (2000) indicates, sets a pattern of responding so that certain distress cues generally—that is, not just on the part just the mother but from anyone— become distress-eliciting. As Eisenberg et al. (1991) are careful to point out, conditioned distress responses cannot be considered compassionate empathy unless the observer links them with another's state or condition; a sharp feeling of aversion at the sight of blood and distressed expressions at the scene of an accident is only compassionate empathy where the viewer interprets his feelings as feelings for the accident victims rather than one's own reaction to the cues (p. 68).

Mimicry, the physical imitation of another person's emotional expression, is another rather rudimentary and automatically occurring process that may provoke compassionate empathy. Mimicry is a phenomenon widely associated with empathy in the cognitive sense (cf. §2.4); who while watching a film, or following a decisive moment during a sporting event, or otherwise engaged in intense involvement in another person's situation has never caught himself or herself involuntarily imitating through subtle changes in facial expression or posture? The question of interest here, however, is not whether such mimicry is the *result* of vicarious introspection or compassionate empathy but rather the somewhat counter-intuitive proposal that there is good reason to suppose that it *triggers* empathic feelings. Hoffman (2000), following Lipps (1906), believes that there is. The hypothesis that imitation stimulates so-called afferent feedback—that is, that imitation produces feelings in the imitator that affectively match those of the imitated—shares a certain affinity with William James' and Carl G. Lange's rather idiosyncratic conception of emotional experience (cf. James, 1884). One way into James and Lange's thesis about emotional experience is to say that their theory reverses the direction of the causal arrow which runs, in most people's pre-psychological view, *from* the affective response *to* some characteristic physiological reaction held to be the result of the affective stimulation: a person cries because she is sad, jumps because she is startled, and so on. Not so, held James: "we feel sorry *because* we cry, angry *because* we strike, afraid *because* we tremble, and [it is] not that we cry, strike, or tremble, because we are sorry, angry, or fearful, as the case may be" (James 1884, p. 190; emphasis added). According to the so-called James–Lange theory of emotions, then, the characteristic feeling tone of a particular emotion is coextensive with the afferent perception of the autonomic and motor functions activated in a particular set of environmental circumstances. Citing a number of studies conducted from the mid-1970s to the early 1990s which aimed to isolate the effect of sheer physical position of the face on affective perception (cf., e.g., Adelman & Zajonc, 1989; Hatfield et al., 1992),[10] Hoffman (2000) concludes that "the evidence is clear that people's emotional experience tends to be influenced by the facial expressions they adopt" (p. 41).

Interestingly, however, Hoffman (2000) notes that these findings are ambiguous. The hypothesis that the studies seemed intended to support is that certain facial postures somehow activate neural processes integral to the experience of an emotion. An equally compatible explanation for the results is that "stage-managed facial expressions", as Hoffman (2000) puts it, coloured the subjects' perceptions

---

[10] One particularly memorable experiment, performed apparently by Strack et al. in 1988, involved taping golf tees to either side of a group of hapless undergraduates' foreheads and, in an effort to have them hold their faces in an unwitting frown, instructing them instructed to "move the tees together". Their emotional responses to photographs of starving children and other sad scenes were then measured and the test group, those with the golf tees taped to their foreheads, were judged by the investigators to have perceived the scenes as sadder than the control group (cf. Hoffman, 2000, p. 41).

via a kind of kinesic association or conditioning. The fact that subjects associate, say, feeling their own eyebrows furrowed or teeth clenched with anger or might contribute to their perceiving themselves as being angry or sad (pp. 41–41). In any case, whether the mechanism involved in mimicry is a type of conditioning or operates by some independent means, for our purposes the main point is that evidence exists to suggest that people's tendency towards empathic imitation is not just a response to involvement in others' situations but may also play some role in setting the emotional tenor of those perceptions. Mimicry is not, in other words, merely epiphenomenal in experiences of compassionate empathy but may carry the experience forward.

The last process to be discussed under the heading of reactive processes underlying what are sometimes referred to rather clinically in the psychological literature as "episodes" of compassionate empathy is "direct association". As the name indicates, this process triggers feelings of compassionate empathy via the direct association either of a particular feature of another person's experience of suffering or the situation generally with some traumatic or distressing event in the observer's own past. To illustrate the latter variety, Hoffman (2000) cites a personal anecdote recounted by one of his students. This student accounted for the great lengths she went to in order to help a man who had fallen and hit his head in terms of very intense feelings of sympathy. The situation evoked such strong feelings, according to her account, because it reminded her of a similar accident where she herself had been the victim (p. 48). Humphrey (1922), one of the earliest psychologist to study direct association, focused on the latter sort, considering typical examples being those where a child picks up on some particular cue of a situation—such as blood—is reminded thereby of having been cut himself, and this evokes an empathic response. Clearly, then, direct association is a subclass of conditioning, the difference residing in the definition of direct association as involving the pairing of distress scenarios or distress cues with the empathizer's own past similar experiences. One can imagine cases of empathy-evoking conditioning where no such pairing holds, as in the case in which one's consistent strong feelings of compassion for, say, homeless people are traceable back not to the memory of being at one time homeless oneself (as it would be if it were mediated by direct conditioning), but rather to some seemingly unrelated and possibly even forgotten shock of, say, seeing some very down-and-out-looking person and believing for an instant that the person was an estranged friend.

One may naturally wonder whether being triggered by the surface features of a situation of a person suffering rather than by a perception or awareness of that person's suffering itself does not somehow disqualify such affective responses as compassionate empathy. Another way of phrasing this would be to say that it seems incorrect to consider compassionate empathy as a caring response to the perception of a person's suffering if what triggers that response is not the person's suffering at all but merely some more or less incidental surface features of the situation, situational cues, or disturbing past personal experience. The most straightforward reply would be to reiterate Eisenberg et al.'s (1991) and Hoffman's (2000) stipulative definition that such processes generate genuine compassionate empathy as long as those feelings are *interpreted* by the empathizer as an attitude or feeling of caring towards another's suffering, regardless of their causal history. In Hoffman's (2000) words, "I consider [conditioning and direct association] empathy-arousing processes as long as the observer attends to the victim and the feelings evoked in the observer fit the victim's situation rather than the observer's" (p. 48). So, for instance, the distress felt by a two-year-old child seeing her mother being violently ill (as witnessed by attentiveness and frightened looks, mimicry, and so on) is still compassionate empathy even though, as it seems safe to assume for the sake of argument, given the cognitive abilities of the average toddler that such feelings are more likely based on surface cues from the situation rather than on what would normally be considered to be empathic insight into the mother's psychological state of suffering.

3.4.2 Introspective Processes

In Hoffman's (2000) estimation, conditioning, mimicry, and direct association deserve to be treated together as a single package principally on the grounds that they are all automatic or involuntary reactions and are of relative cognitive simplicity (pp. 36, 48, 59). Another common feature of these empathy-evoking processes, as Hoffman (2000) notes, is that in each case the state of empathic concern they give rise to is not based on insight into another's state of distress but rather on cues in or surface features of the victim's situation. The processes that will be discussed in this section have the common feature of being central and to borrow Kohut's (1959) term "information-gathering activities"—that is, any compassionate empathy evoked is in response to insight into another person's inner states, namely, mediated association, cognitive networking, labelling, and perspective-taking.

What Hoffman (2000) calls "verbally mediated association" and what Davis (1994) refers to as "language-mediated association" cover a broad set of situations in which language (as opposed to, say, facial expressions, bodily gestures, or other visual or audio cues) plays a central role in communicating a person's feelings or his or her empathy-evoking situation. However, as Hoffman (2000) seems to suggests, language-mediated association goes beyond the mere involvement of language since emotionally charged words—words, perhaps, like "holocaust", "cancer", and "failure"—might trigger empathic responses via conditioning or direct association (cf. p. 49). Rather, what Hoffman (2000) has in mind as typical instances of mediated association involve some form of narrative in which "the victim's emotionally distressed state is communicated through language" (p. 49) either in the form of face-to-face interviews, audio or visual recordings, or written documents. Naturally, in the actual or virtual presence of the sufferer, the empathizer may pick up expressive cues such as facial expressions, tone of voice and posture through conditioning, association, and mimicry. Thus, the most unalloyed instances of mediated association—in the sense of minimizing (but of course not completely eliminating) the intervention of other arousal modes—would appear to be the interpretation of texts.

As for the "associational" dimension of language-mediated association, the question of whether and if, in Hoffman's view, language-mediated association has a unique identity vis-à-vis other arousal modes is not clear. Given what we have seen about direct association (in §3.4.1), one might expect that language-mediated association constitutes something parallel to what Blum (1980b) refers to as "identification". Identification, exemplified by the Hoffman's student's interpretation of her helping response to an injured man mentioned above, is a phenomenon whereby an amplification or facilitation of a compassionate empathic response is attributed to a shared traumatic personal experience or some other salient point in common between the empathizer and the sufferer, thoughts of which the sufferer's narrative or traits and characteristics evoke in the mind of the empathizer (pp. 509–510). In reference to a study by Batson et al. (1996) that measured adolescents' responses to stories recounting peers' upsetting life experiences, Hoffman (2000) states that the result that "the female subjects reported even greater empathic distress if they recalled having a similar experience themselves" (cf. p. 52) illustrates language-mediated association. On the other hand, he seems to allow as well that compassionate empathy aroused by perspective-taking or the imaginative reconstruction of the narrator's feeling elicited by such narratives is some form of language-mediated association as well (see p. 52). The safest interpretation seems to be the most general one and hold, with Gibbs (2003, p. 82) in his discussion of Hoffman's theory, that mediated association refers to the phenomenon where a person's distress or distressing situation is communicated via language (merely as opposed to some other means), while bearing in mind that such communication can coincide with or set off other arousal modes such as perspective-taking or "identification" (i.e., association in the sense of direct association).

Quite rightly, Eisenberg never fails to caution against overestimating the role of perspective-taking in discrimination of others' emotional states and, relatedly, against the assumption that such introspection is necessarily a cognitively complex affair (cf. Eisenberg et al., 1991, 1997; Eisenberg & Strayer, 1987). A case in point, as Eisenberg et al. (1991) see it, is "labelling", the process in which an inference about a person's inner state draws on, in their words, "a basic knowledge of the meanings associated with perceptual cues" (p. 68). So, for instance, a person's assessment of the inner state of someone attending a funeral may reflect the view that attending funerals are generally sad, or extending the idea to groups of people, the average tourist may view, say, a Roma family on a Paris or Barcelona street to be in a state of despair given what is generally believed about the socio-economic conditions of the Roma. Like conditioning, mimicry, and direct association labelling is presumed to be largely involuntary and unreflective (p. 68), but since it characteristically facilitates explicit inferences about others' inner states it seems best regarded as an introspective rather than a reactive process. Also, apparently falling into the category of "labelling" is Higgins' (1981) idea, referred to in §2.3.1, that beliefs about a person's motives, attitudes, and responses are sometimes arrived at by way of a process in which one first categorizes the target person in terms of a known "personality type" or considers him to be psychologically comparable to a person the judger knows well (i.e., a parent or friend) and then draws inferences about the target person's motives, attitudes, and responses on the basis of such comparisons: shy people do not like to try new things; Neil is a shy person; so, Neil must be frightened at the prospect of flying in an airplane for the first time.

Eisenberg et al. (1991) identify a second process mediated by "elaborated cognitive networks", by which inferences about another's inner states are drawn independently of perspective-taking. Quoting Karniol (1982), these authors define elaborate cognitive networking as a process whereby "the observation of social stimuli such as another person's behaviour in a given setting initiates cognitive processes in which the observer attempts to match the observed event with some pre-stored chunk of stereotyped knowledge" (p. 69). As Eisenberg et al. (1991) have it, the "social stimuli" in question can be perceptual or linguistic—that is, the actual sight of some event or action or narrative accounts—and the "chunks of knowledge" commonly take the form of social scripts. Thus, for example, the sight of a person lying in the street surrounded by onlookers triggers inferences about how the various players must feel and what actions people might be inclined to take in such a situation.

Eisenberg et al. (1991) conclude that, in addition to being a common basis for adult's beliefs about others' inner states, cognitive networking and labelling enable young children whose cognitive capacities do not as yet permit them to engage in perspective-taking to introspect and thus possibly to experience compassionate empathy. Nelson's (1981) research is suggestive in this connection: three-year olds are able to recount social scripts about ordinary events like going to a familiar restaurant or to the zoo on which such inferences could be based.[11] In any case, we can see how cognitive networking is clearly close to labelling, the difference being apparently that the former is more sophisticated cognitively.

We know from Chapter 2 that human beings' ability to draw accurate conclusions about another's internal states go under at least three main labels in contemporary social psychology: "role-taking", "perspective-taking" (sometimes as "social perspective-taking"), and "empathic accuracy" (cf. esp. §2.4). All the "introspective processes" discussed in this section would be components of this basic perceptive faculty. For the sake of avoiding a misunderstanding, observe now that the present use of "perspective-taking" is inconsistent with this schema. Here, perspective-taking is understood as being *just one* process among the other processes of labelling, mediated association, and cognitive networking by which people come to make inferences about another's viewpoints, responses, or inner states. What sets perspective-taking in this sense apart from the other processes that may become implicated in other-directed introspection is that, instead of drawing on

---

[11] If the totally unscientific observation of one's own children is anything to go on, whenever the author's own 21-month-old baby hears another baby crying, she screws up her face in a look of mock anguish, taps her head, and repeats, "Head! Head!" suggesting that the reason why the baby is crying is because he is in pain from having bumped his head—although admittedly whether this is in and of itself constitutes evidence of entertaining a belief about other babies' inner states rather than the expression of a causal belief about what makes babies cry is an open question.

such things as knowledge of social scripts, memories of past experiences, and interpretations of linguistic expressions and narratives, it involves what Eisenberg et al. (1997) and Gordon (1996) call "mental simulation" (p. 77), what Blum (1980b) called "imaginative dwelling", what, in Adam Smith's (1759/1976) hands became, "changing places in fancy with the sufferer", and what the vernacular describes as the process of "putting yourself in the other guy's shoes"—in each case actively imagining another person's experiences. Because the point is as crucial as it is easy to overlook, it would not hurt to recall as well that perspective-taking in neither this narrower more technical sense nor the more expansive conception of perspective-taking *necessarily* has an emotional dimension. Awareness of another's aversive state is consistent with a wide range of emotional reactions including joy, smug satisfaction, curious excitement, anxious anticipation. It only becomes compassionate empathy when it is joined with an attitude of care or concern for another's suffering as something to be avoided, as we saw above (cf. §3.3).

All signs point in the direction that the notion that imaginatively adopting the perspective of a person in distress evokes empathy is commonplace and is, hence, unlike the other processes touched upon earlier, hardly in need of explanation or justification. Far less frequently recognized, however, is the fact that there are at least two distinct ways to imaginatively engage with another's experiences: (1) via self-focused perspective-taking, imagining how one would feel or react if one were *oneself* in another's position, and (2) via other-focused perspective-taking, imagining how the other person would or does feel *himself* or *herself* in the situation. Most important for our purposes is the possibility that these two modes of imaginative involvement evoke significantly different affective responses.

Psychological treatment of perspective-taking and related emotions, Batson et al. (1997, p. 751) tell us, frequently fails to acknowledge the distinction (cf., e.g., Aderman et al., 1974; Davis, 1994; Davis et al., 1996). This may come as a surprise, since, as Blum (1980b, p. 510) suggests, there is at least one possibly mundane respect in which the difference in imaginative orientation—self- or other-focused—may evidently connect with a person's perception and affective response to another's situation. To borrow Blum's (1980b) example, take a case where someone's adult child has decided to make a career in the military. If I were, say, a pacifist and if my first reaction is to imagine how I would feel if I were one of the parents, I would very likely feel great sympathy towards them. However, were I to somehow come to learn that the child's parents believe that a military career is as good as a career in any other field, I might, imagining the situation now from their perspective, conclude that they are no longer the appropriate object of my sympathy— or, at any rate, not in quite the same way. However, the kinds of cases that research in social psychology into self- versus other-focused perspective-taking regard as typical are not at all cases where a person's personal beliefs and circumstances would seem to be determinant. To take only Hoffman's (2000) examples to illustrate, the situations he describes are invariably those that putatively anyone, regardless of character, values, or life-situation could reasonably find distressing: the experience of severe physical pain (p. 53), losing a close relative in an accident (p. 55), or from disease (p. 57), discovering one's newborn child has a severe congenital disease (pp. 57–58), and the like. Yet, even in these cases, Hoffman (2000) argues, it is possible to imaginatively engage in a self- and other-focused way with the significant difference being that self-focused perspective-taking correlates with "more intense empathic affect" (p. 55), as he puts it. What evidence supports this claim and what more can be said about the difference between self- and other-focused perspective-taking as precursors of compassionate empathy? In order to answer these questions, Hoffman draws primarily a recent study conducted by Batson et al. (1997), which addresses empirically precisely these questions.

Hoffman (2000) and Batson et al. (1997) agree that Stotland's (1969) seminal empathy research suggests strongly that self-focused perspective-taking and other-focused perspective-taking are indeed significantly different experiences. Stotland's (1969) research subjects, observing through a one-way mirror a confederate undergoing what they were led to believe was a painful diathermic treatment, were divided into a group instructed to adopt a self-focused perspective and another an other-focused perspective. A third control group was asked to pay careful attention to the confederate's physical movements. Briefly, the other-imaginers scored higher on one physiological measure (i.e., vasoconstriction), whereas the self-imaginers scored higher on another (i.e., palmar sweat). In their verbal reports, the self-imaginers expressed, as Batson et al. (1997) summarized it, feeling "more tension and nervousness" (p. 751) than either the other-imaginers or the control group. Batson et al. (1997) study aimed to build on Stotland's (1969) findings by targeting a more nuanced profile of the kinds of empathic responses evoked by the two perspectives. In order to isolate compassionate empathy from other possible emotional responses, their measurements were based, importantly, on the tracking what they called "direct distress"—emotional responses that are *personally* disturbing— and levels of "empathic distress"—emotional responses *for* a person in need— rather than basing the study on a methodological technique called "factor analysis". Factor analysis, in this case, would operationalize the distinction between experiences of empathic distress and direct distress in reference to lists of codeable words of phrases held to be indicative of empathic distressing (e.g., "sympathetic", "moved", "compassionate", etc.) or personally distressing responses (e.g., "alarmed", "troubled", "perturbed", etc.) (cf. p. 752). Although possibly not without some validity—which it is admittedly beyond the competence of the present author to ascertain with any authority—one can nevertheless appreciate how factor analysis, as used in this case, might fail to distinguish instances of personal or direct distress from empathic distress or distress for another person. One may be "troubled" *by* another's situation no less than one may be "troubled" *for* another in his or her situation. Like Stotland (1969), Batson et al. (1997) randomly assigned participants to control, imagine-other, and imagine-self groups and recorded participants' responses to a fictitious interview with a young woman, "Katie", in highly distressing personal circumstances. The control group, rather than being asked to imagine how the woman feels or to imagine how they themselves would feel in the woman's place, were instructed to "remain objective and detached" by avoiding imagining how she feels and what she has experienced (p. 752). To quote from the authors' interpretation of their findings directly, their data analysis showed that:

> [P]articipants instructed to imagine how Katie felt reported more empathy than distress and more empathy than did participants instructed to remain objective. When asked about the nature of their distress, these participants reported a relatively high level of empathic distress for Katie and a relatively low level of direct distress. In contrast, participants instructed to imagine how they would feel in Katie's situation reported high levels of both empathy and distress, more of each than was reported by participants instructed to remain objective. When asked about the nature of their distress, these participants reported relatively high levels of both distress for Katie and direct distress. (p. 756)

In other words, both the self- and other-imaginers showed higher empathic responses when compared with the objective group but the self-imaginers reported higher levels of personal distress than the other-imaginers. More than just being unsurprising, this result is to be expected; focusing on how one would oneself feel in very upsetting circumstances would seem naturally to evoke self-directed feelings rather than feelings for the victim. Be that as it may, Batson et al. (1997) and Hoffman (2000) seem to concur that, owing to the greater affective intensity with which it correlates, self-focused perspective-taking is likely to create a stronger motivation to help than other-focused perspective-taking—although, as Batson et al., (1997) note such a motivation is likely to be tainted from the viewpoint of altruism, being related to a motivation to relieve one's own negative emotional state brought about by self-focused perspective-taking (p. 757, cf. Batson, 1991). Hoffman's (2000) major caveat concerning self-focused perspective-taking is that, while it is more emotionally evocative that other-focused perspective-taking, self-focused perspective-taking is also more susceptible to egoistic drift (p. 56). As mentioned earlier (in §2.2.2), egoistic drift occurs when attention to another person's traumatic experience triggers feelings of personal distress, often evoked by memories of a similar painful experience in the person's past or worries about something similar happening to him or her in the future. Illustrating with excerpts from interviews, Hoffman shows that such feelings of personal distress can continue to occur in conjunction with feelings of genuine empathic distress. But when they reach a certain point of intensity, they may resonate so strongly that the observer actually "forgets about" the victim altogether and ruminates instead on the observer's own personal distress (pp. 56–58). In this way, the initial concern for another person transmutes into feelings of concern for oneself and, becoming thus self-focused, cease to be feelings of compassionate empathy altogether.

3.5   Summary and Discussion

As a point of entry into understanding compassionate empathy as a moral *disposition* susceptible to furthering and support in professional and practical ethics education, this chapter analysed compassionate empathy from the perspective of an *experienced* emotion. To retrace the analysis' main points, experiences of compassionate empathy are characterized by specific propositional beliefs and a distinct but no less characteristic form of caring involvement in another's suffering. The first three of the five cognitive components of compassionate empathy, as I called them, circumscribe

the emotion's appropriate objects. Judgements of compassionate empathy pick out
(1) objects whose well-being is faced with a *serious* threat. Concerning individuals,
or groups or categories of individuals indiscriminately, they are (2) *sufferer-focused*
in that they attend to an object in harmful state not the event, circumstance, or
affliction which has caused the harm in question. Lastly, a judgement of compassionate empathy are not restricted to considerations of overall well-being but may
be directed at forms of harm considered in isolation from the overall well-being of
its object. Otherwise put, they may be (3) *holistic* or *dimensional*. It was observed
further that judgements of compassionate empathy have identifiable knowledge
conditions. Sufferers (4) need not be *aware* of their aversive states in order to be
the appropriate object of compassionate empathy and, perhaps surprisingly, one
need not be right about one's appraisal of the object's state in order to have said to
experience compassionate empathy. Judgements of compassionate empathy, that
is, (5) need not be *empathically accurate*. Supposing, as experiences of compassionate empathy do, insight into another's aversive state merely believing that
another is suffering in some significant way is not compassionate empathy. Caring
about the sufferer in his or her aversive situation, or perceiving suffering as being
in need of alleviation, and (as a possible corollary of caring) experiencing a sense
of human solidarity with the sufferer is definitive of compassionate empathy. For
one may be involved in another's suffering in any number of ways. In *Schadenfreude*,
for instance, one takes some satisfaction in seeing another suffering and a clinician
might view a person's suffering principally as a technical problem. Punch and Judy
shows and similar sadistic entertainments take harm and suffering as cause for
amusement. Compassionate empathy as an emotional experience is the marriage of
other-directed insight into another's suffering *and* an analytically distinct affective
tenor comprising (6) a state of *caring* involvement in that suffering with (7) a sense
of *shared humanity* (see Table 3.1 in §3.3).

Folk psychology tends to hold that the experience of compassionate empathy
involves a more or less linear three-step run-up. Drawing on a process of imaginative

Table 3.1 The cognitive components and affective tenor of compassionate empathy

Cognitive components	**Objects**	(1) *Seriousness*: Judgements attend to an aversive situation posing a serious threat to genuine well-being.
		(2) *Sufferer focus*: Judgements attend to the harmed individual or group not the harmful event, circumstances, or affliction causally responsible for the harm.
		(3) *Holism* or *dimensionality*: Judgements attend to either *somme tout* well-being or a particular dimension of well-being.
	Knowledge conditions	(4) *Awareness*: Judgements attend to states of suffering of which the object may or may not himself or herself be aware.
		(5) *Empathic accuracy*: Judgements may be based on false beliefs about the object's aversive situation.
Affective tenor		(6) *Caring*: The sufferer's aversive state is regarded as something to be removed or alleviated.
		(7) *Shared humanity*: The sufferer is identified with as someone deserving of consideration, attention, and respect.

dwelling on the sufferer's state, the empathizer forms beliefs about a sufferer's aversive state and becomes disposed to alleviate or relive the perceived suffering. Based on a review of the diverse psychological processes known in social psychology to play a mediating role in the experience of compassionate empathy, we found that the pathway to compassionate empathic experience can be *cognitively* much simpler than the folk account supposes but that, at the same time, the overall story of compassionate empathic arousal is *psychologically* more complex. The cognitively simple "reactive" modes of empathic arousal—namely, the processes of (1) "conditioning", where visual cues such as the sight of blood elicit distressing feelings; (2) "mimicry", where the involuntary imitation of a person in distress produces feelings in the imitator that affectively match those of the imitated; (3) "direct association", a process whereby feelings of compassion are triggered via the association either of a particular feature of another person's experience of suffering or his or her situation generally with some traumatic or distressing event in the observer's own past—belie the idea referred to as the "perspective-taking/compassionate empathy hypothesis", the widespread assumption that cognitively demanding psychological processes and in particular mental simulation *necessarily* interpolate in the arousal of feelings of compassionate empathy. In fact, there seems to be broad consensus in social psychology that not just one but *several* cognitively more complex "introspective" modes can be associated with compassionate empathic arousal. There is (4) "language-mediated association" which refers to a very broad set of situations in which language plays a central role in communicating a person's feelings or her empathy-evoking situation, (5) "labelling", and (6) "cognitive networking" where inferences about a person's inner states are drawn from stereotyped chunks of knowledge about perceptual cues and especially social scripts, in addition to (7) perspective-taking. Moreover, perspective-taking itself may in turn be self-focused or other-focused with significant documented differences in the type and intensity of thoughts and feelings evoked (see Table 3.2 in §3.4).

Table 3.2 Multiple psychological processes mediating experiences of compassionate empathy

Reactive processes	(1) Conditioning	Visual cues elicit distressing feelings.
	(2) Mimicry	Involuntary imitation of a person in distress stimulates empathic feelings.
	(3) Direct association	Circumstantial features recalling a traumatic event evokes distressing feelings.
Introspective processes	(4) Language-mediated association	A person's empathy-evoking situation is communicated by language.
	(5) Labelling	An inference about internal states is based on standard social beliefs or generalizations about personality types.
	(6) Cognitive networking	An inference about internal states is based on complex social scripts.
	(7) Perspective-taking	*Other-focused*: Imagining what it would be like to be a person believed to be in an aversive state.
		Self-focused: Imagining how one would feel or react if one were oneself in another's aversive situation.

This study's snapshot view of the experience of compassionate empathy has brought into focus two questions—root and branch conceptual questions each— that puzzle the suggestion to use professional and practical ethics education as a site for the development of capacities of compassionate empathic responding.

The first question, in short, is whether compassionate empathy is indeed a moral emotion. The foregoing account is consistent with the intuitive idea that compassionate empathy is a positive social emotion. It suggests that there is an internal relation between compassionate empathy's characteristic attitude of solicitousness towards others' well-being and a conative disposition to further it. If what it means to experience compassionate empathy is to want to alleviate or avoid a perceived aversive state, it should not be surprising if the people who tend to become compassionately involved in other people's problems are the same people who tend to actually act in order to help them. Indeed, as we saw, 30 years of research on empathy in social psychology confirm this conceptual claim empirically: empathy correlates strongly with pro-social and helping behaviour (cf. §3.3). Helping behaviour is nevertheless not *ipso facto* moral behaviour, or what might be defensibly considered moral behaviour when evaluated from a position of impartiality. Neither is every moral act necessarily a helping act, or at least not in any straightforward sense; just as the best-intentioned carer can do more harm than good, fairness sometimes demands acting in ways that are prejudicial to one person's interests in the name of another's. Furthermore, it is not out of the question for compassionate empathy to motivate manifestly unfair acts, as in familiar cases of giving unjustifiable preferential treatment to friends, relatives, or others with whom one happens to identify—an entirely predictable consequence, perhaps, of the known reactive and especially associative nature of compassionate empathic responding. The *prima facie* prospect that these realities raise is that compassionate empathy is neither necessary nor sufficient for moral performance.[12] But this feature of compassionate empathy is difficult to square with the eulogious terms in which we saw compassionate empathy described earlier (in §1.2); Hilfiker (2001), Callahan (1980), Coombs (1998), Scholz and Groarke (1996), and others clearly single out compassionate empathy for special educational attention in virtue of a special *moral* quality it possesses; were compassionate empathy to have only incidental moral worth—that is, if it motivates moral acts or draws one's attention to morally salient features of situations only if it is directed by some prior and distinct moral intention or judgement—it is hard to see what makes compassionate empathy different from many other emotions in this regard. After all, any number of emotions including anger, indignation, shame, courage, and fear seem no less susceptible, when properly directed by sound moral judgement, to motivate moral acts and sharpen moral perception. Can these conflicting claims be reconciled?

Quite apart from the question of whether or not compassionate empathy is a genuine moral emotion is a second question that the results of this study raise vis-à-vis the prospects of supporting empathic responsiveness in professional and

---

[12] For parallel assessments, see Verducci (1999) and Blasi (1999).

practical ethics education. Is it realistic to think that compassionate empathy as emotional response can be educated in a meaningful sense? Although phrasing the question in these terms might make the matter seem to be first and foremost a *practical* one, the problem, in the first instance, amounts to sorting out what it *means* to morally educate emotions. Peters (1972/1998) once proposed that the educability of the emotions rests on the extent to which they are based on a particular type of cognition he called, following Arnold (1960), "appraisals" (p. 180). On the basis of his analysis of what "education" means in ordinary language, Peters defined it as an activity centrally concerned with developing knowledge and understanding based on public standards of assessment (cf. Peters, 1973). There is scope for educating emotions, he argued, only insofar as they are inextricably bound up with beliefs that are susceptible to such assessment (cf. 1972/1998, pp. 179–181). For instance, a student's feeling of shame after failing a math test can be in Peter's sense "educated" by pointing to the fact that he did the best he could or to the fact that the test was particularly hard and lots of other students failed it too or to some other consideration that is supposed to show that he really has no good *reason* to be ashamed. Applied to compassionate empathy, one might attempt to "educate" a person who fails to experience compassionate empathy towards another in a particular situation by pointing out the relevant features of his situation that *should* evoke the emotion in question. If things are as Peters (1972/1998) sees it, and the only scope for educating compassionate empathy is by way of rational scrutiny of the cognitions underlying such emotions, the account given here would suggest that this scope is modest indeed. Specifically, even if one grants that it is possible to provide reasons that any rational person could presumably accept that, in a particular situation, he or she should be having the kind of judgement that is characteristic of compassionate empathy whether and to what degree that person *reacts* to such a judgement with an attitude of *caring* or, in other words, becomes *compassionately involved* in that person's situation is liable to be highly particular to each individual. For such reactions, as we saw (in §3.4) are dependent on conditioning, personal associations with surface cues, or the narrative structure of the situation, structures which may include past personal experience as a point of identification between an observer and an object of compassionate empathy. In sum, even if one accepts the view that the failure to experience compassionate empathy in conjunction with a characteristic judgement of compassionate empathy and its objects is a failure of practical rationality (of one sort) the answer to the relevant educational question— namely, whether, how, and to what degree one *in fact* responds with compassionate empathy—is to be found less in the structure of judgement as such than it is in such educational intangibles as socialization, will, disposition, and the influence of contextual factors. Even if reason, to paraphrase Hume, is not in every case a slave to the passions, the passions are, in this case, the slave to socialization in the sense that patterns of empathic response reflect its vagaries. Before jumping to hasty educational conclusions, however, bear in mind that the idea of promoting empathic responding in professional and practical ethics education is not merely that compassionate empathic responses should be somehow stimulated then subjected to rational scrutiny when and if they fail to meet reasonable standards of appraisal.

The leading idea seemed instead to involve creating an education climate favourable to the advancement of compassionate empathy as *generalized state of heightened ethical sensitivity* to harms and threats to well-being. Compassionate empathy, in other words, is imagined as a cultivated moral disposition or skill, a moral virtue if you like. Like practical wisdom itself, compassionate empathy in this sense is the result of training, practice, habituation, and reflection but also susceptible to high degrees of variation from individual to individual and, in all likelihood, from circumstance to circumstance—features that make compassionate empathy a rare human achievement (if not an unrealizable moral ideal) and, most importantly for present purposes, an appropriate object of the kind of educational refinement higher education has historically been well positioned to provide. Without denying that it has merits and much interest, the just-in-time, straightforwardly rationalist conception of the moral education of emotions Peters (1972/1998) identifies just does not seem to be quite the right tool for the moral education of emotional *dispositions* and this observation, moreover, raises the distinct possibility that we have in Peters' account just one among a set of plausible conceptions of what the moral education of the emotions consists in.

We will go back to consider the possibility of a pluralistic conception of emotion education when we address educational matters in earnest in Chapter 6. For now, let us study the prior question of what a moral emotion is and whether compassionate empathy is one.

Chapter 4
The Paradox of Compassionate Empathy's Moral Worth

4.1 Introduction

At first blush the question of what is good about compassionate empathy might seem too obvious to be the serious subject of study. Like love, attachment, and concern, compassionate empathy is, to borrow de Sousa's (2001) term, a "nice" emotion; it is one that is generally approved of in virtue of being thought to be conducive to moral consciousness and behaviour and stands in contrast with "nasty" ones—pride, envy, malice, and the like—having just the opposite tendency (cf. also Ben Ze'ev, 2001; and Noddings, 1998). From this perspective, a "moral emotion" is one of the nice emotions just as an "immoral emotion" is one of the nasty emotions and on this basis one might posit the existence a class of "amoral emotions" that have clear tendencies in neither direction. On closer examination, however, the distinction begins to unravel. After all, a "nice" emotion like love can have a hand in destructive jealousy and, as was suggested at the end of Chapter 3, compassionate empathy is not always so nice either—as, for instance, when a benefactor's well-intentioned assistance over time stifles a beneficiary's ability to look after himself or herself or, more generally, when actions aimed at protecting a person from harm lead in the final analysis to more harm than good. Furthermore, a blanket moral injunction against nasty emotions like anger fails to recognize, according to Aristotle (4th century B.C.E./1955), that *not* to feel some anger in the face of a deliberate and unjust attempt to frustrate one's interests is weak-hearted if not foolish (NE, 1126a8). Also relevant, to reintroduce another point made at the end of Chapter 3, is that anger and possibly other emotions that could be considered nasty, when properly channelled by judgement at least, can conceivably play a role in recognizing a situation as one that poses a moral problem and motivate a moral action. Such observations raise legitimate doubts about whether any emotion deserves to be considered a moral emotion categorically and seem to favour instead the proposal that an emotion's moral status may always depend first and foremost on whether the acts it motivates are morally justified and the intentions underlying it are morally sound rather than on some supposed inherent conduciveness to a moral outlook and ethical conduct. While this assessment might seem to hit the mark for emotions generally, it seems to badly overshoot it if only in the case of compassionate empathy. Chapter 3 argued that solicitude towards another's well-being is the characteristic emotional attitude of compassionate empathy and that such a motive contributes to the performance of beneficent—if not in some cases actually moral—actions (cf. esp. §3.3). These qualities parallel a moral orientation close enough so that to begrudge compassionate empathy the status of a moral emotion on the grounds that it issues in moral acts imperfectly seems philosophically cheap. This chapter studies the problem of how and whether it is possible to reconcile these two conflicting but apparently equally convincing ideas about compassionate empathy's moral status. It will be argued that the paradox dissolves in large measure when one recognizes the various and distinct ways in which it is possible to speak of an emotion as being "moral" or at least as being implicated in moral functioning: first, as a constitutive component of excellences or defaults of moral character; second, as a judgement-distorting passion; and third, as being generally conducive to moral consciousness and action (§4.2). What the distinction entails, obviously, is that, in view of being a member of the elite club of moral emotions in the first sense, compassionate empathy has a genuine claim to categorical moral value—and, indeed, *a fortiori* I will argue (in §4.3) that compassionate empathy has a special morally elevated status in that class itself. However, like all emotions, compassionate empathy is liable to become passionate. In this connection, and as demonstrated by a brief review of empirical evidence and related theoretical considerations to the effect that compassionate empathy has an apparently constitutional susceptibility to bias (in §4.4.1), empathy's incompatibility with the ideal of the impartiality of moral judgement is little short of striking. After briefly setting out the meaning of impartiality as a criterion of moral evaluation and arguing that standard objections levied against impartiality as a genuine criterion of a moral evaluation seem to miss the mark (§4.4.2), I conclude that, irrespective of the fact that compassionate empathy is strongly antithetical to one crucial dimension of a moral outlook—impartiality—its attractiveness as a focal point of moral-developmental interest and educational intervention is both explained and justified by the fact that it expresses just as strongly another—the idea of normativity or, loosely, that human needs carry with them binding practical demands on one's attentions and actions.

4.2   Three Positions of the Relevance of Emotions in Ethics

We may consider the first position vis-à-vis the ethical significance of emotions as that commonly associated with Aristotle: excellences of moral character are concerned not just with what one does but also how one feels (Aristotle, 4th century B.C.E./1955, 1104b). Bravery consist not only in facing danger but facing it, as Aristotle puts it, "gladly, or at least without distress", whereas a coward, he held, faced danger in a state of distress (Aristotle, 4th century B.C.E./1955, 1104b). Moderation is willing abstinence whereas licentiousness finds it irksome (Aristotle, 4th century B.C.E./1955, 1104b). An arrogant person, one might add, feels too much self-regard while in a humble or modest person self-regard is properly balanced, and so on. So much, in Aristotle's view, are the virtues concerned with emotions that he suggests that an indispensable component of the definition of any particular virtue was a description of its emotional tenor. Accordingly, he argued, "true education" is habituation from an early age to feel the right emotions to the right degree at the right time (Aristotle, 1955, 1104b; cf. White, 1998; Carr, 1991). The general point, of course, is that emotional responses are commonly the subject of normative evaluation; one *should*, for example, be cheerful when visiting relatives, be respectful when dealing with a legitimate authority, be apologetic towards a person one has hurt, show sympathy in the face of undeserved suffering, and feel guilty when having transgressed a moral rule that one accepts.[1]

In this connection it is worth noting further that the modulation of one's spontaneous emotional reactions so as to achieve the normatively required measure and proportion of emotional response a situation calls for does not aim to achieve mere outward conformity or the impression of virtuousness. Rather, *mimesis*, in this sense, functions as a sentimental-education strategy or technique; by *putting on* an emotional reaction, if done frequently and consistency and under proper tutelage, can over time habituate spontaneous genuine appropriate affective responding (cf. Steutel & Spiecker, 2004). Just as pretending not to be afraid—"pulling oneself together"—in the face of, say, fear of getting on an airplane can in some cases be the first step towards overcoming fear of flying, so too can a pattern of envy towards others' successes be transformed into a pattern of feeling happy for others by the habitual *dissimulation* of envy and the *display* of gladness.[2]

Furthermore, it should be pointed out (de Sousa, 2001, p. 110) that the Aristotelian account, focusing as it does on the characteristic patterns of emotional responding in an account of a well-lived or virtuous life, does not identify a particular class of emotions that play a special or central role in moral life either by motivating moral acts, expressing moral intentions, or distorting moral judgement but views instead *all* emotions as having intrinsic ethical significance. Because requests to imitate target any emotional response that deviates from the circumstantially prescribed norm of good moral character, whatever that response might be, no specific range of emotions seems to be the appropriate object of requests to imitate. That having been said, however, some emotions seem categorically normatively inappropriate and, hence, a coherent object only of attempts to pretend *not* to experience

---

[1] Even if one disagrees with these particular normative expectations, the main point is that such normative standards are probably a universal moral phenomenon even thought the specific content of such expectations will naturally vary to some degree from cultural community to cultural community.

[2] The popular notion of pulling oneself together emotionally is usually discussed in the philosophical literature on the emotions and emotional regulation as "bootstrapping" (e.g., Kristjánsson, 2005). An occasion to present a more detailed picture of the several strategies which may assist in efforts to bootstrap will arise when the discussion returns to examine various conceptions of educating moral emotions in Chapter 6.

them. These emotions would cover, surely, all the "nasty" emotions to which we turn shortly—malice, rage, callousness, and the like—but might encompass such emotions as pride, *Schadenfreude*, and maudlin.

In addition to the fact that the emotions are the subject of normative evaluation in the sense that balance and appropriateness of emotional responding is inextricably bound up with ideals of moral character, it seems unmistakable as well that some emotions, or possibly even emotions generally, are deleterious to the exercise of practical wisdom. This second conception of moral emotions is naturally associable with the Stoics who, in the name of personal enlightenment, exhorted their followers to eliminate emotions to the extent that it is possible. The passions are false, they held, because they ascribe too much importance to external things and render people's happiness dependent on the world (cf., e.g., de Sousa, 2001; Nussbaum, 1994, 2001). Buddhists as well have historically been exercised by the practical-judgement distorting powers of the emotions. Not advocating the total abnegation of feelings, both these eudaimonistic philosophies hold that desires and passions which are based on mistaken beliefs about the world are responsible for personal and social ills; true beliefs tend to issue in emotional moderation that are consistent with sound practical judgement and a virtuous life. It is in Descartes' less ascetic prescriptions in connection with the control of the passions, however, that we find a more familiar version of this thesis which can be referred to for the sake of convenience as the "rationalist" conception of the role of emotions in moral life.

In *Les passions de l'âme* (1649/1984), Descartes asserts that the principal utility of the emotions is to provide motivational force to the desires of the soul or mind, as fear compels a frightened person to flee, anger to fight, and so on (§40). Related, the emotions are necessary to the sustention of the Cartesian mind–body union by motivating the procurance of the body's material needs. In Descartes' words, they "dispose our soul to want the things which nature deems useful for us, and to persist in this volition; and the same agitation of the spirits which normally causes the passions also disposes the body to make movements which help us to attain these things" (§52). In keeping with his self-professed approach to the subject of the passions as being that of the impartial observer, and not as a "rhetorician or even as a moral philosopher", Descartes observes that while the passions, on one hand, contribute to our well-being, they are also prone to harmful excesses (cf. §211). Notorious in this regard are love, fear, jealousy, grief, and anger. Although it is probably not inaccurate to state that Descartes held that the passions could distort the faculty of practical reason, his actual position seems to have been somewhat more sophisticated than this. Because we can never directly control the passions and only with difficulty control them indirectly (§§45–50), for Descartes, practical wisdom *is* in large part nothing other than the ability to control the passions (cf. Garber, 1992). He writes, the "chief use of wisdom lies in its teaching us to be masters of our passions and to control them with such skill that the evils which they cause are quite bearable, and even become a source of joy" (§212).

Just as on the Aristotelian account, then, moral emotions in the passion theory of Descartes comprise a broad palette. Indeed, all emotions are prone to "excesses" and it is difficult to think of an emotion that could not, in some circumstances, lead to harm. However, unlike the Aristotelian account where virtue comprises the moderation of emotional excesses and extremes (as for instance in the Aristotelian idea that courage is a mean between rashness and fearfulness), the general Cartesian supposition seems to be that the emotions pose a singular threat to the proper exercise of practical reason. If it were not for the emotions, in other words, human beings would be in possession of right moral judgement in virtue of their rational faculty. Never free of vulnerability to the passion in virtue of embodiment, the most morally broken human beings can hope for is a degree of mastery over them.

A comparable but more modest (and possibly more credible) take on the judgement-distorting capacities of emotions has been worked out in contemporary interpretation of Kantian views of the role of emotions in moral judgement. According to this view, emotions can play a moral-perceptual role, drawing a person's attention to the morally salient features of a situation and proposing action incentives (cf., e.g., Sherman, 1990; Korsgaard, 1999; Herman, 1984, 1996)—viewing, say, in a bakery a child's repeated request for service being ignored might inspire feelings of indignation which in turn might motivate one to take a stand in the child's defence. However, because this moral-perceptive faculty is highly susceptible to error, one's spontaneous emotional responses are not a reliable guide to what constitutes right action in a set of circumstances and therefore must be subjected to what Sherman (1990) refers to as the "regulative constraint" of practical judgement. Practical wisdom, it follows, constitutes at least in part a mechanism which strives to ensure consistency between one's spontaneous appraisal of a situation and how one would appraise it under conditions of full rationality.[3] In Kantian terminology, one could say that an emotional response can issue in a genuinely autonomous act insofar as the deliberating agent could accept as a law in a "kingdom of ends"—that is, the agent conceiving himself or herself as at once legislator and subject to the law—the justificatory principle on which the proposal suggested by an emotion is based (cf. Hill, 2000; Korsgaard, 1999).

Turning now to the third position on the relevance of emotions in moral experience, given that human beings are both apparently naturally endowed with an altruistic disposition and their singular capacity for cruelty, it should come as no surprise that naturalistic eudaimonistic philosophies through the ages—ideas prominent in the writings of Epictetus (First century C.E./1925, 1928), Seneca (First century C.E./1969), and Lao-Tzu (Sixth century B.C.E./1961) among others—should prescribe the cultivation of a set of "moral" emotions defined in virtue of their inherent objects and affective profile that render them conducive to moral consideration and behaviour.

More recently, and largely as an expression of dissatisfaction with excessive rationalism in ethical theory, later-day proponents of moral sense theory claim that the ability to form moral judgements presupposes the active exercise of sympathy.

---

[3] Full rationality is understood here rather formally in William's (1981) broad sense of being based on no false beliefs, having only relevant true beliefs, and correct deliberation (cf. also Smith, 1994).

Hume (1751/1957), for instance, considered that moral "approval" of an act or character trait just is the feeling that the act or character trait in question is conducive to general human well-being. Analogous ideas are central to Adam Smith's (1790/1976) theory of moral sentiments and Scheler's (1954) "inverted Kantianism" (cf. Vetlesen, 1994). For his part, Schopenhauer (1840/1995) appeals to a class of "other-directed" emotions as the ground of all genuinely moral actions. Parallels are perceptible as well in Blum's (1980) idea of the trinity of "altruistic emotions" of sympathy, compassion, and "human concern" (p. 1) which form an identifiable category of emotions in light of taking as their objects "persons in light of their 'weal' and, especially, their 'woe'" (p. 12) and necessarily involving a conative or motivational aspect directed at the promotion of the object's well-being (p. 13). As mentioned more than once earlier (in §§2.2.2. and 3.3) empathy and its related emotions have attracted the attention of social psychologists seeking empirical evidence for the link between sympathy and helping and to understand the related psychological mechanisms.

Though apparently lower profile members, emotions of guilt and shame seem to deserve a place in this category of emotions prone to motivating moral behaviour as well. In Freud's analysis, for example, guilt is the conscious manifestation of anxiety produced when the standards of the superego are violated (see Freud, 1986, p. 459). In Hoffman's (2000) theory of moral development it is feelings of guilt, a socialized response to the prospect of harming another person (p. 151), that helps to explain the workings of the process of "de-centration" in moral development theory whereby children come to be willing to negotiate and compromise their own claims in the face of other's conflicting claims (pp. 130–132). The inclusion of shame and guilt in the category of moral emotions, however, might seem to suggest the need to revise the idea that "other-directedness" is the category's defining criterion. Guilt being the feeling of regret and responsibility for having caused some unjustified harm, and shame being distress at being seen failing to live up to some serious or important public expectation (cf. similar definitions in Stocker, 1996, pp. 3–4, 217–219; Nussbaum, 2001, pp. 215–216; Wallace, 1994, pp. 38–39; Williams, 1993; Taylor, 1985) are, in Taylor's phrase, "emotions of self-assessment". Nevertheless, where feelings of guilt and shame are connected with some harm done to another and especially when, in such cases, they motivate rectification, reconciliation, or otherwise have a hand in motivating "niceness" they seem to remain concerned, albeit indirectly, with promotion of others' well-being.

Putting the question of which particular emotions might make up the most defensible list of *the* moral emotions, some basic level of moral-affective responsiveness seems to be almost universally regarded as a psychological precondition of normal social functioning.[4] Post-Darwinian explanations of the apparently natural human disposition towards this "fellow feeling", in Smith's (1759/1976) phrase,

---

[4] An exception might be Nietzsche and kindred spirits who seem to regard the moral emotions as a form of human frailty (cf. Nietzsche, 1954, 1999).

appeal to the adaptive value of this trait in small groups of human beings who must cooperate with one another in order to survive, social conditions though to characterize all but the tiniest fraction of human evolutionary history (cf. esp. Hoffman, 1981). Seen in this way as a broad, general, and quasi-perceptive *disposition*, the problem of regulation is primarily a problem of socialization—that is, of identifying which social conditions or social interactions favour, support, reinforce, and enhance the emergence of sympathetic responding and which impede it (cf. Hoffman, 2000). It does not seem entirely beside the point, either, to observe the connection between perspective-taking, imagination, and the moral emotions. Chapter 3 recorded the persistent moral psychological folk belief that "empathizing" or vicarious involvement in another's experience of suffering spontaneously generates feelings of sympathy, compassion, and concern for the suffering person—insofar, of course, as the state of woe in question is held to be undeserved.[5] For this generalization to be acceptable it must be qualified by the condition that it applies only to moral agents whose disposition to respond to others with care falls within a psychologically normal range.

In sum, the "moral" emotions are morally significant because they contribute to moral motivation and, at least according to some philosophical accounts (esp. Hume, 1751/1957 and Smith, 1759/1976), they are inexorably bound up with the phenomenon of moral appraisal insofar as it seems difficult to explain why anyone would be interested in morality if they were not somehow operating under their influence. In regards to moral motivation, moral emotions may: (1) provide a motivational counterweight to a harmful intention by contributing to feelings of guilt or shame either at the prospect of harming another (cf. Hoffman, 2000); or (2) motivate actions that are intended to alleviate perceived suffering (i.e., "pro-social", "helping", or "altruistic" behaviours; cf. esp. Batson, 1991; Davis, 1994; and Eisenberg & Miller, 1987a).

4.3 Compassionate Empathy as a "Quasi-ethical Achievement"

The foregoing discussion of three interpretations to which emotions are susceptible in the context of discussions of moral appraisal and conduct clarifies, perhaps, how it is that the common sense notion of a specific class of inherently nice emotions can be sustained in the face of suggestions to the contrary. To reintroduce the counter-examples raised above, the claim that love is not an inherently nice emotion because it can lead to destructiveness overlooks the fact that there is nothing inconsistent in holding that love is a nice emotion in virtue of its characteristic objects and intentions *and* that it is, like all emotions, susceptible to distorting one's

---

[5] For an in-depth discussion of the role of perceived desert in emotions involved in the appraisal of others' conditions of well-being, see Kristjánsson (2003).

judgement when excessive or otherwise unregulated. Similarly, to hold that anger is not an inherently nasty emotion in light of the fact that in some circumstances anger is appropriate fails to recognize the fact that anger, understood as the feeling of aggressive ill will directed towards another person, does sometime motivate harmful actions does not preclude that it might be praiseworthy or even virtuous to be angry, as Aristotle put it, "at the right things, and with the right people, and, further, as he ought, when he ought, and as long as he ought" (NE, 1125b32)—that is, in the right circumstances. In sum, there seems to be little doubt that the notions that (1) balanced and appropriate emotional responses are part and parcel of any defensible conception of good character; (2) emotions can become passionate and in this capacity sometimes motivate harmful behaviour and cloud moral judgement, and; (3) certain emotions have a categorically good status in light of being characteristically directed at human well-being. These are distinct but nevertheless entirely mutually compatible views of the role that the emotions play in ethical life.

It might seem superfluous, then, to state that the moral worth of compassionate empathy relates to its membership of the privileged class of moral or nice emotions whose moral worth derives in turn from their contribution to moral behaviour and moral consciousness. But what more can be said about what it means for a moral emotion to *tend towards* or to be *conducive to* moral consciousness and moral actions?

Most obviously, compassionate empathy's moral significance might seem to consist in nothing more than the fact that it motivates helpful behaviour, however imperfectly. We know already that there is a broad consensus in social psychology that "empathy" or "empathic distress", terms understood as functional analogues to compassionate empathy as it is understood in this work, correlates positively with, precedes, and contributes to beneficent acts (cf. §3.3 and Hoffman, 2000; Batson, 1991; Davis, 1996). Such pro-social and helping behaviour, even if sometimes motivated by consideration of extrinsic reward, frequently and commonly procures socially desirable ends (cf. Eisenberg & Miller, 1987a, pp. 91–92). Blum (1980b) argues, however, that this cannot be the whole story about the moral worth of compassionate empathy. Compassionate empathy has *non-instrumental* moral worth, Blum (1980) says, and he supports this claim by pointing to the fact that there are situations where it is appropriate, rational, and possibly obligatory to experience compassionate empathy quite independently of any role the emotion might play in motivating beneficent actions in the circumstances.

At first appearance, the idea of experiencing an emotion for its own sake, be it compassionate empathy or any other, may be recommendable and is easily dismissed as a kind of kitschy Romanticism which self-consciously revels in the experience and enjoyment of emotions. But as both Blum (1980a, 1980b) and Sherman (1990) illustrate in slightly different ways, there seems to be widespread pre-philosophical agreement that, in some circumstances, people do appear to have an obligation to feel compassionate empathy (or at least to *pretend* to feel compassionate empathy) even when it serves no clear instrumental–pragmatic ends. As Sherman argues the point, in ordinary language at least, an act's moral quality can be assessed by reference to a distinction between the mere performance of an act and the *way* that the act is performed (cf. pp. 150–151). She concedes that there are acts, most prominently acts performed in emergency situations that call above all for immediate and effective response. Here, emotional tone is extraneous to the act's moral quality. All the same, a doctor, for instance, who fails to adopt an appropriately compassionate tone in communicating to a patient a diagnosis of a serious and life-threatening medical condition can legitimately, it seems, be charged with some kind of moral shortcoming. This suggestion, however, seems open to two objections.

First, one might simply propose that the performance/tone distinction can be explained away and indeed Sherman admits (1990, p. 51) that an act performed with and without a tone of beneficence could be considered not a single act but two altogether different acts. From this perspective, emotional tone would be viewed as something like a function, expression, or indicator of good intention. An unfeeling action is not the right action performed with the wrong tone. It is just a different action. Even granting this, there are nevertheless times when it is important to distinguish between the action performed and the way it was performed. At such times, it would be viewed as excessively formalistic, if not confusing, to fail to recognize that the same action can be performed in different ways. One can appreciate, for instance, a physician's frankness about a bad prognosis but object to his matter-of-factness about it, just as one can agree with a critic's comments on some piece of written work but resent his arrogant delivery of them.

Second, and somewhat more problematically, one could object that if one can reasonably state that the doctor *should* adopt a compassionate tone, it is because such an expression of concern is valuable to the sufferer and so is valued for its consequences not "in itself" (cf. Blum, 1980b, p. 515). What seems to buttress this objection further is that, in this case at least, what is crucial to the moral quality of the act is that the doctor convincingly *displays* compassion and not the doctor's genuine experience of compassion. Blum (1980b), indeed, faces this objection directly when he argues by appealing to certain carefully circumscribed cases which, he appears to believe, make the non-instrumental values of compassionate empathy inevitable. His counterfactual argument can be summarized as follows. If it were the case that compassionate empathy is only of instrumental value, it would be unreasonable to say that a person *ought to* feel compassionate empathy towards those he or she is powerless to help (e.g., a friend with a terminal illness). These are the cases in question: (1) where the provision of such help would be highly impracticable, as would be, to borrow Blum's example, dropping everything and flying off to assist the victims of some natural disaster (p. 514); (2) where it is not within one's power to remove the suffering caused, for example, by terminal illness or another irreversible affliction (p. 515); and, (3) where inaction is necessary in order to respect a person's autonomy (p. 514). This last case seems to correspond with actions describable as paternalistic in the pejorative sense: intervening in a troubling personal dispute between one's adolescent child and a peer, for instance, or perhaps arranging a job for a friend whose unemployment is due to chronic irresponsibility and who, accordingly, is thought to be most in need of support in learning how to help himself. The fact that it is entirely fitting, if not morally required, by basic standards of humanity to experience compassionate empathy towards others' suffering even where it is impossible, impractical, or inappropriate to act on desires to relieve their aversive condition shows, in Blum's words, "that compassion's sole significance does not lie in its role as motive to beneficence" (1980, p. 515). In sum, if the display of compassion has instrumental valuable to the sufferer because it communicates a sense of solidarity or a willingness to help if one could, the rational grounds of the experience of compassionate empathy should fall away in situations where the object of the emotion can or will never know that he or she is the object of compassionate empathy. However, it *does* still make sense in such cases, at least in Blum's reading of the situation, to say that a person should feel compassion and so, he claims, it remains only to identify the non-instrumental justificatory grounds of such obligations (cf. Blum, 1980a, pp. 146–149 and 1980b, pp. 515–516).

Now it may well be that most or even many people would concede that in the cases Blum sketches, an absence of compassionate response is inappropriate. However, even universal agreement—a point Blum does not seem to appreciate— would probably not be considered convincing to someone like Kant, for instance, who thought otherwise. In an oft-quoted passage from the *Doctrine of virtue*, Kant (1797/1996) argues that the obligation to experience "sympathetic feelings" pertains only insofar as such feelings are (1) "used as a means to promoting active and rational benevolence" (6: 456) and (2) as long as they are freely chosen and not merely passively received (6: 456). Failing this connection with action and choice, sympathy is in Kant's estimation at best a kind of sentimentality or pity. He writes:

> It was a sublime way of thinking that the Stoic ascribed to his wise man when he had him say "I wish for a friend, not that he might help *me* in poverty, sickness, imprisonment, etc., but rather that I might stand by *him* and rescue a human being." But the same wise man, when he could not rescue his friend, said to himself "what is it to me?" In other words, he rejected compassion.
>
> In fact, when another suffers and, although I cannot help him, I let myself be infected by his pain (through my imagination), then two of us suffer though the trouble really (in nature) affects only *one*. But there cannot possibly be a duty to increase the ills of the world and so to do good *from compassion*. This would also be an insulting kind of beneficence, since it expresses the kind of benevolence one has towards someone unworthy, called *pity*; and this has not place in people's relations with one another, since they are not to make a display of their worthiness to be happy. (6: 457)

Kant makes two points in this passage which provide material for an argument to the effect that, rather than viewing non-instrumental compassionate empathy as a disposition to be cultivated and fostered, it is in fact a kind of mawkishness which should be discouraged. First, there is the claim that non-instrumental compassionate empathy would add to unnecessary suffering in the world because the suffering experienced by the sympathizer could not be put to use as a motive to help the sufferer. Second, he claims that rational grounds for the sympathizer's affective involvement in the sufferer and his situation are weak because, again, nothing can be done to help him. Sympathy, in such cases, is merely futile or superfluous.

Notice, however, that the claim that compassionate empathy in these circumstances is irrational turns on a decidedly instrumental interpretation of that concept; for Kant, apparently, the rationality of compassionate empathy in any circumstances stands and falls with its potential contribution to a preconceived end, the relief of suffering. As long as we conceive of the rationality of compassionate empathy in these terms, Kant's conclusion would seem to be inevitable. However, by viewing the problem from a broader and (ironically) rather Kantian conception of rationality which in principle embraces publicly accessible standards of acceptability—that is, standards comprehensible to human beings in virtue of their shared capacities and common interests (cf. Habermas, 1990a, 1990b)—things arguably look quite different. From this broader perspective, it seems just as inevitable to say that the mere awareness of a person who is facing (1) some serious misfortune that (2) is undeserved while (3) taking into consideration the relevance of the relationship between the observer and the sufferer and the nature of the sufferer's misfortune is sufficient grounds for a compassionate empathic response (cf. Nussbaum, 2001, esp. pp. 335–342, 414–425).[6] To think otherwise and, most important for present purposes, to hold that compassionate empathy is only appropriate where one can help is a gross misunderstanding of what compassionate empathy is. That is to say, compassionate empathy is not first and foremost a motive to beneficent acts, although it clearly can be such a motive as well. What it is, instead, is a perfectly appropriate and rational response to witnessing the undeserved plight of a person one is concerned about. As for Kant's Stoic, his "rejection" of sympathy for the friend he cannot help, far from showing him up as a paradigm of practical rationality, simply demonstrates that he does not care about his friend or, one might be tempted to claim, that he is in fact *not* a friend. From this perspective, a disposition of compassionate empathic response at the right time, to the right degree, towards the right objects is not saintly, supererogatory, or a handmaiden to moral motivation but is a *demonstration of* maturity in the exercise of the faculty of practical wisdom.

Both Blum (1980b) and Nussbaum (2001) provide accounts of the characteristic interest in the well-being of another gives compassionate empathy its inherent moral content, which are instructive in filling out this idea. As Blum puts it, "any interest in the welfare of others is morally good, especially when it promotes the sense of equality is (*ceteris paribus*) morally good" (p. 515). The "moral force of compassion", Blum says, stems from the simple and often spontaneous recognition of another person's suffering as the kind of thing that could happen to any human being, including oneself (p. 511). In Nussbaum's (2001) assessment, as in Blum's (1980b), the notion that the very experience of compassionate empathy represents a

---

[6] The relationship between the observer and the sufferer is often a relevant factor in determining the appropriateness of response. For instance, the kind of distress that it is appropriate for me to have when my child becomes gravely ill is not the same if my neighbour's child becomes ill. However, relationships are one factor to be balanced with the other factors. For example, if my child is in bed with a low fever but the neighbour's child has been hospitalized with a suspected case of avian influenza it would be absurd for me not to be more intensely concerned for my neighbour's child than for my own. See also the discussion of special obligations and impartiality later in §4.4.2. The general point, of course, is that how much and towards whom one compassionate empathic involvement is appropriate is a delicate question of the application of practical judgement in a set of particular circumstances and thus can only be decided on a case-by-case basis.

sense of communion with others in virtue of *shared* human vulnerability has nothing to do with self-regarding sentiment whereby the other's plight is taken as a lucid and troubling illustration of "what could happen to oneself" (Blum, p. 517) or of "one's own vulnerability" (Nussbaum, 2001, p. 335). That is, compassionate empathy is not, in the language of social psychology, "personal distress" (cf. esp. Eisenberg & Strayer, 1987 and §3.2.1). While it may be sparked by a sense of personal vulnerability or, no less plausibly, by fantasies about the existence of a moral economy in which one can buy insurance against future hardship with the currency of concern for others, the emotion itself is not self- but other-regarding. Nussbaum writes:

> A compassionate person does not help a beggar simply because he or she does literally think that he may shortly be in a similar position. Entertaining that thought, feeling one's own vulnerability, is an important route to the emotion for many people; but the emotion itself acknowledges the pain of another separate person as a bad thing, because of what it is doing to that other life. The compassionate person remains fully aware of the distinction between her own life and that of the sufferer, and seeks the good of the sufferer as a separate person, whom she has made part of her own scheme of goals and ends. (pp. 335–336)

It is in valuing another person as part of one's own "scheme of goals and ends" that makes the very experience of compassionate empathy, as Nussbaum (2001) aptly puts it, a "quasi-ethical achievement" (p. 336).

A comparison between compassionate empathy and other moral emotions seems to support the idea the very experience of compassionate empathy has moral worth independently of any of its practical consequences and indeed suggests that compassionate empathy might be rightly considered the moral emotion *par excellence*. Notice that the other members of any rough and ready list of nice emotions—love, shame, concern, attachment—can clearly be directed at objects outside the moral domain. One can, for instance, love architecture or gardening, feel shame in connection with the violation of a rule of etiquette, be concerned about the state of one's financial position, and feel attachment towards a sports team or one's car. One can only, however, feel compassionate empathy for suffering beings.[7] The moral flavour of compassionate empathy, then, seems to derive from the fact that it is directed towards the weal and woe of another as a conceptual given. And it is precisely this basic and abstract interest of compassionate empathy—an interest in promoting well-being and avoiding harms—which links compassionate empathy with the *moral domain* at least as this concept has traditionally been interpreted in the social sciences: the range of human "value" understood as a discrete area of

---

[7] In a session of an educational conference I once attended, a pair of delegates argued passionately but unpersuasively, to my mind, that fostering a sense of compassion towards the natural environment was an essential ingredient in any defensible programme of environmental education. Nature is the proper object of many fine and noble emotions—awe, respect, care, love, gratitude, and others—and one can certainly feel compassion towards animals and other sentient forms of life. It seems to me clearly idiosyncratic, however, to claim that one should feel compassion towards the environment for the simple reason that the environment cannot feel or suffer (except of course in a derivative metaphorical sense).

social interest pertaining to the protection and promotion of fundamental human needs and interests rightly understood.[8]

The claim that compassionate empathy has an in-built moral content, however, is by no means equivalent to the claim that it is unconditionally good, which is why, of course, Nussbaum considers its experience as being just a *quasi*-ethical achievement rather than as an ethical achievement *tout court*. When understood as a moral emotion in connection with character, its deficiency is insensitivity or callousness in the face of another's suffering and, in excess, sentimentality, maudlin, or mawkishness. Having proposed a settlement to the question of why it seems to have inherent worth as a member of a privileged class of moral emotions, we turn now to the question of, as Descartes might have put it, the endemic excesses of compassionate empathy of which moral judgement needs to be wary.

4.4 (In)Compatibility Between Compassionate Empathy and Impartiality

Identifying how compassionate empathy can contribute to the failure of practical reasoning seems as easy as the problem of identifying it as a moral achievement complex: morality is impartial and universal whereas compassionate empathy is typically, if not inexorably, specific and particular. This section presents distinct psychological and philosophical perspectives on this problem. First, existing and relevant empirical evidence that empathic bias, more than just an *idée reçue*, is scientifically credible. Then, in §4.4.2, I will consider empathic bias in its conceptual significance and, in particular, its tendency to bring to moral agents' attention *pro tanto* special obligations that seem to be strongly at odds with impartiality as an ideal of sound moral judgement.

4.4.1 Empirical Evidence for Empathic Bias

The average person's basic stock of anecdotal evidence to the effect that people tend to respond with stronger feelings of compassionate empathy with sufferers who are familiar to them or who are immediately present is consistent with existing empirical evidence, recently summarized by Hoffman (2000, pp. 206–213).

Hoffman analyses what he naturally labels "familiarity bias" into three subcategories: (1) in-group bias, (2) friendship bias, and (3) similarity bias. The form of

---

[8] For characterizations and defences of the moral domain in these terms, varying in their degrees of depth and strategic approaches, see Frankena (1973), Peters (1981), Turiel (1983), Nunner-Winkler (1994), Warnock (1996), and Nucci (2001).

empathic bias most thoroughly studied seems to be similarity bias, expressible as the hypothesis that people tend to empathize more strongly with those with whom they consider to have some affinity of social import, such as skin colour, sex, or personality type. For instance, Feshbach and Roe (1968), studying 6- and 7-year-old children's verbal responses to pictures of other children in sad, happy, and frightening situations, found that boys responded more empathically to pictures of boys and girls to pictures of girls. A study by Klein (1971), for all intents and purposes identical to Feshbach and Roe's except that it studied skin colour rather than sex, reached parallel conclusions. Studies by Krebs (1975) and Houston (1990) focused on personality affinity. Krebs paired subjects with confederate "victims" and found that subjects who believed they had a similar personality profile to victims "showed more pronounced physiological responses when the other appeared to be experiencing pleasure or pain [and] reported that they identified more with the other and felt worse (had more empathic distress) while the other was waiting to receive an electric shock" (Hoffman, 2000, pp. 208–209). More explicitly studying what is commonly called "identification" and its role in heightening compassionate empathy, Houston (1990) observed that subjects who described themselves as "shy" and who viewed their shyness as a deviation from their "ideal" self-description reported feeling comparatively high levels of anxiety in connection with reading an account of another student recounting his own distress and unpleasant experiences related to his own shyness. In a 1992 study, Costin and Jones found evidence for what Hoffman calls "friendship bias" among pre-schoolers. After watching a series of puppet shows depicting protagonists in different dangerous or stressful situations, the subjects reported more empathic distress towards—and, when asked what they would do if they were in the story, were more likely to say they would help—the puppets which represented friends than puppets representing acquaintances. Representation was achieved by asking the children to imagine the different puppets as a particular close friend or acquaintance and pictures of these individuals were affixed to the puppets to support the vicarious involvement. The distinction between in-group bias and similarity bias is not in all cases clear. Superficially, one could regard those with whom one shared relevant affinities and a particular "in-group" are one and the same and, accordingly, Klein's (1971) study of empathy and racial identification just mentioned is evidence for both. However, studies by Katz et al. (1973) and Meindl and Lerner (1984) on the rationalization of criminal behaviour are stark reminders of the role that, if not straightforwardly *in*-group, at least *out*-group perceptions can play in situational moral perception. These studies document the familiar phenomenon whereby perpetrators of violent crimes morally derogate their victims on the grounds that they belong to some group with which the transgressor does not identify—old people, rich people, gays, immigrants, or whatever—and in so doing temper their feelings of guilt if not exculpate themselves entirely.

In Hoffman's (2000) estimation, the "reactivity" of empathic arousal, that compassionate empathy is medicated by involuntary psychological responses to immediate situational and personal cues (cf. §§3.4.1 and 3.5) goes some distance towards explaining the "here-and-now bias" (p. 209). As familiar as the notion that people tend to respond with greater emotional intensity to the suffering of those present to them is, this psychological phenomenon has been the subject of only very sparse empirical examination. Perhaps the claim that first-hand experience with others' suffering is incomparably more evocative of compassionate empathy than hearing about it second-hand has been considered too obvious to warrant it? Even though nothing like direct empirical evidence is forthcoming, a pair of relatively recent studies by Batson et al. (1995) published in a single paper on empathy-induced immorality seem to speak of the problem indirectly. In the first study, groups of college student subjects were tasked with assigning desirable and undesirable jobs to two anonymous "workers". The subjects were reminded the fairest way to do was randomly, by the toss of a coin, but that the experimenters did not oblige them to adopt this procedure (p. 1044). The main experimental group was given a personal statement written by one of the workers recounting some unfortunate recent life event and encouraged to vicariously identify with the person's travails. Another group read the statement but were instructed to "try to take an objective perspective" and to "not get caught up in how he or she feels" (p. 1044). The control group had no communication with either worker whatsoever. Unsurprisingly, in the first so-called high-empathy group, half the subjects expressly chose to assign the desirable task to the victim worker and the other half assigned them tasks randomly. A much higher percentage of the second "low-empathy" group, 85% by contrast, employed a random method of task assignment as did no less that *all* members of the control group. The second study, indistinguishable from the first except that it involved the more serious problem of reassigning patients on a waiting list for some life-saving intervention, produced very similar data.

Do these studies provide evidence for the existence of the here-and-now bias of compassionate empathic responding? Hoffman's (2000) claim that they do not, seems unambiguously convincing. As with familiarity bias, the here-and-now bias seems susceptible to categorical analysis. More specifically, it is analysable into two distinct sub-forms of bias, one which corresponds to the "here" part of the here-and-now bias and the other which corresponds to—wait for it—the "now" part. The "perceptual immediacy bias", a more elegant alternative to label of the "here bias", takes in cases where an observer is aware that two people are suffering equally but becomes more compassionately involved with the person who is immediately present. The "temporal immediacy bias", rather than the "now bias", describes the phenomenon whereby people feel greater compassionate empathy towards a sufferer in direct proportion to the vicinity of the suffering to the present moment, a kind of statute of empathic limitations if you will. The distinction is suggested by Slote (2003), for example, who has postulated that "agents are more empathically concerned with what they *perceive* than with what they do not; and they are also empathically more sensitive to what *they know to be going on at the same time as their decision making and choices*" (p. 136; original emphasis). Problematically for Hoffman's claim, the relevance of the Batson et al.'s (1995) studies to the here-and-now bias is far from being clear. The situation the studies construct is not relevant to its "here" dimension because the study participants do not come into direct perceptive contact with the sufferer, either physically or virtually. All communication between the subject and confederate–victim is language-mediated. However, evidence that people react more empathically to others with whom they have become *familiar*, as in these studies, is not evidence that they will react more empathically to people with whom they are in *perceptual contact*. What would be relevant to know if we are interested in finding out about perceptual immediacy bias as an analytically distinct variety of empathic bias, in other words, is comparative data showing, say, that language-mediated exposure to a normally compassionate empathy-evoking situation (e.g., reading a newspaper article describing a tragic car accident) correlates with weaker responding than witnessing a normally compassionate empathy-evoking situation directly (e.g., being present at the scene of a tragic car accident). The relevance of these studies for the temporal immediacy bias is equally questionable and for precisely the same reasons. The study subjects, it is true, are made aware that the unfortunate event in the worker's life occurred "recently" but, again, only *comparative* data showing that subjects were more biased towards people thought to be the recent victim of a traumatic event (e.g., someone who lost a dear friend after a long struggle with cancer last week) than towards people though to have been the victim of the same kind of traumatic event further in the past (e.g., someone lost a dear friend after a long struggle with cancer last year). In light of these considerations, the most we can say about the Batson et al.'s (1995) studies as evidence for empathic bias is that they provide further evidence for familiarity bias. Like Stotland's (1969) early research, however, they also demonstrate that imaginative involvement in another's woe generates stronger feelings of compassionate empathy and, perhaps most significantly, that it is possible for human beings to regulate, by a willed act of perspective-taking with another person in an aversive situation, their disposition to care about and help another in need. As for the here-and-now bias of compassionate empathy itself, it appears to be a notion of moral folk psychology still awaiting empirical scrutiny.

In any case, even though the various forms of empathic bias are not usually associated with the noblest of human social tendencies, some have argued that empathic bias, when viewed from an evolutionary perspective, has a certain adaptive value. Familiarity bias, for example, would seem to lend to the survival of the small social groups on which individual humans were thought to be materially dependent over the course of most of their evolutionary history and which were frequently in competition for scarce material resources with other groups of humans (cf. Hoffman, 2000, p. 206; and Gibbard, 1990). Without having to rely too heavily on such just-so stories to explain the apparent fact of empathic bias, it is also true that people seem to have a *general* familiarity bias—not only can they *get used to* just about anything, no matter how bad or unpleasant it is, they actually *get to prefer and enjoy* what they get used to whether it is a person, an experience, a type of house pet, or, as it is most commonly observed, a style of music. The phenomenon has been documented by Zajonc (1968) and Harrison (1977) and is a staple of the Aristotelian tradition in moral education (cf. Steutel & Spiecker, 2004). Put otherwise, the familiarity bias, as Hoffman (2000, p. 206) suggests, could be a special form of human beings' general tendency to "like what they know".

Slote (2003) has offered a functionalist rather than directly evolutionary explanation for both the temporal and perceptual immediacy biases in terms of the "natural flow or evocation of human empathy" (p. 133). He writes:

> Agents are more empathic and more empathically concerned with what they *perceive* than with what they do not; and they are also empathically more sensitive to what *they know to be going on at the same time* as their decision making and choices. And these differences correspond to what we naturally think of as the greater immediacy of dangers that we perceive or that are contemporaneous with our concern. (p. 136; original emphasis)

Slote's suggestion seems to be that there is a distinct practical advantage of being more acutely concerned with immediate and present suffering: being in close physical and temporal proximity to some instance of suffering, the agent has a better chance of actually being able to do something to relieve it (pp. 132–136). This suggests, of course, that it might be something of a mistake to consider the tendency of compassionate empathy towards partiality as a limitation or problem in need of rectification. Indeed, as Hoffman (2000) observes, to see that the Clintonesque moral ideal of empathic promiscuity—understanding everyone's point of view and feeling everyone's pain—is impracticable, one need only consider what would happen if it were realized in practice. People would be immobilized. Being a form of attention, compassionate empathy can provide motivational back-up for helping, but if one attended to everyone's suffering equally, one would obviously become unable to help anyone (pp. 214–215). Even in a world with far less suffering than in our own, some kind of filtering mechanism must be in place in order to frame and direct empathic attention in order to render it cognitively manageable. More than likely, empathic bias in its diverse forms has a hand in this.

4.4.2 Ethical Universalism and Ethical Particularism

If compassionate empathy is a strange moral phenomenon, it is so because it seems to both encapsulate the one attitude that is essential to a moral outlook—concern for others—yet to be singularly at odds with the other—impartiality. Justice and caring; benevolence and fairness; the dichotomy runs tirelessly through modern discourse in moral philosophy from Schopenhauer's (1840/1995) critique of Kant's ethics down to the Kohlberg–Gilligan debate (cf. Flanagan & Jackson, 1987). The apparent tension has been variously elaborated by numerous recent authors (see, e.g., de Sousa, 2001; Ben Ze'ev, 2000; Nussbaum, 2001; Sober & Wilson, 1998) but Ben Ze'ev's (2000) account, whose structure is loosely followed here, is attractive in its frankness.

The universality of morality can be stated thus: if one person has a moral obligation in a set of circumstances, anyone in the same circumstances has the same moral obligation. Sidgwick (1902/1988) held that the universality of morality is trivially true by the principle of non-contradiction, a basic law of logic according to which no predicate can at once possess and fail to possess some property. This seems to be quite ungainsayable as long as it is taken at face value. First and most, obviously, it is not a statement about moral motivation. That is to say, the claim does not imply that two different people under the same circumstances will necessarily desire to act in accordance with the moral obligation, only that they are categorically *under* it. Universality, in this sense, is not unique to morality but shares this characteristic with rules of etiquette and pointers for playing sports (cf. Foot, 1972; and Sober & Wilson, 1998). Second, the claim should not be conflated with the more controversial Kantian idea of universalizability as a justificatory criterion for moral principles. The principle of universality as a feature of moral judgement is silent on whether any particular claim that some set of circumstances generate a genuinely binding moral obligation is justified. The idea is merely that if someone *really does* have a moral obligation in some set of circumstances, all others *would have* the same obligation as well.

The main difficulty that the application of the principle of universality poses for practical reasoning is not, as Ben Ze'ev (2000, p. 249) observes, the fact that no two situations are identical. The problem is rather how to correctly identify relevant similarities. For instance, unlike being in a rush to deliver a critically ill passenger to the hospital, a person's, say, red hair or bushy black moustaches to no degree absolves him of the responsibility for driving at a dangerously high speed. In this regard, the principle of fundamental moral equality of persons poses a special problem for compassionate empathy as a moral emotion. Compassionate empathy notoriously discriminates on the basis of such things as whether the object of compassionate empathy happens to be known personally, belongs to a familiar group, or is in one's physical presence, differences which are *prima facie* irrelevant when it comes to the question of the principle of universality's application. At risk of stating the obvious, although the physical assault and robbery of a neighbour before one's very eyes is no worse than the physical assault and robbery of a perfect stranger on the other side of town, a stronger compassionate response in the former case is reliable to the point that strict neutrality of moral perception in such circumstances would by most people be considered something of an aberration, if not actually morally offensive. "Tis natural for us to consider with most attention such as lie contiguous to us, or resemble us", as Hume expressed the point (1751/1957, pp. 340–341). Empathic bias, in other words, is not just predictable but also comprehensible, or at least it is widely held to be so. Accordingly, the *psychological* difficulty that compassionate empathy poses in the context of moral judgement is that of maintaining impartiality (Ben Ze'ev, 2000, p. 253). Indeed, how difficult it is (or is thought to be) is witnessed by the fact that where standards of fairness are highest, such as in law courts and in the selection of candidates for important professional functions, any personal relation between party and adjudicator is strictly prohibited (Ben Ze'ev, 2000, p. 253).

The apparent tension between compassionate empathy's genuine moral content and its inclination to prioritize in moral perception, the needs of kith and kin leads straight to a thorny debate in normative ethics over what exactly to make of such apparent obligations, obligations that are labelled variously special obligations (e.g., Jeske, 1998), role obligations (e.g., Goldman, 1980; Hardimon, 1994; Luban, 2003) and associative duties (e.g., Brink, 2001). The difficulty is that of how and whether it is possible to reconcile the ideal of moral impartiality whereby obligations follow from the imperative to respect persons *qua* persons with the sometimes conflicting obligations internal to particular relations between family members, friends, clients, and compatriots. On the face of it, and perhaps even in what Luban (2003) calls "common morality"—ordinary, everyday, and widely shared moral standards (cf. p. 585)—I have an obligation to feed and clothe my own children which I do not towards your children (or at least not quite in the same way) even though neither of us thinks (or at least would admit publicly) that our children are more deserving of respect and moral attention than anyone else's children. Proponents of the normative ethical position known as "particularism" or "partialism" characteristically argue that it is not possible and, add further, that if moral impartiality requires us to consider special attachments as morally irrelevant, all the more reason to reject impartiality as an ideal of moral assessment.

What is sometimes called Godwin's dilemma—a misnomer because Godwin himself did not see the problem as being dilemmatic at all—is often taken by partialists as a case in point that the demands the moral ideal of impartiality imposes on us are absurdly high. The thought experiment begins by asking us to imagine that we are standing in front of a burning building (Godwin, 1926, p. 26). In this building are trapped two individuals: someone of great social importance, the archbishop of Cambray as Godwin has it, and someone of supposedly little social consequence, the bishop's chambermaid. There is enough time to save only one of them. For Godwin, at any rate, the question of whom to save is supposed to be at this point a proverbial no-brainer, justifiable on straightforward consequentialist grounds. Because the archbishop's life is conducive to more general good than that of the chambermaid, one should save him and not her. Next, Godwin asks us to consider how our moral assessment of the situation should change were the chambermaid our sister, wife, or "benefactor". Now, of course, even the most dyed-in-the-wool utilitarian would immediately *want* to save the chambermaid and might even think that he *should* save the chambermaid. Alas! Godwin considers this shift in perspective to be the effect of a familiarity bias skewing correct assessment of the morally relevant features of the situation, in particular that the chambermaid happens to be *my* mother and not somebody else's. "Of what great consequence is it that they are mine?", Godwin (1926) asks, "What magic is there in the pronoun 'my' to overturn the decisions of everlasting truth" (p. 42). Some critics, quite understandably, have not viewed Godwin's thought experiment as revelation of the grimly rigorous standards of judgement moral theory hold us to. Rather if moral theory asks us to consider the attachments to people who are especially important in our lives as morally irrelevant, as it suggests we do, that is a good reason to suspect that there is something deeply flawed in the ideal of moral impartiality itself.[9]

---

[9] For discussions of Godwin's dilemma and parallel critiques to the effect that theories of normative ethics frequently prescribe unacceptably high standards of judgement and action see Toulmin (1981), Cottingham (1983), MacIntyre (1983), Baron (1991), Blustein (1991), Flanagan (1996), and Ashcroft (2001).

This critical hunch has been developed into two main directions. The first seems to involve the strong claim that impartiality should be *rejected* as a general principle of moral appraisal on the grounds that it is just too demanding to be of much practical use in the actual lives and practical dealings of imperfect "creatures like us", as Flanagan (1996) memorably put it. The point is made, following Williams (1976), using a *reductio ad absurdum*: the principle of impartiality entails that before proceeding to rescue one's own mother from conflagration (Godwin, 1926), one's wife from drowning (Williams, 1976), or staying up all night looking after one's sick child (Cottingham, 1983) one must consider whether there are not others who might be in greater need of one's attention. Only when one has reasonable grounds to believe that there are not, is acting on one's inclination to come to assistance justified. But conceding to this demand requires one to unreasonably distance oneself if not altogether repudiate the kinds of attachments and relationships that are essential to human fulfilment and happiness. This is moral reasoning for machines or, if not, it is moral reasoning for people who think too much (cf. Williams, 1976; Williams & Smart, 1973; Cottingham, 1983; Nagel, 1986, esp. pp. 200–204). The second general particularist response to the problem of special obligations, rather than rejecting the principle of impartiality out of hand, defends the thesis that there are "two realms" or standards of ethics, a social morality which applies to strangers and a personal one which applies to kith and kin, or in Toumlin's (1981) phrase an "ethics of intimacy" and an "ethics of strangers" (cf. also Hardwig, 1997; Deigh, 1989; McFall, 1987; and Kekes, 1981). Acknowledging that the two realms can sometimes conflict, practical wisdom consists partly in knowing when to apply which standard (cf. Blustein, 1991, p. 218).

Baron (1991) argues persuasively that both lines of attack on the ideal of moral impartiality quite badly miss the point of the principle of impartiality as a principle of moral justification. In her assessment, not even the hard-bitten utilitarian Godwin wanted to claim that personal relations are *never* morally relevant; the general problem for practical judgement is rather to discern in what circumstances personal relationships or personal preferences for particular persons *are* morally relevant and when they are not. As a case in point, everyone can agree, even the most staunch particularists, that there are some circumstances—judging competitions or student's work, the guilt of a person accused of a crime and so on—in which strict impartiality is called for—and where accordingly personal relations should be treated as irrelevant considerations (Baron, 1991, p. 837). That is to say, even the strong partialist does not seriously propose to reject impartiality as a principle of moral judgement. Her claim is at most that in some circumstances it should be outweighed or overruled by morally relevant features of a situation. Furthermore, Baron's suggestion that critiques of the principle of impartiality are sometimes built on straw-man versions of their target gains further credence when one attempts to actually name anyone outside a small coterie of philosophers, such as Singer (cf. esp. 1972), out on what is widely regarded as a utilitarian lunatic fringe who would seriously demand as a condition of sound moral judgement that one consider every human being's well-being equally before proceeding to execute such *pro tanto* associative duties as cooking the children supper, a doctor doing rounds on a hospital ward, or helping a friend move. By far and by contrast, most philosophical attention to the problem of special obligations positively accepts them as a fact-like surface feature of moral discourse and tries to *justify* them and square them with other "platitudinous" moral commitments, to borrow Smith's (1994) expression, such as the principle of impartiality. A recurrent consequentialist tack, for instance, is to understand special obligations as ensure the efficient and approximately equal provision of social goods.[10]

In any case, the decisive point for our purposes is hard to deny and it is this: there is no *necessary* correlation between the conation built into any particular experience of compassionate empathy and whatever *pro toto* or all-things-considered moral obligation one might happen to have in a set of circumstances. Even in people's most important personal relations, Baron (1991) reminds us, there are times when being practically wise in a situation involves taking a step back from one's attachments and submitting feelings of attachment to the impartial scrutiny of "an outsider's eye". "A loving parent", she writes,

> may see his overweight child as adorably plump and fail to see that the child has a problem and needs his parents' help. More serious, a mother may fail to detect signs that her lover or her father is molesting her daughter. In each case, the problem is not that the parent is too partial—it is not that they would be better people if they were less partial—but that they never try to view the people in question with an outsider's eye. (p. 853)

The present relevant question, in other words, is not when and whether compassionate empathy brings to light genuine special commitments to others and motivates the performance of special obligations. It is clear that often it does. If, however, part spontaneous feelings of concern and compassion for so-called significant other are for the most part consistent with both the associative obligations which attend to such relationships and with one's obligations to strangers in ordinary morality, practical wisdom would not seem to demand that we justify those obligations every time we set out to meet them. Rather, what practical wisdom does quite urgently demand is something subtly but crucially different—namely, that one understands and recognizes *when circumstances dictate* that one needs to submit naturally arising feelings of attachment to others, and the *pro tanto* obligations they illuminate, to the court of practical judgement.

4.5   Summary and Discussion

To restate the problem this study set out to consider, no one can reasonably deny, apparently, that an *affective* response of caring involvement at the perception of a prospective or actual threat to another's well-being is at most an incidentally

---

[10] Cf. Sidgwick's classical formulation of this argument in 1907/1981 (pp. 434ff). For an overview of the range of positions currently defended in contemporary ethics vis-à-vis special obligations, see Jeske (2002).

connected with a morally appropriate *action* response when judged from a position of impartiality. After all, an action's *moral* status is determined in relation to whether the action meets certain criteria of a *moral* action. If it is unclear that being motivated by compassionate empathy is a necessary criterion—for any number of other motivations, emotions, and desires, could potentially motivate a moral act—it is plainly obvious that merely being motivated by compassionate empathy is not sufficient either for the good and simple reason that compassionate empathy can motivate morally questionable acts. To paraphrase Blasi (1999), compassionate empathy has to expresses moral concerns in order to be correctly considered a moral motivation. But then the moral meaning of the action motivated by compassionate empathy derives not from the characteristic concerns which give the emotion its meaning but from the features of the action and its circumstances which give it *its* moral meaning. If the moral value of compassionate empathy as a moral motivator is wholly contingent on being directed by practical wisdom, as it seems to be, the *prima facie* attractive views of Callahan (1980), Hilkfiker (2001), Coombs (1998), and others, presented in Chapter 1 (§1.2), that a compassionate empathic disposition is recommendable as a stable agentic factor suspected of correlating positively with moral motivation is either chimerical—unjustified but explainable, perhaps, in terms of a cultural prejudice to exalt compassionate empathy and feelings of concern for others in their basic humanity—or some crucial moral feature of compassionate empathy has been overlooked.

In my assessment, advanced at the beginning of this chapter, both rival claims—as the matter was put crudely, that compassionate empathy seems to at once possess and to lack inherent moral worth—are strongly compelling, so much so as to warrant describing compassionate empathy's moral character as paradoxical. The chapter studied this paradox and argued, in effect, that it results from equivocating the analytically distinct, mutually compatible, and indeed, once appreciated, rather mundane roles that emotions play in moral assessment and moral functioning: the Aristotelian idea that emotions are constitutive elements of moral virtue and vice, the rationalist notion that emotions intervene in moral deliberation processes primarily as judgement-distorting passions, and what I called the "naturalist" suggestion, that there exist a specific set of moral emotions which favour moral outlook, moral attitudes, and moral behaviours (cf. §4.2 and Table 4.1). Excess of compassionate empathy is recognizable in character traits such as sentimentality, mawkishness,

Table 4.1 Three conceptions of the relevance of emotions in moral life

Aristotelian	Emotions are constitutive elements of moral virtue and vice and should be modulated in accordance with virtue and vice as normative ideals of character and conduct.
Rationalist	Emotions are passions susceptible to distorting situational perception and sound appraisal and should be subjected to the regulative constraint of moral judgement.
Naturalist	Human beings have an inherent moral capacity mediated by a specific set of "moral" emotions (sympathy, compassion, concern for others) which socialization should support.

maudlin, and its insufficiency in callousness and insensitivity. At the same time, and like probably all other emotions, compassionate empathy is susceptible to being passionate, responsible for incorrect or otherwise distorted situational moral appraisal. Regarded as a moral emotion like love, concern, and perhaps guilt, compassionate empathy is broadly—but by no means irreproachably—conducive to morally good acts. The fact that feelings of compassionate empathy are appropriate even in circumstances where the possibility of helping is out of the question is telling because it implies that the moral worth of compassionate empathy derives not just from its causal connection with demonstrable positive social consequences. Compassionate empathy's state of concern, the kind of involvement that is typical to it, and which gives it its unique meaning and distinguishes it from other emotions, reflects characteristically moral concerns for others' weal and woe. Viewed as a moral emotion in this sense, it is easy to see what Nussbaum (2001) means when she says that the very experience compassionate empathy is a "quasi-ethical achievement" (cf. §4.3). Compassionate empathy and the moral domain have connate concerns with the promotion and protection of human well-being as such, as I put it. But whereas viewing a problem from a moral point of view demands scrupulous attention to the weighing competing claims fairly (cf. §4.4.1), compassionate empathy's proclivity to skew one's perception of the needs of others and the urgency of those needs in favour of those with whom one identifies or who happen to be in one's close perceptual or temporal proximity—that is, its susceptibility to the familiarity bias and the here-and-now bias the evidence for which was presented in §4.4.2—is such that it seems to be constitutionally incompatible with the ideal of impartial moral appraisal. Bias in compassionate empathic appraisal, we saw, is not just predictable and apparently inevitable but, when regarded from the practical angle and seen as a means of focusing an agent's attention on the suffering of those he or she is in a position to easily help, possibly desirable. As I suggested at the end of §4.4.2, however, recognizing compassionate empathy's strong partialism—that in the moral court, it should be treated more with the circumspection worthy of a party than with the authority worthy of the judge—does not for all that make it *any* less recommendable as a "moral emotion". However biased compassionate empathy can be and, perhaps, even when it is mere self-indulgent other-directed sentimentality, if a person is even *capable* of feeling compassionate empathy that demonstrates something significant about him or her as a moral agent: that is to say, that he or she has grasped the fundamental moral notion that others' needs are *normative*—that they make categorical demands on one's attentions. From the perspective of moral development this is no small accomplishment.

At this juncture it is apposite to reiterate that precisely this capacity has been the focus of one of a range of lines of inquiry in moral psychology aiming to round out, if not correct, Kohlberg's classical theory of moral development. It will be recalled from Chapter 1 (§1.1) that empirical evidence brought together and summarized by Blasi in a 1980 review article demonstrated, astonishingly and counter-intuitively, only the most feeble of correlations between cognitive moral development and moral action. These results suggested something very important about moral development. The gain in question was not empirical confirmation of a point that is a staple of conceptual critiques of the classical Kohlberg theory—namely, that the theory "overlooks" affect or, stated more precisely, that it fails to acknowledge that moral development, in the Kohlbergian understanding of the construct, presupposes the growth of concern for others.[11] Kohlberg's account of moral development in and of itself is certainly not inconsistent with the possibility that moral development *has* an affective dimension and, for whatever it is worth, the present author has never seen any indication in Kohlberg's writings that he ever once denied this point. What Kohlberg actually did seem to think was rather that the growth of the ability to think about moral problems in increasingly differentiated ways and the propensity to care about morality—or "the growth of moral motivation" in Nunner-Winkler's (1993) expression—went quite unproblematically hand in hand. It was this assumption, the doctrine of cognitive-affective parallelism as it has become known, that Blasi's (1980) review helped put into question.

The danger is great, especially in a context where moral reasoning (i.e., the process of justifying a course of action vis-à-vis an abstract moral problem) and day to day *in situ* moral functioning are for all intents and purposes taken as one and the same phenomenon, that one sees the realization that cognitive moral development and affective moral development follow two distinct trajectories as providing, at long last, decisive grounds for admitting "benevolence" or concern for others as a legitimate criterion of moral justification alongside considerations of fairness, right, or justice—loosely, that human beings are in their heart of hearts both consequentialists and deontologists. While it is almost certainly true that considerations of both benevolence and justice are sometimes relevant to problems of moral justification,[12] seeing the matter this way—seeing it, that is, as having implications for an understanding of moral *reasoning*—badly overlooks the potential significance of the collapse of the doctrine of cognitive-affective for an understanding of moral *functioning*. It is a mistake John Gibbs makes, I think, in his recent book *Moral development and reality* (2003).

Gibbs adds his voice to the chorus calling for theoretical reconciliation between the perennially dichotomized moral concepts of right and good, justice and caring, cognition and feeling. His suggestion, in particular, is that a healthy appreciation that neither justice nor caring alone is capable of capturing the "core of the moral domain" (p. 6) might bring an end to the endless jostling in both moral psychology and philosophical ethics over the question of which set of concepts is conceptually prior to the other one. In this regard, his position resembles a view defended in one version or another by, for instance, Frankena (1973), Beauchamp and Childress (2001), and O'Neil (1996) that "both justice and beneficence collectively comprise the substance of the moral point of view" (Gibbs, 2003, p. 6). In Gibbs' (2003) hands, the debate is played out between two rival theories of moral development

---

[11] For examples of this critical position, see Trainer (1977), Fraenkel (1978), and Peters (1981).

[12] See Carr (2001) and Wringe (2006) for persuasive and, in the latter case, elaborate and protracted arguments to the effect that, indeed, skill in moral reasoning in large part consists itself in the judicious assessment of when and to what extent different and possibly incommensurable justificatory criteria are relevant to a particular moral problem.

whose incompatibility, as he sees it, is more apparent than real: Kohlberg's (1981, 1984) theory of cognitive moral development and Hoffman's (2000) theory of moral development based on the growth of empathic, rather than on primarily cognitive, capacities. Far from being at odds, Gibbs (2003) argues, these two theories are in fact integral to any balanced comprehension of moral maturation and moral maturity. Gibbs (2003) attempts to capture the spirit of the process of moral maturation with the phrase "growth beyond the superficial" (p. 8). The Kohlbergian theory articulates the growth of a "deeper" or more differentiated understanding of the meaning of fairness and reciprocity—thus capturing the justice dimension of the moral domain—whereas Hoffman's theory articulates the emergence of feelings of benevolence and interest in the avoidance of others' suffering as a fundamental aspect of moral experience, or the empathy dimension of the moral domain (p. 78). The specific relationship he posits between justice and caring in the moral point of view appears to be that they are, if you will, equal but separate. That is to say, the moral domain is divided into two distinct realms: (1) the realm of empathy which is concerned with the most important aspects of human weal and woe; and (2) the realm of reciprocity whose interests—impartiality, equality, and universality—seem not to be explainable in terms of empathy. In Gibbs' view, then, justice and empathy are mutually complementary but not mutually dependent. As he puts it, "ideal and 'necessary' moral reciprocity [...] has a place in moral motivation that affective primacy fails to capture" and "if reciprocity is akin to logic—'the morality of thought' in Piaget's famous phrase—then reciprocity and its violation generate a motive power in its own right" (2003, p. 108).

Hoffman himself, I suspect, would have been unwilling to settle for Gibbs' happy compromise—and this, as I have already insinuated, because he views the problem from the perspective, not of moral reasoning, but of moral functioning. As Hoffman (2000) has indicated, his theory of empathic development was never intended to sit quite so comfortably alongside theories of cognitive moral development. According to Hoffman, the Piagetan tradition in moral development theory suffers from a rather gross inadequacy in connection with the problem of explaining moral motives and moral engagement. All sides agree that the underlying process of cognitive moral development is something along the lines of "decentration". This term, which incidentally Gibbs' work (esp. 1991) seems to have done much to popularize as a term of art in moral-developmental circles, captures the developmental shift from moral judgement based on the child's own egocentric perspective through judgements that begin to consider the perspectives of others to a possibly ideal end-state where the perspectives of all are progressively coordinated (cf. Hoffman, 2000, p. 129; Gibbs, 1991). However, what Hoffman (2000) considers to be its "exaggerated focus on rational, cognitive processes" (p. 131) of the Kohlbergian schema rides roughshod over a crucial moral phenomenon that badly needs explaining. That is to say, to quote Hoffman (2000) directly:

> Why [should] the knowledge of others' perspectives that is gained in the context of conflicting claims [...] lead children to take others' claims seriously and be willing to negotiate and compromise their own claims, rather than use the knowledge to manipulate the other? That is, why should perspective-taking serve pro-social rather than egoistic ends? (p. 131)

Hoffman's (2000) own account of moral development, in other words, is distinguished from the cognitive developmental tradition of Piaget (1932) and Kohlberg (1969, 1984) precisely with regards to the claim that moral development does not occur spontaneously in minimally constrained attempts at moral conflict resolution between peers, as he claims these authors held, but necessitates direct adult intervention or moral socialization. The ability to comprehend and the coordination of others' perspectives, of course, only becomes a *moral* competence when it leads children to take those perspectives as a legitimate reason to negotiate and compromise their own demands. Hoffman's (2000) theory of empathic development is intended to address this very problem. Drawing on an impressive array of empirical evidence and theoretical considerations, Hoffman (2000) arrives at the conclusion that: (1) human beings have a biologically rooted adaptive disposition towards concern for others or "empathy" (cf. Hoffman, 1981); (2) the process of empathic moral development consists in the transformation of this basic disposition into the feelings of guilt and states of moral internalization, which regulate children's egocentric motives, thereby enabling the decentration process; and (3) in direct opposition to the ethical naturalist assumptions of cognitive developmentalism, this process depends on successful moral socialization. In sum, the disposition to care about whether others get what is owed to them as persons, takes place against a backdrop of a general concern for human well-being. Again, in sharp contrast with the Piagetan constructivist, Hoffman (2000) argues that an interest in morality is not spontaneously constructed in the course of free peer interaction, but requires support in the form of adult intervention or socialization. In particular, it requires what Hoffman (2000) calls "induction", a discipline encounter, where adults attempt to "make the connection, necessary for guilt and moral internalization, between children's egoistic motives, their behaviour, and their behaviour's harmful consequences for others—and put pressure on children to control their behaviour out of consideration for others" (p. 142). Induction is probably familiar to most parents and caregivers and many use it pre-psychologically or spontaneously: when a child hurts another person, the adult attempts to "induce" feelings of guilt or a sense of conscience by pointing out the nature of the harm and to the fact that the child is uniquely responsible for it.

With the possible exception of point (3), all this has a familiar ring. Indeed, the claim that the very fact that human beings ever are interested in morality at all presupposes an active interest in others' well-being is arguably the core thesis of a philosophical persuasion opposed to ethical rationalism as (putatively) epitomized by Kant. From the perspective of moral sense theory, a particular affective disposition or moral emotion which has been labelled variously empathy (Hoffman, 2000; Vetlesen, 1994), sympathy (Smith, 1790/1976; Hume, 1751/1957), and altruism (Blum, 1980a) is the foundation of moral experience writ large. Understood in this sense, empathy's relevance is not restricted to situations where another's suffering is at stake—as Gibbs (2003) seems to hold—nor is its main moral interest connected with the motivational support it can give to the cold deliberations of duty—as Kant (e.g., 1797/1996), according to Allison's (1990) interpretation, seemed to hold—but it is, to borrow Vetlesen's (1994) phrase, the core "precondition of moral performance" which consists in the recognition that others' well-being is the source of normative *demands*.

For whatever it is worth, it is likely not just Hoffman who would have been dissatisfied with Gibbs' attempt to neatly analyse the moral domain and moral development into two discrete components corresponding to justice and empathy, if one of his last statements on the question is anything to go by, so would Kohlberg. Kohlberg (1990), in fact, seems to have come around to viewing, and publicly endorsing, an interpretation of the moral point of view that is not altogether inconsistent with that brought to us by moral sense theory. Briefly put, the idea is that the fundamental moral notion "respect for persons" idealized in Kohlberg's stage 6 presupposes the *co-primacy* of justice and benevolence or empathy. Kohlberg and his co-authors Boyd and Levine explain that benevolence views situations through the lens of *attachment*—that is, with a view to promoting goodness and preventing harm—whereas the viewpoint of justice is that of *detachment*—that is, with an eye to respecting the rights of individuals conceived as autonomous agents, an interest which, in situations where incompatible claims compete, may lead to harm of the interest of some in order to satisfy the rights of others (Kohlberg, Boyd & Levine, 1990). The two principles can be understood as being in tension in virtue of being mutually constraining. Justice constrains benevolence by ensuring that the interest in promoting the good for some respects the rights of others. Benevolence constrains justice by ensuring that the interest in promoting the rights of individuals is consistent with the best for all (cf. pp. 157–158). Bracketing the question of whether heads or tails can be made of this position, if it is defensible, the idea that benevolence and justice are co-primary in the moral point of view would seem to have the implication that an active regard for the weal and woe of others is neither peripheral to moral experience (as in some versions of Kantian ethics) nor one distinct department of it (as Gibbs seems to hold) but, much as moral sense theorists have long argued, a *sine qua non* thereof.

Chapter 5 studies this postulate or at least the version of it that recurred in the justifications for using professional and practical ethics education as a site for promoting the development of compassionate empathic capacities of response reviewed in Chapter 1: compassionate empathy is an essential ingredient of moral perception.

Chapter 5
Compassionate Empathy, Moral Perception and Moral Conscience

5.1 Introduction

The suggestion that moral functioning and the subsidiary act of moral appraisal actively engage compassionate empathy is deceptively simple. Just what does the claim mean? If one supposes with Vetlesen (1994), for instance, that the issue concerns the nature of moral *motivation* and, in particular, whether all actions and behaviours that one might evaluate as morally good or right are *in fact* motivated by concern for the well-being of others, the role of emotionality moral functioning in this sense seems highly questionable. Much of the behaviour that is usually qualified as being moral is the result of more or less thoughtless habituated reflex.[1] Perhaps, then, the idea is instead that a genuine moral *intention* supposes a regard of compassion. If this is what the claim means, the answer appears to some degree to depend on what one takes as a typical moral act. At least on the face of it, and acknowledging the possibility of a countervailing Kantian position, at least deliberate helping acts would seem, again, to obviously involve concern for the beneficiary's well-being; to the extent that a helping act is motivated by some other intention – personal advantage or even arguably as a matter of duty – it is to that extent at least less morally good. By contrast, when an agent is charged with delivering some contractual or professional obligation, for example, or in a simple case of distributive justice, then the moral goodness of the intention would seem to turn rather on a regard of respect for the legitimacy of the principle of fairness or professionalism or consistency and, accordingly, seem to involve minimally or perhaps not at all a sense of concern for preventing harms and promoting basic human goods. Now these considerations point to two rich and difficult general conceptual questions about the moral psychology of mature moral agency: the *evaluative* question of whether it is a prescriptive requirement of distinctively moral acts or intentions to be motivated by or based on an attitude of concern for others and the separate

---

[1] An appreciation of this fact, commentators observe (cf., e.g., McLaughlin & Halstead, 1999 and Narváez & Lapsley, 2005), is one of the strengths of the character education approach to moral education which advocates the habituation and early moral socialization of children into pre-established and putatively uncontroversial patterns of moral responding.

B. Maxwell, *Professional Ethics Education: Studies in Compassionate Empathy*,
© Springer Science+Business Media B.V. 2008

analytical question of whether the very act of formulating a moral intention or performing a moral act cannot be adequately explained in the absence of such a state of affective involvement. The focus of this study will be on a third one: whether and to what extent an affective engagement of caring for others might be a presupposition of the very ability to consider a moral problem from the moral point of view. Not to act on a moral judgement or to formulate a moral intention, but just to deliberate over a moral problem.

More specifically still, my first concern will be with what is sometimes referred to as the faculty of moral perception, the moment of moral judgement, if you will, at which one perceives the moral issues that are at stake in a situation, issues that become the basic terms of a moral problem. The purpose of this chapter is to submit to scrutiny the claim that moral perception is predominantly an affective capacity. The strategy adopted here is admittedly just one of any number of different routes one could take to tackle the question of whether a failure to empathize compassionately might entail an impairment of the general exercise of the faculty of moral judgement. One notable alternative approach is that of Deigh (1995) who has examined this problem from the point of view of the presuppositions of the ability to universalize moral judgements.

The choice to focus on moral perception, however, is not arbitrary. We saw in Chapter 1 (cf. §1.2) that one suggestive reason cited as grounds for encouraging the development of the moral imagination and related capacities of empathic response in the context of practical ethics education was because it is in a person's initial emotional responses to a situation that his or her attention is drawn to its morally salient features and the moral problem itself, the object of moral deliberation if you will, is constructed on the basis of these first impressions. I begin by presenting in §5.2 what I consider to be a clear and plausible account of the basic role that moral perception plays in the construction of moral problems. In what I will refer to as the "Kantian situation of moral deliberation" we have, I will argue, such an account and, furthermore, one which has the important strategic advantage of being a hard case. An analysis of the role that emotions play in constructing moral problems, which is consistent with the basic Kantian prescriptive story of principle-based moral justification would seem to be better placed to please even the heartiest of ethical rationalists. After responding briefly, in §5.3, to the worry that the moral perception, occurring prior to moral deliberation, does not constitute a dimension of moral deliberation as such – and hence that a deficiency of moral perception would not entail a deficiency of moral judgement – I turn, in §5.4 to the nub of the matter: an examination of the postulate that the faculty of moral perception necessarily depends on active affective involvement. Here, I will argue that relevant and existing knowledge about the moral psychology of the diagnostic category of "psychopathy", a personality disorder characterized by full cognitive integrity coexisting with emotional stagnancy, and corroborating empirical research on psychopathy and moral development, speak convincingly against the claim. As I argue in §5.5, while the evidence on moral functioning and psychopathy *denies* Callahan's (1980), Coombs' (1998), and Hilfiker's (2001) hypothesis about the affectivity of moral perception, it *corroborates* their view that an affective disposition of concern for others underlies not just the ability to grasp the notion of normativity, the "bind-ingness" of valid moral rules, and the notion of moral obligation, but also plays an important role in what Callahan (1980) referred to as "the drive to get moral problems right", or "moral conscience" under one interpretation of this term.

5.2 Moral Perception in the Kantian Situation of Moral Deliberation

When in search of an account of moral judgement, which pictures moral judgement as being the exclusive purview of the cognitive faculties, the collective gaze turns naturally towards Kant. The emergence in recent years of a body of Kantian scholarship showing that the Kantian interpretation of the basic situation of moral deliberation actually helps clarify one indispensable role that affect and concern for others play in the exercise of moral judgement – that is, in the constitution of moral problems by drawing an agent's attention to the morally salient features of a situation – is an intriguing development. Although Kantian scholars themselves increasingly reject the notion that Kant's (1785/1987, 1797/1996) ideal of the mature moral agent as a steely eyed calculator of duty in favour of interpretations that show that Kant had in fact a rather rich appreciation of the affective side of moral life (cf., e.g., Hill, 2000; Sherman, 1990; Baron, 1997; Herman, 1984, 1985), so-called Kantian ethics remains a favourite foil for those wishing to illustrate the various pitfalls of excessive rationalism in ethics (cf., e.g., Vetlesen, 1994; Williams, 1985; Blum, 1980a). Blum's (1980a) sketch is particularly germane to our present purposes since it narrows in on the general conception of emotions and feelings of the Kantian view and seems to accurately depict the Kantian (though not necessarily Kant's own) view of the place and significance of the emotions in moral judgement and moral motivation (for a more recent and very similar summary see Vetlesen, 1994) and so it is with an outline of this position that we begin.

With the caveat that his depiction should not be taken for Kant's view proper but instead "some lines of thought associated with him, which have been influential in moral philosophy" (Blum, 1980a, p. 2) Blum enumerates three general suppositions about emotions involved in the Kantian view. First, emotions are capricious and transitory. They are subject to variation according to one's mood and particular inclinations (p. 2). Second, feelings are beyond our direct control. That is to say, we are "passive" with respect to our emotions in that we generally have no choice about whether and how we experience them (p. 2). Third, altruistic emotions such as compassionate empathy are highly partial in respect of being felt more strongly towards people we know or otherwise identify with and are typically triggered by unique features of a set of circumstances which have personal resonance (p. 2). They are, in Blum's words, "directed towards and occasioned by particular persons in particular circumstances" (p. 2).

With the exception of the second assertion, which fails to appreciate the ways that emotions are susceptible to *indirect* control – one can avoid experiencing an emotion by avoiding situations that arouse it and the ability to "pull oneself together" or "bootstrap", as it is sometimes labelled, when in the grip of a strong emotional experience by diverting or refocusing one's attention are both common-place (for discussions of this point see Steutel & Spiecker, 2004; Maxwell & Reichenbach, 2007; Peters, 1981; Ben Ze'ev, 2000) – these claims seem both hard to deny on the face of it and are consistent with the foregoing characterization of compassionate empathy (see esp. §§3.4 and 4.4). More perplexing issues emerge, however, in consideration of what these characteristics of the emotions entail with regards to the role of the emotions in moral judgement and moral motivation.

From the capriciousness of the emotions and, in particular, from the fact that compassionate empathy is subject to empathic bias, the Kantian inference, in Blum's (1980a) assessment, is that the incongruity between the deliberative stand-point of impartiality characteristic of the moral point of view and this feature of emotions demands that we repudiate or distrust their council. To consider a problem from the moral point of view, on this conception, involves, in Blum's (1980a) words, "abstracting oneself from one's own interests and one's particular attach-ments to others" (p. 3) in the name of the principle of universal equality. Otherwise put, since emotions are so notoriously unreliable as a guide to what is right in a given situation, a problem discussed in Chapter 4 under the heading of "empathic bias" (cf. §3.4 earlier), the demand of moral impartiality suggests that the source of moral justification must lie elsewhere. The passivity of the emotions, further, raises doubts about whether acts motivated by an emotion could be considered to be genu-inely moral. If emotions and their concomitant action tendencies are not willed or chosen, and if we can only be held responsible for acts which are free in this sense, any action motivated by an emotion falls afoul of the Kantian criterion of the inten-tionality of moral acts – i.e., a morally good act is one that is motivated by "good will". This, or something closely related to it, was almost certainly Blasi's (1999, p. 13) point when he asked:

> [C]an emotions provide moral motivation, giving origin to moral action and ultimately to a sustained moral life? [...] As emotion is normally understood in psychology, the answer would have to be negative. [In psychology], emotion is seen as arising in us unintentionally, as generating its action tendencies automatically and unintentionally, and as being regu-lated by processes that are considered to be mostly unintentional and unconscious. Thus conceived, emotions cannot give origin to intentional actions, to actions that are performed for conscious reasons and fall in the realm of the agent's responsibility.

I suspect that Kant himself would have considered this last point to be the most important one, but that he would have expressed it rather differently.

It is well known that Kant took autonomy of the will as a presupposition of morality as such and moral autonomy consisted, in one of his formulations, in being a member of a "kingdom of ends": both the author and subject of the principles that govern his actions. A free will, in other words, is one which is not determined by any cause foreign to itself; a will otherwise governed is, in Kant's term, "heterono-mous" rather than autonomous. To act on the basis of one's natural or spontaneous inclinations is to choose on the basis of an external principle – a hypothetical rather than a categorical imperative – and this constitutes a failure vis-à-vis the autonomy requirement of morality, motivation by a good will. Kant's proposal for screening the potentially confounding influence of external bases of choice (and these included, for Kant, not just emotions but the influence of others, tradition, and – causing great scandal in his time – divine law as well; cf. Kant, 1785/1987, pp. 59–60) was to verify whether any ostensible duty or action principle could meet the criteria of being a "law of a free will", or a categorical imperative. If the policy or principle of action can be rationally willed to be a law governing anyone in a similar situation, one is under a categorical imperative, understood as a universal practical demand of reason.[2]

In sum, considering (1) its scepticism towards the epistemological reliability of spontaneous human caring responses and, in particular, (2) its apparent demand to abstract oneself from the kinds of attachments characteristic of significant human relationships in considering moral obligations, and, finally, (3) its cognitivist assumption that valid norms are distinguishable from invalid ones in terms of their predication of a certain rationally discernable property – willability (if you will) as a universal law – the Kantian view of feelings and emotions in moral judgement does indeed seem to constitute a powerful line of thought which would appear, in Blum's (1980a) words, to "deny a substantial role to sympathy, compassion, and concern in morality and moral motivation" (p. 3).

Without wading too far out into the treacherous waters of Kantian interpretation, there seems to be good reason to suspect that the position just sketched, most notably the idea that acting in accordance with an emotionally generated action impulse is morally out of bounds in the sense that it is inconsistent with the ideal of a good will, is something of a straw man version of not just Kant's position. It also seems to be out of step with the basic features of a moral deliberation situation and the idea of compassionate empathy as a "quasi-ethical" achievement discussed earlier (in §4.3). As Hill (2000) reminds us, Kant's principal ethical writings take as their central theme the questions "What should I do?" when it is asked, "sincerely […] from a first-person deliberative standpoint by more or less mature and rational moral agents faced with significant moral questions" (p. 19).[3] That is to say, the "categorical imperative" understood as a principle which enables one to distinguish on rational grounds between valid and invalid action norms, is addressed to moral agents understood as being *in medias res*: faced even now with a moral problem or conflict in a particular and possibly unique set of circumstances. It was emphatically not intended first and foremost, and this is contrary to the way it is sometimes portrayed in textbook discussions of deontologism, as a handy tool for generating in the abstract a list of categorically inviolable moral rules interdicting killing, lying, stealing, and so on.

The Kantian deliberation situation has been vividly described in a relatively recent article by Korsgaard (1999, pp. 10–12) and her analysis is consistent with

---

[2] For recent discussions of these issues see Hill (2000), Secker (1999), and Korsgaard (1999)

[3] Habermas (1993b) and Korsgaard (1999) argue for similar interpretations.

Baron's (1984) and Herman's (1984) older treatments. Human beings, in virtue of being able to ask the question "What should I (from a moral point of view) do in this situation?", have a free will, at least inasmuch as the question itself is coherently raised only by agents who understand themselves to possess the ability to select between action alternatives. (cf. Hill, 2000, p. 20). If we understand a deliberation situation as one where the need for moral judgement arises and such a need arises in two characteristic situations: (1) when an agent is faced with an apparent moral dilemma; and (2) where an imperative to satisfy some need or desire appears to conflict with some putative moral norm (cf. Herman, 1985, p. 418). Deliberation situations of the latter sort are probably the most common and in such cases the will is presented with at least two incompatible action proposals. A common source of such action tendencies is, in Kant's term, "inclinations" grounded in incentives. The latter are the features of the object of an inclination that make the inclination an attractive ground of choice, like the prospective enjoyment understood as the consequence of the choice to drink a glass of wine (cf. Korsgaard, 1999, p. 11). Action proposals generated by compassionate empathy would seem to qualify as an inclination in this sense. On the most general level, the incentive in which compassionate empathy is conceived of as an inclination in the relevant present sense is the relief of suffering. Imagine, then, that you are a teacher faced with an ambitious student who, up until the last evaluation, has done quite well in your course. She can offer nothing to account for her poor performance, except for complaining that she had been "feeling kind of weird lately", but nevertheless, and between sobs and moans, begs you to assign at least a passing grade. Otherwise, she firmly and apparently rightly believes, her chances of getting into the accounting programme of her choice will be jeopardized. Alternatively, consider a situation where you are sitting on a very crowded subway train at rush hour. Adjacent to your seat is a man holding two heavy shopping bags and, unable to grasp a handrail, is struggling not to fall down as the train jerks along. You feel terrible for him but you have a long journey ahead of you and you are quite certain that if you offer him your seat, you will travel the rest of the way home standing. In both these deliberation situations, inclinations – here, feelings of compassionate empathy – present the free will with proposals each of which makes a specific recommendation for a course of action: in the first circumstances to pass the student on the assignment and in the second to offer your seat.

Now a heteronomous will, on Korsgaard's (1999) reading of Kant, would unreflectively follow its inclinations and do these acts. An autonomous will submits the proposal to what Sherman (1990) refers to as the "regulative constraint" of moral judgement (pp. 161–162). In strictly Kantian terms, this means asking whether one would be willing to submit oneself to the principle on which such an action decision is based as a universal moral law – in other words, whether the principle in question is a categorical (rather than a mere hypothetical) imperative. As Korsgaard (1999, p. 12) puts it, in an autonomous will:

> [...] nothing is a law to you except what you make a law for yourself, you ask yourself whether you could take *that* to be your law. Your question is whether you can will the maxim of doing act-A in order to produce end-E as a law. Your question, in other words, is whether your maxim passes the categorical imperative test.

Let us suppose now for the sake of argument that in the student case the inclination fails the categorical imperative test and that in subway case it passes. In the student case, the will rejects the specific action proposal suggested by the inclination (i.e., to comply with the student's wish to be assigned a passing grade) on the grounds that the application of moral judgement confirms the suspicion that it provided, in these circumstances, *mis*guidance as considered from the moral point of view. As mentioned above (in §§4.1 and 4.5), this is precisely the kind of case that is frequently cited in order to shatter the illusion that compassionate empathy has inherent moral worth in any straightforward sense; the point is often put by saying that, despite many good reasons to suspect that it is a good and noble thing, compassionate empathy is not "necessary" for moral motivation since it can motivate morally questionable or even morally bad acts unless checked by sound moral judgement (cf., e.g., Snow, 2000; Sober & Wilson, 1998; Verducci, 1999; Eisenberg & Miller, 1987b; Blum, 1980b).

For our purposes, more telling than the student example where the will *rejects* an inclination's action proposal is the subway example in which the will *accepts* it. A seemingly solid classical Kantian interpretation of such cases is that, when an agent judges that he has a moral obligation to act in accordance with an inclination, while the inclination may provide a secondary support for the motivation to act, if the decisive consideration is the action's consistency with a categorical imperative, in the final analysis, it was considerations of duty, not inclination, which motivated the act. This question is the subject of some controversy. Baron (1984), for instance, regards duty in such cases as a "counterfactual condition" which provides merely a limiting condition or control on what can be done from motives other than duty (cf. pp. 207, 216–217). Arguing along similar lines, Herman (1984) suggests that Kant's schema requires only that we act morally "permissively" and "where there is an obligation to help, we are required to acknowledge this moral claim, even though we may give help out of compassion, etc." (p. 376; quoted in Sherman, 1990). Sherman (1990), however, seems sceptical of these claims. The question of whether or not duty has to be the primary motive in order for such an act to be considered moral in some strict Kantian sense aside, the fact remains that the inclination in this case, in virtue of having submitted the action proposal to give up the seat on the bus out of compassionate empathy for the man, *got it right*, as confirmed by the application of moral judgement. Furthermore, and as Herman (1985) argues, in cases such as the student example, even though the inclination was constrained by moral judgement, it remains a *sine qua non* of the exercise of the faculty of moral judgement in the sense of having played a central role in creating the practical problem as object of moral reflection. One could, presumably, object that any consistency that might be found to pertain between an inclination and a duty in a particular set of circumstances is merely incidental. However, this suggestion seems to overlook a problem that is so obvious that it is difficult to discern. Akin to something discussed by cognitive scientists under the name of the "frame problem", in any given problem situation an agent is faced with a potentially infinite number of possible solutions. So, there must be some mechanism which eliminates most strategies *a priori* and thus reduces its complexity to a manageable level (cf. e.g., de Sousa, 2001). In the examples discussed in this connection, compassionate empathy would appear on the face of it to play this perceptual role of drawing the agent's attention to features of the situation that have genuine moral salience.

In light of these considerations, it might seem increasingly difficult to sustain, with Blum (1980a) that, on this putatively Kantian picture of moral deliberation, sympathy, compassion, or concern plays "no substantial role" in moral judgement and moral motivation. On the contrary, and indeed in both examples above, compassionate empathy has an indispensable hand in *generating* the moral problem as such by presenting the will with prima facie obligations and drawing the agent's attention to action proposals as candidates for a solution. Spelling out the role of affective engagement in the faculty of moral judgement in terms of its contribution to the constitution of moral problems, however, generates two further difficulties. First, the fact that moral perception in this sense comes on the scene prior to moral judgement might be taken to imply that such perceptive capacities are not part of moral judgement itself. Second, the question seems to remain open as to whether the operation of moral perception is primarily and necessarily achieved through the implication of affective psychological process. The next two sections (§§5.3 and 5.4) address these issues in turn.

5.3   Moral Perception and Moral Judgement

Whether moral perception involves capacities encompassed by moral judgement depends above all on how moral judgement is defined and delineated. As Vetlesen (1994) observes, theories of moral judgement in normative ethics typically take the object of moral judgement, the content, and structure of the deliberation situation as given and are not concerned with the conditions under which the moral dilemma or moral conflict arises in the first instance (p. 158). This appears true. For instance, in principle-based normative ethics, moral judgement is centrally concerned with the identification and application of moral principles as justificatory grounds for action choice. In virtue ethics it involves measuring action alternatives against the choice a person of ideal moral character would make in the circumstances; an act is morally justified or "morally right" to the extent that it is consistent with what a virtuous agent would do. Consequentialists, by contrast, characteristically hold that a process of considering which action alternative in a particular set of circumstances would lead to the best overall consequences for all those affected captures the substance of moral judgement.[4] Seen from this perspective, the broad intent of a theory of normative ethics is not far to seek: they propose prescriptive justificatory frameworks for resolving moral problems with which a moral agent is already faced – i.e., how a person *should* deliberate over moral problems. They are not intended

---

[4] See Baron et al.'s *Three methods of ethics* (1997) for authoritative accounts of each of these theories of normative ethics and the differences between them.

to provide explanatory insight into how moral problems *in fact* psychologically arise for agents as practical problems. And so it is that if we follow normative ethics and understand the purview of moral judgement as encompassing more or less formal process of deliberate rational moral reflection, the faculty of moral perception, coming into play as it putatively does primarily in the psychogenesis of moral problems, is indeed something outside and other than the process of moral judgement itself.

This picture of a tidy division of labour between moral judgement and moral perception is muddied, however, if we attend to another trait that is definitive of a theory of normative ethics. Be it a monistic theory such as consequentialism and deontologism – a theory which prioritizes a single moral category as having overriding moral relevance in moral deliberation – or a pluralistic theory like Ross' (1930) intuitionism and possibly virtue ethics – a theory which depicts moral assessment as appealing to a range of moral categories that do not always fit together in a neat hierarchy of value – they all naturally take it as given that moral judgement makes reference to *some* moral category.[5] When notions such as "harm", "virtue", "dignity", "beneficence", "fairness", and "happiness" operate as moral categories, they represent human or social goods in whose name one has reason to act. To formulate it otherwise, such goods make sense as justificatory grounds for action choice considered from a moral point of view if promoting them is an imperative, a compelling reason for action. Moral perception and moral judgement are linked up in this respect: the mastery of substantive moral categories seems to be a precondition of both.

Because of the predominantly tacit workings of such categories in everyday moral discourse and reflection, the point is perhaps easy to overlook. So in order to help appreciate their necessity Herman, in her searching and yet sparklingly insightful essay on moral perception titled "The practice of moral judgement" (1985), invites one to consider how a "computer" would have to be programmed for it to pass moral judgements on events:

> Just to recognize that it should present the event "A punching B in the nose" for moral judgement, the machine would have to know, for example, that such actions involve injuries and that injuries are morally salient features of human events. (Imagine how much more complex its information would have to be to pick up the harm of an insult or demeaning remark.) (Herman, 1985, pp. 416–417)

The computer, in other words, would have to be provided with some means of isolating from the indefinitely many possible descriptions of an action situation just which features are morally salient. Herman calls this knowledge that enables agents to perceive the features of a set of circumstances or action proposals that require moral attention "rules of moral salience" (p. 418). The application of the rules of moral salience constitutes a species of moral appraisal, even though conclusions arrived at come quickly and unreflectively. In this regard quite unlike the plotting

---

[5] This distinction between monistic and pluralistic theories of moral judgement follows Hill (2000, pp. 11–12, 21–24).

and considered processes of evaluation usually associated with moral judgement. This is why Herman can speak of moral judgement as embracing moral perception. "Moral judgement", she writes, "is not the first step in moral deliberation" (p. 417).[6]

Herman draws attention to several features of the rules of moral salience that are worth attending to. But to forestall confusion, it is important to underline that she views the rules of moral salience from the perspective of what was characterized in §5.2 as the Kantian standpoint of moral deliberation: an agent faced even now with the question of what she should do in the face of what she regards as a significant moral question. In her view, a "routine" or "characteristic" situation where an agent recognizes the need to exercise moral judgement is one where some feature of that situation signals to the agent that the normal hypothetical or instrumental grounds for action justification might need to be overridden by some moral ground of action. "The need for [moral] judgement characteristically arises", Herman says, "when an agent has what he takes to be a good compelling reason to act to satisfy some interest or need and yet realizes that what he would do violates a known moral precept" (1985, pp. 418–419). Presumably, the rules of moral salience understood as moral categories enabling agents to perceive morally salient features of a situation are rallied in other ordinary situations where there is no question of *deliberation* over whether some moral right or wrong has transpired. While one might not speak of moral judgement in Herman's normative-ethical sense in observing, say, someone telling a bald-faced lie to or in realizing that one is witnessing an openly malicious act, the ability to formulate such appraisals seems equally to presuppose the same set of moral categories captured by the rules of moral salience.

With the idea in mind that the rules of moral salience, in Herman's (1985) analysis, are mental categories whose existence moral appraisal presupposes, one is better placed to grasp what she means when she says that the rules of moral salience (1) "do not themselves have moral weight" (p. 419). The rules of moral salience, that is, do not instrumentally serve moral ends, say, as some kind of adaptive feature of human psychology which permits human beings to recognize forms of human harm so that they can help to relieve them (pp. 419, 424). Rather, if the rules of moral salience are instrumental, it is in the role they play in signalling to the agent when moral judgement is needed or, in cases of distress, "whether their help is morally appropriate or called for" (p. 424). In this sense, as she puts it, "the rules of moral salience constitute the structure of moral sensitivity" (p. 419) but not part of the structure of moral *judgement* as such. The second feature of the rules of moral salience she wishes to draw attention to is this: in virtue of signalling to the agent the need to suspend the normally hypothetical-prudential grounds for action justification they (2) are a presupposition of what is ordinarily called "conscience" (p. 419). To illustrate the point, following Herman's (1985) own example of deceit

---

[6] Similar accounts of moral perception are to be found in Blum (1991), Vetlesen (1994), and Rest (1986). All respect that moral perception and moral judgement are analytically distinct components of moral functioning and all concur that the two components overlap at least insofar as they both involve moral appraisal.

(p. 419), consider a business executive who is keenly interested in increasing his company's share value. He learns at a board meeting that profits for the coming quarter are projected to be down and that public knowledge of this would lead to a drop in the share price. Only for the executive equipped with a particular rule of moral salience covering cases of deceit would the question of whether or not to release the figures publicly become a matter of conscience; he would be able to recognize, in other words, that *here* is a case where a moral precept makes a demand on his decision-making. Finally, if, as Herman has it, the function of the rules of moral salience is to enable agents to perceive morally salient features of a situation as a preliminary to moral judgement, such rules must (3) be rather simple and general (p. 420). This third feature of Herman's rules of moral salience invites comparison with the Kantian idea of an imperfect duty. One thing that distinguishes perfect from imperfect duties in Kant's schema is that whereas a perfect duty requires or interdicts specific acts, imperfect duties are general; there is a perfect duty not to commit the specific act of suicide whereas there is an imperfect duty to act in ways that are generally benevolent to others (cf. Kant, 1797/1996 and, e.g., Mathias, 1999). Similarly, the rules of moral salience, on Herman's account, can never function independently of other rules of judgement because it is moral judgement, not the general rules of moral salience, which enables agents to identify such things as exceptions and limiting cases and to propose the specific candidates for morally appropriate action. That is, she says, they "encode a *defeasible* solution to questions about the nature of moral agents, the appropriate descriptive terms that capture morally salient features of our situations, our decisions and so on" (p. 429). Moral perception, in Herman's sense, sets the stage for moral judgement but does not, if you will, write the script.

Herman's attempt to draw a clear distinction between the rules of moral salience and moral judgement in this way stems, obviously enough, from her paper's avowed aim of arguing that moral perception and its concomitant features – one of which is possibly affective involvement – is both an inalienable dimension of what she calls "the practice of moral judgement" and consistent with a rather orthodox reading of the "categorical imperative" as a formal principle of moral judgement in Kantian ethics. Her point is that critics are simply wrong to suggest that acknowledging the phenomenon of moral perception commits one to rejecting some or all of Kant's prescriptive account of moral justification. The question of whether one wishes, with Herman, to stipulate that the term "moral judgement" is to refer exclusively to explicit processes of moral justification or it should be taken more broadly to refer to all forms of moral appraisal is neither here nor there from the perspective of this study. Moral judgement, defined in either way, depends on moral perception, the faculty which enables people to pick out morally relevant features of situations and, in situations where conflicts between moral demands are perceived, the insights of moral perception are the building blocks of a moral problem.

It might on the face of it appear that the phenomenon of moral perception is itself sufficient evidence to support the claim that the kind of involvement characteristic of compassionate empathy, seeing others suffering as something to be alleviated, is a *sine qua non* of the exercise of the application of practical wisdom to moral problems.

If the possession of certain moral categories is a presupposition of the ability to perceive morally salient features in a situation – that is, to recognize and frame moral problems when they occur – and if such categories connect up on a basic level with human needs, welfare, and interest, it would seem that the ability to perceive morally and the affective capacity of moral sensitivity are of a piece. A moral agent, as Herman (1985, p. 424) articulates it:

> *must* have a characteristic way of seeing if he is to judge at all. To be a moral agent one must be trained to perceive situations in terms of their morally significant features. [...] Gross failures of perception – e.g., the inability to realize that unprovoked injury is morally significant – would be counted as marks of moral pathology. A person will be less than a *normal* moral agent unless he achieves a certain level of moral sensitivity.

But a few lines above this passage, Herman (1985, p. 424) asks, "might not the ability to discern distress require the development of affective capacities of response? I do not know the answer to this". Herman's agnosticism on this point demonstrates rare insight. Scholars in both psychology and ethics who work with the construct rarely seek grounds for the claim that moral perception is an affective faculty, tending either to assume moral sensitivity's affectivity or to carefully skirt the question. Among the apparent believers, for example, is Sherman (1990) who, in her treatment of moral perception, asserts that it "involves a sensitivity cultivated through emotional dispositions" (p. 150); in a recent major empirical study Morton and her colleagues stipulatively characterize moral sensitivity as the regulation of other-directed emotional responses (Morton et al., 2006, p. 390).[7] There are also agnostics who wish to study only the observable face of moral sensitivity, with little regard for the nature of its underlying psychological process. Volker (1984), for one, defines moral sensitivity as "merely the tendency to recognize that moral [problems] exist".[8]

For the purposes of the present work, the question of whether moral perception or moral sensitivity is a predominantly affective process is of the utmost significance. If it is an affective capacity, we have in moral perception, first, one promising and rather concrete response to the otherwise uncertain call, petitioned in Chapter 1, concerning how to pedagogically "expand beyond" traditional judgement-focussed terrain of most professional and applied ethics (see §1.2) in the improvement of situational moral perception. What is more, a growing body of evidence indicates that this ethical competence can be taught and improved through techniques practicable in classroom instructional contexts and, *a fortiori*, that even standard forms of ethics education in universities have a positive impact on moral sensitivity (cf. review in You & Bebeau, 2005, pp. 11–12 and Clarkeburn, 2002; Liebowitz, 1990;

---

[7]Others in ethics who could seem to fall into the "believers" camp are Murdoch (1970), Blum (1980a, 1991) and Vetlesen (1996). For representatives of this position in the field of moral psychology see Rest (1986), Bebeau (1994, 2002), and Pizarro (2000).

[8]Quoted in You and Bebeau (2005). For similarly agnostic views on the affectivity of moral perception see Hébert et al. (1990, 1992), and Akabayashi et al. (2004).

Myyry & Helkama, 2002; Ofsthun, 1986; Sirin et al., 2003). Second, moral perception has the added advantage of being relatively uncontroversial as a domain of affective functioning in moral life. The idea that emotional engagement sets the stage for moral reasoning is consistent with, as Herman (1985) and Korsgaard (1999) take pains to demonstrate, dominant cognitivist or "realist" accounts of moral reasoning and moral justification, those which take normative claims to be analogous to assertoric claims insofar as they are susceptible to assessment in terms of publicly accessible criteria of justification.[9] The next section (§5.4) confronts the problem directly: if "moral sensitivity" understood the ability to pick out morally relevant features of a situation and construct dilemmas *does* draw on affective capacities of response, that would predict that psychopaths, those who have been diagnosed with a psychiatric condition characterized by full cognitive integrity and abnormally low affective responsiveness to others, should also be characteristically morally insensitive.

5.4   Are Psychopaths Morally Sensitive?

5.4.1   Psychopathy and Its Nosological Controversy

Psychopathy has long been a rather indeterminate expression used to denote a wide range of psychological disorders and syndromes related to antisocial behaviour. These included neuroses, phobias, and schizophrenia. As a medical term, it is absurdly broad; etymologically, "psychopathy" is a disease (*pathos*) of the mind (*psyche*). Nevertheless, in what are now classic works such as Cleckley's (1950) *The mask of sanity* and *The psychopath* by McCord and McCord (1964), the foundations of the current, more specific clinical concept of psychopathy were laid. In these works, it is argued that the clinical concept of psychopathy should be reserved for a particular deficiency frequently encountered in the professional lives of many psychologists and psychiatrists. Typical and distinctive of this disorder is a lack of conformity to social norms, and the sheer absence of the so-called moral emotions of guilt, shame, and empathy.[10] This low emotionality, however, seems to affect social understanding or social skills in curiously ambivalent ways. The title of Cleckley's book, "the mask of sanity", refers already to what the author considered to be the psychopath's singular adeptness at masking his disorder by mimicking the reactions of normal and sane people. Owing to the psychopath's fully functioning rational faculty or what Cleckley (1950) calls his "unimpaired peripheral abilities"

---

[9] On the distinction between cognitivist and non-cognitivist conceptions of moral justification see, for example, Habermas (1993b) and Smith (1994).

[10] Cf. also Spiecker (1988b). For a recent interpretation and defence of the controversial idea of a "moral emotion", see de Sousa (2001).

(p. 413) the psychopath comes across, at least on the first few encounters, as being perfectly sane even to the most experienced clinical eye. This, further, marks psychopathy off dramatically from other documented psychological disorders whose outward manifestations are immediately apparent to any observer (cf. Cleckley, 1950, pp. 411–413). Cleckley writes:

> In the simple schizophrenic or the seriously schizoid personality, an inadequate or impaired affective participation appears in outer signs of indifference, withdrawal, oddity, queer tastes, etc. [...] In contrast the semantically disordered psychopath with the peripheral mechanisms for adjustment functioning accurately does not show on the surface similar indications of trouble within. (p. 413) [...] Functionally and structurally all is intact on the outside. Good function (healthy reactivity) will be demonstrated in all theoretical trials. Judgment as well as good reasoning will be apparent at verbal levels. Ethical as well as practical considerations will be recognized in the abstract. A brilliant mimicry of sound social reactions will occur in every test except the test of life itself. (p. 411)

In short, Cleckley's core hypothetical diagnostic interpretation is that a psychopath is in essence a fully functioning person in every respect except that he cannot *feel* (cf. 1950, esp. pp. 398–399).

The observed lack or extreme shallowness of emotional response characteristic of the psychopath explains, Cleckley (1950) held, many of the other recognized traits such as: (1) an inability to maintain long-term relationships such as friendship and marriage; (2) proneness to boredom; and, (3) persistent failure to formulate and execute long-term life plans (cf. Hare, 1991). If friendship is reciprocal concern (cf. Blum, 1980a, esp. pp. 67–70) and interest in some activity or other is sustained by some significant degree of involvement or engrossment in it (cf. Heller's 1979 definition of "emotion"), it is perhaps not so surprising that a person with grossly impoverished emotional reactions can make friends but cannot keep them, and is easily bored. As Cleckley (1950) suggestively puts it, "if the 12-year-old boys could enjoy King Lear or [Beethoven's] Ninth Symphony as much as some people do, they would not be so reckless and unruly" (p. 421). As for the psychopath's poor judgement about how to formulate and achieve personal goals, a possible explanation is that an absence of appropriate concern for *himself* renders him incapable of arriving at an adequate conception of his own interests and advantage (cf. Elliott & Gillett, 1992, p. 58; cf. Cleckley, 1950).

In the decades that followed the publication of *The mask of sanity*, psychopathy became a widely researched subject in various fields. The portrayal of the psychopath as an unemotional but socially skilled and intelligent individual has ever since been the subject of psychological and philosophical disputes about the nature of moral agency, the intrinsic motivational force of moral reasons or judgements, the rationality of immorality or amorality, the responsibility of evil-doers that lack moral emotions, and the concept of insanity itself (e.g. Blair et al., 1995; Glannon, 1997; Milo, 1998; and Nichols, 2004). The psychopath's utter lack of sensitivity to others' suffering – while committing heinous criminal acts as in mundane day-to-day interactions with others – has led some to describe psychopaths as being "morally indifferent" (Milo, 1984), "moral imbeciles" (Spiecker, 1988a), and even "morally dead" (Murphy, 1972).

Despite the widespread interest in the phenomenon of psychopathy, standard psychiatric diagnostic manuals, the DSM-III (1980) and the DSM-IV, do not include an entry for "psychopathy"; according to current received wisdom, the DSM diagnostic category of "Antisocial Personality Disorder" (ASPD) is the equivalent of psychopathy. This position has been questioned on conceptual and empirical grounds.

Lilienfeld (1998), for example, argues that with the development of a "behaviour-based" approach to describing and categorizing psychological and psychiatric disorders, not directly observable "internal" aspects of pathology are ignored. This means that attempts are made to write characteristic traits and criteria in behavioural terms – such as "aggressiveness" in the case of ASPD. What this inevitably leaves out are the "inner" emotional states and personality traits – remorselessness, manipulativeness, glibness, and so on – so central to Cleckley's (1950) and McCord & McCord's (1964) interpretation of the psychopathy concept.

For the express purpose of marking out psychopathy from ASPD, the psychologist Hare and colleagues developed the Psychopathy Checklist and its successor the Psychopathy Checklist-Revised (PCL-R) (cf. Hare et al., 1991). The PCL-R is today considered to be the most valid and reliable diagnostic tool to determine psychopathy. In contrast to the category of ASPD, the PCL-R explicitly includes personality traits in addition to behavioural characteristics.

The psychopathy construct is regarded as being composed of two or more "clusters" comprising a set of traits which are also referred to individually as "factors" (Blair et al., 2005). The PCL-R distinguishes aspects related to emotions or interpersonal relations (e.g., lack of emotions, lack of intimate relationships) from aspects related to behaviour (e.g., antisocial behaviour). The first cluster of factors is commonly referred to as Factor 1 and the second as Factor 2 (see Table 5.1).[11] Put simply, Hare's idea is that a psychopath will score high in clinical assessments on *both* factors, whereas a person with ASPD will score high on Factor 2 only. Research seems to support the thesis that the PCL-R does track two significantly different psychological disorders: ASPD and psychopathy (e.g. Hare et al., 1991; see also Blair et al., 2005).

Table 5.1 Hare's two-factor model of psychopathy (Hare, 1999, p. 34)

Emotional/interpersonal	Social deviance
Glib and superficial	Impulsive
Egocentric and grandiose	Poor behavioural controls
Lack of remorse or guilt	Need for excitement
Lack of empathy	Lack of responsibility
Deceitful and manipulative	Early behaviour problems
Shallow emotions	Adult antisocial behaviour

---

[11] More recently, a three-factor model has been developed in which Factor 1 is subdivided into a personality or emotional factor (e.g., "shallowness") and a relational factor (e.g., "narcistic") (Cooke & Michie, 2001). There is even a four-factor model that subdivides the behavioural component into lifestyle and antisocial behaviour factors (Neuman et al., 2005). Most research on psychopathy, however, adopts as its theoretical frame the two-factor model. I follow this convention.

The early work on psychopathy by Cleckley (1950) and McCord and McCord (1964) postulated a causal relation between a lack of guilt and empathy, and impulsivity and the strong antisocial desires. More recent research complicates this picture significantly: Factor 2 correlates with high anxiety and emotional distress, while Factor 1 correlates with low anxiety (Hicks & Patrick, 2006). Furthermore, it is established that Factor 1 correlates highly with proactive, controlled aggression aimed at achieving an end that the aggressor perceives to be in his interest (e.g., in the context of a racketeering operation, breaking a shopkeeper's arm as a means of encouraging the owner to make timely "protection" payments), but that Factor 2 correlates with impulsive reactive or "expressive" aggression which typically occurs spontaneously as a response to a perceived threat (e.g., a jealous man who assaults his girlfriend's male friend) (Blair et al., 2005). What is more, Ishikawa et al. (2001) found that "successful" psychopaths, psychopathic individuals who did not get arrested for their crimes, perform better on tasks measuring delay gratification and impulse control not only when compared with "unsuccessful" psychopaths, those who did get caught. Indeed, the "successful" psychopaths even performed better than the non-psychopathic control group on the tasks! The importance of these findings from the present perspective is that they suggest that the moral-affective deficiency of the psychopath is a rather isolated deficiency: it differs from ASPD, and seems independent of other deficiencies, such as cognitive deficiencies or deficiencies of impulse or aggression-controlling skills – deficiencies, if you like, of self-control.

Psychopathy, then, being a moral-emotional deficiency which leaves intact social understanding and social skills, clearly provides us with an intriguing test case for the hypothesis that moral sensitivity is correctly characterized as a predominantly affective capacity. And as already advanced earlier, if it is, a reasonable prediction is that diagnostic psychopaths will show a marked *in*capacity in the *in situ* perception of morally relevant facts. But evidence that diagnostic psychopaths *do not* have impaired moral perceptive abilities would seem to belie the assumption.

This claim is susceptible to empirical scrutiny and established measures of moral sensitivity do exist and could, presumably, be straightforwardly used to test it.[12] If empirical research had been conducted using a psychological measure which elicits the construct of moral sensitivity well and psychopathy turned out to be associated with moral *in*sensitivity, this would be good evidence that moral sensitivity is indeed a predominantly affective process. Pending direct empirical evidence, we can only attempt to deduce conclusions regarding the psychopath's competency in moral sensitivity on grounds of other investigations that provide insight into the moral (dis)functioning of psychopaths. Doing so is the task of the next sections.

---

[12] Since the early 1980s, at least 20 psychological measures of moral sensitivity have been developed for the purpose of educational evaluation in fields as diverse as business, counselling, dentistry, journalism, medicine, and in pre-university schooling and the stronger measures, in You & Bebeau's (2005) assessment are based on the early Dental Ethical Sensitivity Test (Bebeau et al., 1985).

5.4.2   Psychopathy and the Moral/Conventional Distinction

Blair and colleagues (1995), using as a theoretical-framework domain theory of moral development (cf. esp. Turiel, 1983; and Nucci, 2001), claim that, when compared with a control group, psychopaths or children with psychopathic tendencies tend not to appreciate that there are some universal moral rules that exist independently of mere social conventions. Based on the results of a question eliciting "subjects' justification categories", Blair found that psychopaths are more likely to give "conventional" rather than "moral" justifications for transgressions (e.g., it is wrong to steal because "That's not what's done"). In other words, psychopaths do not seem to perceive that moral norms such as those forbidding stealing are not contingent on the existence of rules (cf. Nucci, 2001, p. 8; Keefer, 2006, p. 370). Diagnosed psychopaths tend as well to have a flat view of the seriousness of rule violations. When probed, a psychopath will typically assert that, say, jaywalking is not much less serious than robbing a bank. According to domain theory, in addition to rule contingency the criterion of "seriousness" also distinguishes moral norms from conventions; violations of moral norms are far more serious than violations of conventions (cf. Nucci, 2001, p. 8; Keefer, 2006, p. 370).[13]

From the point of view of the psychopath's moral-perceptive abilities, Blair's reported findings that psychopaths consistently omit welfare or justice considerations when asked to explain why some act is sanction-worthy would seem to be of no small significance. Certainly, such conceptual oversight on the part of an adult is, according to domain theory, a grave impairment of moral functioning. Even children as young as 3 years (Smetana & Braeges, 1990) and those with serious cognitive disabilities (e.g., autistic children; cf. Blair, 1996) make reference to justice and welfare considerations when prompted to justify a moral rule.[14] But does this failing constitute a failing of moral *sensitivity*?

On one hand, it might seem that it does. Blair's research shows that psychopaths tend to miss that moral norms are distinct from conventions in this crucial respect: that moral norms are ultimately concerned with protection of other persons'

---

[13] These results are confounded by the fact that the experimental group did not, contrary to Blair's (1995) expectations for the study, regard both moral norms and conventions as being equally *un*serious but rather claimed to regard violations of both as being very serious indeed. Parallel surprising results were collected with regards to the authority–contingency criterion. Apparently unsure exactly what to make of this, Blair posits that incarcerated psychopaths tend to give socially desirable answers. Yet, this raises immediately the question of why other incarcerated persons do not, and some non-incarcerated psychopaths do, respond identically (cf. Blair & Cipolotti, 2001).

[14] Drawing on, for instance, Baron-Cohen's (1989) work on people with autism's deficient theory of mind, Blair's (1996) claim about autistics' ability to make the moral–convention distinction might seem highly implausible. But bracketing the possibility of methodological errors on Blair's part, here one has little choice but to assert the Aristotelian principle that whatever exists is *ipso facto* possible.

well-being and interests. In light of the standard classification of the moral domain in terms of "human welfare, justice, and rights" (Nucci, 2001, p. 7), it might not be unreasonable to interpret this failing as a lack of moral sensitivity insofar as it demonstrates an inability to perceive that the violation of a moral norm harms the well-being and interests of others. Rest (1983), for example, characterizes moral sensitivity as constituting in large part an awareness of the consequences of actions on "the welfare of someone else" (p. 559). If the conclusion can be sustained that the psychopath is in the Kohlbergian–Piagetian sense "egocentric" (i.e., unable to perspective-take), it would seem to corroborate the prediction that the psychopath's lack of moral emotions *does* impair competency in moral sensitivity, and subsequently, that moral sensitivity *might very well* draw importantly on affective capacities of response. On the other hand, the claim, which this suggestion seems to imply, that psychopaths are blind to the fact that certain actions (such as aggression, lying, cheating) might be detrimental to others' interests and welfare is difficult to square with the psychological portrait of the psychopath that emerges in Cleckley's (1950) and Hare's (e.g., 1999) studies. For in the view of both these authors, psychopaths are characteristically equipped with at least normal and by some accounts exceptionally good social perspective-taking skills. How, in fact, could one account for the characteristic psychopathic manipulativeness and deceitfulness in the absence of the assumption that psychopaths are well able to take the perspective of their victims and gain insight into what motivates them, including fear of harm? Precisely this ability, coupled with very low concern for others needs, is what makes psychopaths so adept at taking advantage of other people.

5.4.3 Psychopathy and Social Perspective-Taking

Considering the intuitive plausibility of Cleckley's (1950) and Hare's (1999) claims about the social perspective-taking abilities of psychopaths, it comes as no surprise that research on perspective-taking abilities and psychopathy does not indicate impairment in this respect (e.g., Blair et al., 1995). It is true that psychopaths' physiological and emotional responses to distress cues are very different from the responses of non-psychopathic controls. For instance, unlike control subjects, psychopaths show few measurable physiological signs of distress when viewing pictures of distressed people (e.g. Blair et al., 2005). But belief attribution and emotion recognition is not deviant. In these experiments the research subjects were tested on rather simple and general perspective-taking tasks. This leaves open the question of whether these measures are fit to detect a more complex context-specific impairment. Although advanced testing of the capacity to construe an adequate theory of mind and to recognize complex emotions has been carried out only very recently and is still limited to a small number of investigations, the findings of these investigations, however tentative, tend not to show disability of perspective-taking or of distress-clue detection.

Research conducted by Richell et al. (2003) and Dolan and Fullam (2004), for example, do not point to impairment in complex theory of mind construal and emotional recognition in adult psychopaths and in similar research Blair and colleagues found no lower recognition of emotions, except for fearful expressions (e.g., Blair et al., 2005). For their part, however, Dolan and Fullam (2006) concluded, in a later study, that psychopaths show lower recognition accuracy for sadness. Research by Dads et al. (2006) also demonstrated that psychopathic individuals were less capable of recognizing fearful facial expressions; however, these problems disappeared when test subjects were instructed to attend to victim's eyes in the images used in the experiment. Finally, Glass and Newman (2006) show that psychopathic offenders performed similarly to or better than non-psychopathic controls on facial recognition tests which included fearful expressions, in conditions where their attention was directed to the facial expressions – and, contrary to Dads and colleagues' (2006) findings, even when it was not.

As stated earlier, owing to the paucity of direct studies on the capacities of other-directed insight among psychopaths, their results are necessarily provisional, but at least three sources of corroborating indirect evidence on the perspective-taking competency and psychopathy exist.

First, there is the research into psychopathy and cognitive moral development. According to classical cognitive moral-development theory, development parallels a growth away from cognitive (i.e., Piagetan) "egocentrism" and towards cognitive "decentration" (cf. Gibbs, 1991). On this basis, one may assume that weak decentration – be it of pathological origin as in psychopathy or just as a natural feature of development as in young children – would in principle translate into low measured levels of cognitive moral development. Yet the research on cognitive moral development among psychopaths does not indicate significant differences between psychopaths and non-psychopaths in respect of cognitive moral development.

Both Lose (1997) and O'Kane et al. (1996), using the same measures and similar groups of incarcerated inmates – namely, Hare's PCL-R (Hare et al., 1991) and Rest's (1979) Defining Issues Test (DIT) – concluded that when IQ is partialled out there is no significant difference between the DIT scores of psychopaths and those of normal adults. One study conducted in the 1970s, albeit using a different set of measures, saw that psychopaths even scored higher than the control group. The investigators interpreted these results as showing that psychopaths' characteristic lack of guilt enables them "to reason about morality with less influence from emotional forces; as a result, their moral reasoning is better" (Link et al., 1977).

Another empirical approach to the same problem hypothesizes that, since psychopaths seem to suffer not from a deficit of theoretical understanding but poor practical judgement, a comparison of psychopaths' responses to highly hypothetical problems to their responses to the kinds of problems that are more likely to arise in real life should provide a more accurate depiction of psychopathic cognitive moral functioning on the ground, as it were. The results of the small number of studies available on this question are as follows: while Simon, Holzberg, and Fisher, according to Cleckley (1950, pp. 414–416) found that psychopaths do score lower on tests of moral reasoning in "real-life" dilemma problems, Trevethan and

Walker (1989), using Hare's (1991) Checklist and this time studying children not adults, observed that psychopaths' answers to real-life dilemma problems tended to be more egoistically oriented.

The results of Self et al.'s (1995) study of medical students – masochists perhaps but certainly not psychopaths – also seem highly relevant to the present problem. If it is the case that affect does have an impact on moral reasoning abilities one might expect, as these authors did, a positive correlation between scores on measure of empathy to correlate positively with scores on the DIT. The authors reported disappointment: "empathy was found not to have any correlation to moral reasoning as assessed by the DIT" (p. 451).

Finally, research on so-called acquired sociopathy or ventromedial damage – the cases of Elliot and Phineas Cage have been classic examples since the publication of the neurologist Damasio's *Descartes' Error* (1994) – suggests that people whose emotional reactions to the distress of others are deficient (in a similar way as the psychopath) due to brain damage later in life, are not affected in moral reasoning skills regarding hypothetical as well as real-life problems. His patient Elliot, Damasio remarks, is a case of "to know, but not to feel" (1994, p. 45).

The second set of studies worth considering in connection with the question of perspective-taking in psychopathic individuals deals with the relation between social perspective-taking ability and patterns of antisocial behaviour. Surely, one might surmise, if the moral defect of the psychopath is causally related to defective perspective-taking capacities, the enhancement of these capacities would lead to a decrease in antisocial behaviour. Although apparently legitimate doubts may be raised about the methodological soundness of the various investigations into the re-offending of psychopaths who followed treatment programmes (D'Silva et al., 2004), the overall picture is that treatment and especially social skills and social perspective-taking treatment programmes do not lead to a decrease but, astonishingly, rather to an *increase* of criminal behaviour (cf. Rice et al., 1992). Moreover, Hare et al. (2000) report on findings that show the phenomenon to be stronger among Factor 1 psychopaths. Offenders, that is, with high Factor 1 scores that followed treatment programmes – for instance, anger management and social skills programmes, or educational or vocational training programmes – had higher reconviction rates than offenders with low Factor 1 scores. Furthermore, treatment that was "designed to produce insight and promote the development of co-operation, responsibility, caring, and empathy" (Rice, 1997, p. 414) seemed to lead to increased criminality. Rice advanced that this might be due to the fact that in such programmes "the psychopaths simply learned how to appear more empathic. They used this information so as to better manipulate and deceive others" (p. 415).

Thirdly and finally, recent insights from social information processing theory seems to shed light on relevant perception and interpretation capacities of psychopathic individuals. According to so-called social information processing models (e.g., Crick & Dodge, 1996), behaviour is determined by one's understanding and evaluation of a situation, and positive and negative consequences of one's act will in turn influence one's representation and evaluation of that situation. Such social information processing proceeds by distinct sequential steps: "encoding", "interpreting", "goal-selection or clarification", "response construal and evaluation", "response decision", and "behaviour enactment".

Empirical studies on aggressiveness using this paradigm (e.g., Dodge & Coie, 1987) demonstrate that two different types of aggression – reactive aggression and proactive aggression – correspond with important differences in social information processing. *Reactive aggression* is attributed to mistakes at the level of encoding and interpreting, the first two steps of this process. That is, the reactive aggressive child's proneness to interpret others' behaviour is part of a snowball effect, where the perception of threat triggers aggressive behaviour on the part of the child which in turn elicits hostile and aggressive reactions of other persons in return – reactions which only reaffirm the hostile expectations of the reactive aggressive child. By contrast, *proactive aggressive* children do not show deficiencies at the level of encoding or interpreting. It is rather at the levels of goal-selection and evaluation that these children show deviant responses. In short, they expect more positive outcomes of antisocial behaviour, and they assign less value to pro-social or relational goals and more value to instrumental egoistic goals. In Arsenio and Lemerise's (2004, p. 993) assessment, "proactive aggression involves a combination of an amoral or even immoral Machiavellian view of one's own victimizing behaviours (e.g. "It's easy and it works") with a focus on morally relevant knowledge regarding the encoding and interpretation of others' intentions". As we observed earlier, it is proactive or "cold-blooded" aggression that tends to correlate highly with psychopathy Factor 1, while reactive or "hot-blooded" aggression correlates strongly with ASPD or psychopathy Factor 2 (Blair et al., 2005). The instrumental antisocial behaviour of the Factor 1 psychopath then seems not to entail deficiencies at the level of detection and interpretation of morally relevant situational distress cues such as expressions of harm, sadness, or fear but instead a deviant evaluation of anticipated outcomes of harmful behaviour.

In sum, the empirical research on psychopathic moral functioning reviewed here paints a complex picture but it does point clearly to the conclusion that psychopaths are morally sensitive in the relevant sense of being able to pick out morally salient situational cues and to predict actions' effects on various relevant forms of human need and desert. This evidence, I conclude, shows the conceptual characterization of moral sensitivity as a predominantly affective capacity to be largely incorrect.

5.5   "Conscience" as a Dimension of Moral Judgement

Cleckley's original interpretive hypothesis that psychopaths are touched by an emotional impairment, rather than a cognitive or volitional one, raises difficult questions about the traditional legal and moral criteria of moral and legal responsibility, questions to which Cleckley himself was very much alive. Standard forensic tests for sanity, as Deigh (1995) notes, turn on "the agent's moral knowledge and his capacity for self-control" (p. 745). That is, the question of whether the principle of "ought implies can" holds in criminal cases is assessed with regards to the agent's knowledge of what is right and wrong for her to do and whether the control she has over her behaviour is sufficient to enable her to conform to such knowledge. If, however, psychopaths have a clear understanding of the content of social norms, as witnessed among other things by their proficiency in the mimicry of social responsibility, love, remorse, and moral intentions, and other basic emotional responses of a normal person and, further, they suffer from no pathological volitional condition (i.e., the are, unlike people subject to maniac episodes, not governed by impulses and can thus be considered to have reasonable mastery their behaviour), then for all intents and purposes they can be held responsible for whatever criminal or immoral acts they might come to perform. Indeed, in Samenow's (2004) assessment, while their criminal behaviour is doubtless that of an exceptionally cruel human being, psychopaths, along with sociopaths and those diagnosed as having an ASPD, are not insane, at least according to a broad consensus in the field of criminology. In any case, the recognition of a third affective criterion of legal insanity – i.e., not just (1) knowledge that an act performed was wrong and (2) the possession of a reasonable degree of self-control, but also (3) the capacity to feel remorse, guilt, or shame for having violated some serious norm – might serve to clarify the question of the psychopath's criminal responsibility and, as Cleckley (1950, p. 487ff.) notes, open the way for safer (and arguably fairer) practices in the legal supervision of psychopaths.[15]

The thorny question of responsibility aside, by all accounts a psychopath appears to know that he is doing wrong in hurting another person. He is simply unmoved by that fact. As Murphy (1972) once put it, "Though psychopaths know, in some sense, what it means to wrong people, to act immorally, this kind of judgement has for them no motivational component at all. [...] They feel no guilt, regret, shame or remorse (though they may superficially fake these feelings) when they have engaged in harmful conduct" (quoted in Deigh, 1995, p. 746; cf. also Elliott and Gillett, 1992, p. 56 for a similar assessment). The suggestion that the psychopath "knows right from wrong" but fails to act on that understanding might seem to suggest that the psychopath suffers from nothing other than a severe case of weakness of the will. This, however, misses the point. Unlike the *akratic* moral agent, the psychopath's particular predicament is not that he professes to seriously believe himself to be under some normative obligation but lacks a corresponding motivation. The psychopath is better compared to a very young child; both are severely egocentric in the sense that they entirely lack recognition there are situations where they need to place restrictions on their own behaviour in consideration of others (cf. Atkinson et al., 1983).

Viewed from another perspective, one might say that the psychopath suffers from having a purely *anthropological* view of morality and moral norms. That is to say he has an expert's knowledge in the moral rules that govern the social world he

---

[15] I admit to almost total ignorance of the current state of research and policy on this question. Although Elliott and Gillett (1992) speak of a putative references to "a flaw in moral structure" (p. 54) as constituting a form of disease, it is not clear whether this is or may be used in legal proceedings as grounds for an insanity plea. It is entirely possible, of course, that current law in some or even many jurisdictions now recognizes an affective deficit as relevant to the assessment of criminal responsibility.

lives in and their related moral categories. Recall that psychopaths typically come across as attractive, intelligent, and charming people with a great facility in manipulating others.[16] He just does not acknowledge any moral rules, and is possibly constitutionally incapable of such an acknowledgement, as having *normative* validity – i.e., as a norm from the perspective of moral evaluation rather than the perspective of the outside observer (cf. Nunner-Winkler, 1994, p. 3915). Elliott and Gillett (1992, pp. 56–57) state the point this way:

> Although the psychopath clearly knows what moral norms are operative in society, he does not seem to have endorsed such moral norms for himself. He appears to realize that moral rules and values govern the lives of others, and he is not blind to the fact that others expect him to abide by such rules and values as well. But morality involves more than simply knowing what society's moral norms and values are. It also involves endorsing and internalizing them, "making them one's own". This is the sense in which the psychopath lacks socialization. He does not seem to internalize norms and values.

Let us now try to put this idea in terms of our discussion of moral perception and judgement earlier as opposed to Elliott and Gillett's framework of the internalization of social rules and norms. In short, a psychopath is a living instantiation of Hume's (1751/1957) "sensible knave" or the Nietzchean "amoralist": a human being who is in full possession of cognitive powers, who recognizes that moral norms exist, but shows no interest in conforming to those norms and no remorse or guilt or shame when he does not.

By dint of his apparent mastery of the moral rules and connected moral categories, the psychopath would be able to recognize the morally salient features of situations and understand the validity of the moral categories underlying the rules of moral salience that connect up with various forms of human need and interest. Given his full cognitive integrity the psychopath can not only identify and construct moral problems, but can also reason about moral problems: weigh evidence, employ criteria to identify limiting cases and exceptions, consider the consequences of actions and their relevance, assign responsibility, and so on. The inability of psychopathic personalities to experience moral emotions such as guilt, shame, and compassionate empathy in coexistence with intact cognitive and other social faculties would seem to suggest that processes of moral *reasoning*, as has long been the default view of in philosophy and psychology, do not draw heavily on affective capacities of response.

I would now like to assert that just as strongly as the case of the psychopath seems to show little necessary involvement of affective capacities in moral reasoning, it also draws attention to one way that moral judgement is very much an affective matter. To put it bluntly, while there seems to be nothing out of place in attributing

---

[16] It should be noted that this account holds only for one category of psychopath, the so-called primary psychopath who, according to Cleckley (1950) are characterized by intelligence, charm, and social skill. Cleckley's cases analyses identify also a category of "secondary" psychopath who are, in sharp contrast with primary psychopaths, characteristically socially inept and withdrawn (cf. also Elliott & Gillett, 1992, p. 55; Blackburn, 1988).

to the psychopath full moral-*reasoning* capabilities it seems very semantically odd indeed to say that someone for whom moral reasoning is never a matter of conscience is capable of moral *judgement*. To engage in moral judgement, as opposed to moral reasoning, seems to supposes (first and foremost but among other things) conditional self-submission to the outcome of the assessment of a moral problem. Indeed, Herman (1985) apparently takes this for granted throughout her paper but it comes out most clearly in one statement: "In addition to picking out the morally significant features of actions, then, the rules of moral salience indicate a burden of justification. The agent [who makes a deceitful promise] understands that normal prudential or instrumental justifications of action will not do in the case of deceit. This is the mark of conscience" (p. 419). Moral judgement, as opposed to moral reasoning, that is, seems to presuppose adopting a *normative* view of the ideal outcome of a particular instance of its application to a situation. In other words, it is a propensity to *care about* the object of moral reasoning – in the sense of being willing to suspend and sacrifice one's own interests in order to promote the kinds of goods and avoid the kinds of harms that are at stake in moral problems – that is distinctive of moral judgement. This is precisely the point of view the psychopath is unable to adopt (for a similar assessment see Elliott and Gillett, 1992). Moral judgement becomes a matter of conscience, then, only when one understands oneself to be *burdened by* its outcomes. Moral reasoning implies no such orientation. Moral judgement is moral reasoning taken seriously and what seriousness means, in this case, is to be disposed towards viewing the results of moral deliberation as placing practical demands on persons, being disposed to act in accordance with moral judgements one comes to regard as right.[17]

It might be objected that, while perhaps good as far as it goes, the stipulated distinction between "moral judgement" and "moral reasoning" does nothing to change the fact that the moral point of view is a concept which falls squarely under the heading of *moral reasoning* in the sense intended. To consider a problem from the moral point of view means, by the basic standard and broad definition of the term, to attempt to arrive at an impartial resolution to a moral problem (cf., e.g., Baier, 1965; Habermas, 1990b). The psychopath who, according to the present analysis and as supported by the empirical evidence cited above, is no more or less adept in perceiving, comprehending, and assessing moral problems in the abstract than are persons free of his affliction. That is to say, the psychopath presumably suffers no limitations in his facility to assess a problem from the moral point of view and,

---

[17]This position does not entail a commitment to one side or the other of the thorny internalist–externalist debate in ethics. Internalists and externalists do not disagree over the question of whether (basically normal or rational) moral agents have a motivating reason to act in accordance with their moral judgements. What they battle over instead is the question of precisely what kinds of reasons those reasons are and, in particular, whether the motivating reason in question is (1) logically entailed by the use of the use of terms such as "should" and "ought" a moral sense (i.e., the rough position of naturalism, descriptivism, and realism); or (2) a reflection of the agent's prior values, moral beliefs, or mere preferences (i.e., the position of emotivism, prescriptivism, and projectivism). Cf. discussions of these issues in Smith (1994), Darwall et al. (1992), and Deigh (1995).

therefore, contrary to what we seem to be trying to maintain, the moral point of view does *not* in fact rally the kinds of insights characteristic of compassionate empathy at all. Simply stating that the psychopath is capable of moral reasoning but not moral judgement does nothing to change this fact. At best, my claim is that affect plays some kind of role in motivating actions in accordance with moral judgements – e.g., by supporting or underlying desires which accord with moral judgements or by or feelings of shame, guilt, or repugnance at the prospect of not doing so – understood as the outcome of a process or moral reasoning.

This I do not deny. However, the objection seems to mis-comprehend the significance of this reading of the moral judgement/moral reasoning distinction. It is not first and foremost the fact that a moral judgement happens to coincide with a corresponding moral motivation that marks the faculty of moral judgement off from that of moral reasoning but rather the way that a certain (true or correct) understanding of what moral judgement is or what is at stake in a moral deliberation situation that underlies a corresponding conation. In other words, the moral point of view understood as the point of view of moral maturity (as opposed to being *just* the point of view of impartiality) goes beyond scales of differentiation in assessing moral problems. It touches on an understanding of moral concepts, what morality is, and what it is for as well.

It is a commonplace especially in the social sciences to observe that morality, in anthropological terms, is a social institution that exists as a bulwark or safeguard of fundamental human needs and interests. As Nunner-Winkler (1994) has stated it:

> [Moral rules ...] can be derived from assumptions about universal physical and social features of humankind. Physically human beings are vulnerable and no instinct keeps them from killing or hurting one another. If humans were immortal or moral saints there would be no need for a (universal) rule against direct harm. Socially, humans need institutions for survival and thus are dependent on others to do their duty, that is, to follow specific rules and avoid indirect harm (p. 3915; see also Habermas, 1990b, p. 199).

In a similar vein, Vetlesen (1994) suggests that the failure to recognize a particular problem as suited for moral judgement, in the sense of rallying both an agent's cognitive and emotional faculties, constitutes, as he expresses it, a "breakdown" of morality as a social institution. He writes, "Needless to say, morality – precisely when it is depicted as a precarious institution – breaks down as soon as people stop being moral, that is, to use my own terms, as soon as they cease to perceive, judge, and act with a concern for the weal and woe of fellow human beings as at stake in some situation" (p. 312; cf. also his discussion on pp. 157–160). Morality is in this regard, Vetlesen remarks, an inescapably *inter-* as opposed to intra-personal affair. Failure to be appropriately concerned with others in a moral deliberation situation is, again, not just a matter of being "insensitive to other people's feelings". It constitutes a failure to grasp this basic fact. For all his adeptness in moral reasoning, the psychopath's abilities are parasitic on the existence of widespread and genuine concern for others that is characteristic of morality; a "moral community" of psychopaths, in the intended sense, is unthinkable.

The question of why this is the case is worth briefly pursuing because it seems to illuminate another important way in which compassionate empathy is involved in moral judgement as an ideal of moral maturity and form of intersubjective engagement. In this connection, the psychopath is the very model of gross moral immaturity. Again, by all clinical accounts, in spite of his unimpaired capacity of theoretical judgement, the psychopath is singularly devoid of practical wisdom. The indications that he might be able to arrive at some sensible conclusion in the abstract about what might be in the best interests of all involved in a moral situation, in "the test of life", as Cleckley (1950) put it, the psychopathic personality seems neither to be the least bit disposed to applying his faculty of reasoning nor to be motivated by anything but his most immediate and narrow first-person interest – and even his perception of what in fact is in his interest, even in a closely circumscribed sense, is often highly questionable. Now according to the standard interpretive hypothesis, this inability is not the manifestation of a cognitive disorder. Rather, it is due to the psychopath's lack of conscience which we have characterized in rough and ready terms as an acknowledgement that some situations, in particular morally significant situations, call for the abandonment of the ordinary instrumental grounds for action justification. Of course, in ordinary situations, such as putting down an interesting book to go see why one of the children is crying in the other room, most people do so without explicit reflection. It should be added that, in situations where what one should do is unclear, conscience, in this broad sense of an acknowledgement that others' needs and well-being make demands on us, would clearly have a hand in disposing one to attempt to determine through intentional, explicit reflection and assessment what might in fact be morally called for in that situation. To rework the example just given, if when I get up from my interesting book to go see why the 3-year-old is crying in the other room and then I notice that the other one is at risk of falling out of her highchair, conscience, apparently, raises the question, "what, from the moral point of view, should I do?"

As Hill (2002) has accurately observed, however, the characterization of conscience as being nothing but, as he puts it, "our capacity and disposition to acknowledge the moral law and to apply the moral law through 'judgment'" (p. 301), is not entirely consistent with the way that people normally talk about conscience. The legal conceit used to describe the operations of the conscience – one speaks commonly as if the conscience passes verdicts and imposes fair punishment in the form of unpleasant but deserved guilty feelings – suggests that it is a second-order faculty of moral judgement: not the faculty by which we make moral judgements but rather the faculty which *judges* moral judgements, if you will. Like the basic capacity of moral judgement in morally unambiguous situations, conscience acts immediately and involuntarily, imposing an awareness that an act we have done, are doing, or propose to do is divergent from what we ourselves would sanction in our own judgement. This is attested to by familiar expressions like "I was struck by feelings of guilt" and "I felt a sudden pang of conscience" and references to conscience as an "inner voice" (cf. Hill, 2002, pp. 297, 301–302). Because conscience makes reference to some criterion of better judgement it clearly draws on the basic capacity for practical reasoning but this, again, is not its principal function. Conscience is more accurately identified as playing a *regulatory* role of ensuring reasonable conformity between the will and the demands of practical reason.

This comes out more clearly, perhaps, when it is unclear what moral rightness demands in a situation. In this connection, Hill (2002) speaks of Kant's idea of conscience as imposing a "duty of due care" (p. 302). Quoting Kant, he says:

> "[C]oncerning the act I propose to perform I must not only judge and form an opinion, but I must be sure that it is not wrong." This is a special, but quite broad, duty of due care; that is, we must undertake and diligently carry out a moral appraisal of our projected acts (presumably unless we are already sure, from previous appraisal, that the acts are permissible). Metaphorically speaking, "judgement$_1$" (one sense of "judgement") is what is responsible for appraising the act diligently, and 'conscience' then "passes judgment$_2$," (a second sense of "judgment") on judgment$_1$ as to whether it has fulfilled that responsibility. (p. 302)

Seen from this perspective, a weakness of conscience (as when one becomes immune to the prodding of conscience by repeatedly ignoring it) or a wholesale lack of conscience (as in the psychopathic or antisocial personality) is not an error of moral reasoning or the *capacity* of moral deliberation as such. It is not a failure to select or apply the correct general moral principle in the circumstances, or a lack of insight into the likely consequences of various action alternatives. It is not an error of fact, a failure to pay adequate attention to the problem at hand, or a case of self-deception such as wishful thinking or special pleading (cf. Hill, 2002, p. 300). It is not, in other words, an *inability* to get it right, from the moral point of view, but rather an failure to be *concerned about* getting it right, with regards to both one's action choices and with regards to the competent exercise of moral reasoning.

As we have seen, the psychopath's lack of conscience is consistent with this schema. While his capacity for moral reasoning is no better or worse than that of a normal person, his behaviour and the patters of reflection that this behaviour suggests demonstrate not merely a want of respect for others' needs. The psychopath is also apparently not the least bit interested in applying this faculty of moral reasoning to real-life situations. At this juncture there may be a temptation to float the objection that the claim that the psychopath is not given to the exercise of moral reasoning is not obviously inconsistent with the observation, noted above, that, all things being equal, psychopaths are neither more nor less competent in moral reasoning, at least when gauged by standard psychological measures such as the DIT. On the contrary, psychopaths' lack of interest in moral judgement could be taken to predict that they would score relatively *lower* owing to their presumed lack of opportunities to exercise the cognitive functions connected with cognitive moral development. Bear in mind, however, that psychopathy is characterized by the habitual manipulation of others and that effective manipulation requires keen insight into others' internal states: their expectations, feeling, preferences, and the like. If one of the core competencies of moral judgement is vicarious other-directed introspection – indeed, Gibbs (1991), Edelstein and Fauser (2001), and others seem sometimes to go so far as to *equate* cognitive moral development with "de-centration", or the ability to gain insight into another person's point of view through some form of vicarious other-directed introspection – then the day-to-day life of the psychopath would furnish ample opportunities for perspective-taking in this sense. These, presumably, would compensate generously for any such absence occasioned by his disinterest in moral problems. In any case, and assuming, once again, that the interpretive hypothesis about the moral psychology of the psychopath we have been working with is correct, the psychopath's apathy about exercising moral reasoning in real-life situations would seem quite clearly to identify a crucial role of compassionate empathy and other moral emotions in moral judgement. That is, an active attitude of caring towards others is a necessary condition not of the ability to consider a problem from the point of view as such – what we called above "moral reasoning" – but rather the *willingness* to adopt the moral point of view in considering practical problems and to apply diligently moral reasoning to a practical problem.[18] From this perspective, it looks very much as if Callahan (1980) was right: empathy, compassion, and concern for others are instrumental to, as he put it, "the drive to get moral problems right".

5.6 Summary and Conclusion

This chapter has sought to probe the broad question of compassionate empathy's involvement in the faculty of moral judgement by examining the subsidiary phenomenon of moral perception. Taking the lead from Coombs' (1998), Callahan's (1980) and Hilfiker's (2001) hunch that concern for others intervenes in the process of moral judgement less in the course of deliberation over moral problems than in the prior step of recognizing and psychologically constructing moral problems, I tried to get some firm footing with regards to this issue by studying the moral psychology of psychopathy as a test case. In short, this study's central working hypothesis was that the postulate that moral perception is a predominantly affective process predicts that psychopaths, those who suffer no characteristic cognitive impairment but who show strong deficiencies in the experience of moral emotions, will have disabled capacities of moral perception. The study began by trying to substantiate the phenomenon of moral perception by showing (in §5.2) that, first, far from providing an insurmountable objection to the involvement of affective faculties in moral judgement, the Kantian account of the situation of moral deliberation is in fact compatible with the possibility that compassionate engagement is pre-required by situational moral perception. Next, in §5.3, I argued drawing on Herman's (1985) analysis of moral perception and her

---

[18] Peters (1981) and Hoffman (2000) both arrive at comparable conclusions though they argue for the point differently. In both cases, they can be seen as arguing that concern for others or "empathy", in Hoffman's term, as a presupposition of the process of "decentration" underlying moral development (cf. Gibbs, 1991) which, in the context of moral practice, requires that "children to take the other's claims seriously and be willing to negotiate and compromise their own claims, rather than use the knowledge to manipulate each other" (p. 13; cf. Peters, 1981, pp. 172–173). Neither, however, distinguishes between a first-order concern for others' well-being and the second-order interest of conscience in checking the reliability of one's moral judgements.

idea of the "rules of moral salience" that, whether or not moral perception is an affective capacity, it cannot be regarded as psychologically distinct from moral judgement because both seem to demand a working understanding of some basic moral categories. Though it did seem prima facie plausible that these categories connect up with a general notion of human well-being and interest, and thus that their mastery would entail engaged affective involvement, triangulating evidence for this claim was pursued in §5.4. Nothing that could be considered direct evidence exists which sheds light on the question of whether psychopathy correlates positively with impaired capacities of moral perception. Available indirect evidence, however, suggests that it should not. Exceptional social perspective-taking abilities witnessed by the trait of skilfulness in the manipulation of others to their own ends indicates an apparent theoretical facility among psychopaths with moral concepts, as does corroborating evidence on the performance of psychopaths on standard psychological measures of moral judgement. But, as discussed in §5.5, the test case of the psychopath hints at something else about the mediation of compassionate empathy and concern for others in moral functioning: that it might very well play a role in both grasping that others' needs and interests sometimes demand that one suspend ordinary instrumental-prudential grounds of action justification (that valid moral norms, to put a complex issue in loose terms, are motivationally binding) *and* in the operation of moral conscience understood, in Hill's (2000) sense, as a concern for getting moral problems right. Psychopaths are disposed to view moral norms from an anthropological rather than a normative perspective, as I put it, and despite the fact that they indeed possess normal moral reasoning skills, they seem singularly bereft of practical wisdom in the course of day-to-day social interaction.

With these observations on compassionate empathy and moral perception we arrive at an important turning point in these studies. Three main claims for empathy and moral imagination as basic aspects of moral functioning (as opposed to a dimension of professional role morality) that were teased out of the review in Chapter 1of calls to promote empathy in the literature on professional and practical ethics education have now been covered. All purporting to be highly relevant to ethical practice and sound ethical decision-making they were: (1) empathy is a moral emotion insofar as an empathic disposition is conducive to a moral outlook and moral behaviour; (2) moral perception and moral sensitivity draw on empathic capacities of response to others' weal and woe; and, (3) such forms of concern for others are part and parcel of caring about resolving moral problems well. The results of attempt to critically examine these claims in light of a characterization of empathy as a moral-psychological construct and relevant current knowledge in social psychology on empathic responding and empathic development come down to this: the idea that empathizing is a moral emotion and that concern for others is important in the drive to get moral problems right are well founded but moral perception is not in fact a predominantly affective faculty. The next chapter (Chapter 6), and the final study in this series (Chapter 7), consider the insights which these studies have afforded into the moral psychology of compassionate empathy in terms of what they mean for contemporary professional and practical ethics education and sketches out too a set of pedagogical principles compatible with them.

Chapter 6
Intermezzo on Moral Emotion Education: Imagination, Imitation, and Reappraisal

6.1 Introduction

Despite the virtual consensus in the broad field of emotion research that rigid dichotomies of emotion and cognition are no longer tenable (cf., e.g., Arnold, 1960; Lazarus, 1966; Lazarus and Launier, 1978; Averill, 1973; and Weiner, 1995) and the widespread recognition of the importance of emotions in education and learning (cf., e.g., Nucci 2001, p. 108; and Piaget, 1981), the question of what it might mean to "educate the emotions" still seems to be far from clear in most people's minds. It is one thing to recognize the importance of emotions in learning and in personal and social development, which is the thrust of such popular ideas as "emotional intelligence" (Goleman, 1995) and "social and emotional learning" (e.g., Cohen, 1999), but quite another to suggest that educators set out to actually try to "educate" emotions. This situation justifies a brief departure from this work's central concern with the educational promotion of compassionate empathy as a *basic* moral capacity in professional and practical ethics education in order to pause and consider briefly the perplexing idea of emotion education.

Education understood as an ensemble of techniques, devices, strategies, and approaches used by educators to attain their educational goals has the unusual characteristic of being purposely and perhaps even constitutionally deficient. It has, as Luhmann and Schorr (1894/1982) put it, a "technological deficit": to the extent that education approximates the ideal of efficiency and effectiveness in attaining its goals the ideal of an autonomous learner or of a subject endowed with a free will, a central supposition of the modern liberal "pedagogies of autonomy", is put into question. If in fact such educational technology were possible, it would not just be undesirable but would be subject to what Benner (1979) called the "technology constraint". This ethical limit imposed on contemporary educational practice is an expression of the pedagogical antinomy of modern educational thought which Kant (1803/1992) famously formulated in the question: "How can freedom be cultivated through constraint?" (*Wie kultiviere ich die Freiheit bei dem Zwange?*). The question has always been one of how to get children and adolescents to voluntarily do the things that they ought do and voluntarily avoid doing the things that they ought not to do. The answer is, of course, that we do not really know and the modern ethical insight that goes along with it tells us that we might not want to know. The techno-logical deficit and technology constraint in contemporary pedagogy do not of course render attempts at education, moral or otherwise, entirely *in*effective or even pointless. We have enough empirical evidence to regard this as false (cf. Lempert's 1989 review). But the distinction between educational strategies and strategies of social control still goes a long way towards capturing the substance of the peda-gogically permissible. In short, if it is *possible* to educate emotions, the question of whether it is ethically *acceptable* to engage in emotion education turns on whether there can be genuinely *educational* strategies of emotion education. This chapter identifies three broad classes of moral emotion strategies which seem to fit this bill: requests to *imagine* other's emotional reactions, requests to *imitate* normative emotional reactions, and requests to *reappraise* the features of a situation that are relevant to an emotional response.[1] In the next and last chapter of this work (Chapter 7), the distinction is reintroduced as an organizing principle. There I com-ment on the foregoing studies' implications for contemporary practices of profes-sional and practical ethics education in terms of their relevance to each of these dimensions of emotion education.

6.2   Pedagogy of Autonomy and Pedagogy of Control

The line between educational strategies versus strategies which merely aim at social control is notoriously confused and confusing; one thing that makes the two types of strategies easy to run together is that, when they succeed at least, their effects on behaviour are for all intents and purposes indistinguishable. Where they are crucially different, however, is in the means employed to achieve those effects and, in particular, the evaluative status of those means.[2]

To borrow Hügli's (1999) compelling contrast between "pedagogies of auton-omy" and "pedagogies of control", pedagogies of autonomy are an expression of a characteristically modern perspective on the morally legitimate and socially desira-ble aims and corresponding means of education. From this perspective, the aim of education is personal and moral autonomy which seems to come largely down to a person's ability and disposition to reflect upon and judge her own inclinations and desires. A morally autonomous person, as Frankfurt (1971) saw things, establishes second-order desires; she asks whether and how desirable her own desires are and

---

[1] This "praxiological analysis" of moral emotion education, as it has been called, was developed in two related papers: Maxwell and Reichenbach (2005, 2007) and Reichenbach and Maxwell (2007). This chapter is based on material from these papers.

[2] For a recent treatment of this distinction see Wringe (2006). The thrust of Wringe's argument against what he perceives to be an incipient movement in the United Kingdom to regard value education as the socialization into community or national values is that it mistakes what is essen-tially an attempt at social control for an educational project in the present sense.

whether it is good to want what she wants. The consequence of this view is as straightforward as it is easy to fail to fully appreciate: the internalization of moral norms is not the *non plus ultra* goal of a pedagogy of autonomy. Unless one admits that the internalization of certain moral norms is *also* in some sense an educational necessity, perhaps as a means to maintaining certain basic levels of social stability, moral autonomy does not seem very attractive as an aim of moral education (cf. Peters, 1981). At the same time, the internalization of moral norms is not "proof" of moral heteronomy any more than it is proof of moral autonomy; it can, in fact, be a result of *either* autonomous moral reflection on morally desirable ends in life *or* the result of mere social control, be the latter intended, say, as some part of an educational regime or just as a haphazard fact of socialization.

The point of pedagogies of control is not, of course, to support autonomy or reflective judgement but are mainly intended as interventions that more or less guarantee (what are held in advance to be) socially desirable *behavioural outcomes*. The effectiveness of pedagogies of control can be measured, or at least observed, since their target is something observable: behaviour and not intangibles like "ability" or "insight". They are interested in, one might say alternatively, performance not competence. The decisive educational question of pedagogies of control is not, "How can we help young people become morally autonomous or moral selves?" but rather, "How can we arrange things so that young people behave as they should behave?". Insofar as pedagogies of control have at their disposal some kind of technical knowledge, the effectiveness of which can be "measured" at least in a probabilistic sense, pedagogies of autonomy, by contrast, suffer from a "technological deficit" in Luhmann and Schorr's (1894/1982) meaning. Their effectiveness is limited and their outcome uncertain. Pedagogies of autonomy endeavour to strengthen insight and reflection and are fully aware that the person as object of educational intervention is not yet morally autonomous. The *aim* is autonomy but the means try to bring the child up to the level of autonomy by operating *as if* the child were already autonomous: *as if* the child could already understand, *as if* the child were able to transcend his or her precarious desires, *as if* the child had the ability to "role-take" (Selman 1980) or to imagine himself into another person's shoes, *as if* the child were rationally motivated and mainly interested in becoming a good person, and so on.

Such "as if" structures are representative of the fact that the educational relationship involves first and foremost communication *between subjects*, and that educational communication is *intersubjective* communication. Pedagogies of control prioritize subject–*object* relations instead: the child is the more or less passive object of educational strategies, the object of reinforcement plans, and sometimes even outright manipulation. It is true, pedagogies of control are more effective, and their effectiveness may indeed render services for the good, but from the perspective of pedagogies of autonomy, they are morally precarious. If they were fully effective, if an education system could produce the "morally good person" designed and shaped exactly according to plan, its product would be heteronomous agents—that is, human beings that fail to possess what is unquestionably *the* central characteristic of moral agency in the Kantian tradition in ethics

(Hill, 2000). Proponents of pedagogies of autonomy, thus, do not lament of education's "technological deficit". On the contrary, they advocate in favour of strict constraints or even prohibition, in Benner's (1979) sense, on educational technology.

The tensions between pedagogies of control and pedagogies of autonomy do not imply, for all that, that educators who view the ideal of autonomy favourably must renounce social-control strategies altogether. The fact that the belief that education can somehow do without behaviour modification is still so widespread does not make it any less naïve. Many acts performed in educational contexts, and surely all the ones judged to be "necessary" (providing positive feedback for instance) can be understood in one way or another as reinforcement strategies. However, what makes matters significantly more complicated is that just as pedagogies of autonomy cannot, in one regard, do without pedagogies of control, neither can pedagogies of control do without pedagogies of autonomy. The popular television show "Super Nanny" and the well-known "Triple-P" approach to education (i.e., the "positive parenting program") both put forward models of control pedagogy which are not sensitive to the demands and complexities of pedagogies of autonomy. They work. For this reason alone they are highly regarded and valued positively. However, they suffer from two defects that are relevant to the present discussion. First, they ride on the confusion between education and social control. People find them attractive because they seem to identify ways of getting children to freely choose what they ought to choose. But what one fails to notice—and this feature is of course never made explicit—is that they trade almost exclusively in the currencies of emotional manipulation and the systematic deployment of Hobson's choice. Second, they ignore the significance of *presupposing* autonomy *as* an educational act. While behaviour modification is necessary in education, *reducing* education to behaviour modification leaves one blind to the need to strengthen basic social competencies appropriate to contemporary society, central among which is undoubtedly the willingness to act *as if* one were autonomous in full knowledge that one is not.

Pedagogies of autonomy do not try to directly act on the child but are characterized instead by their expression of *requests* or reason-based *appeals* to change in one way or the other. It should come as no surprise, then, that the education of the moral emotions might consist centrally in *requests* to alter, regulate, or otherwise adapt emotional responses.

To illustrate, consider the way that perspective-taking is commonly used in everyday moral education. As we saw in §2.3, perspective-taking in the strict cognitive sense of other-directed introspection has no inherent moral value in and of itself for it can be used for morally dubious goals. But perspective-taking, as a tool of moral education as it were, cannot be fully understood without reference to emotion. Indeed, whether it is self-focused (i.e., involves imagining how one would feel *oneself* in another person's situation) or other-focused (i.e., how another person would feel in a particular situation given that person's beliefs, desires, and so on) social perspective taking as education *just is* a request to put oneself into the *emotional* situation of the other.[3]

Take, for example, the case of Larry and Carol, two preschoolers playing together with blocks. There is only one *really good* reason why Carol should not destroy the tower that Larry has built: Larry would *feel* bad about it. The children's mother, seeing Carol's intention to destroy Larry's tower, might say: "Carol, you wouldn't want Larry to destroy your tower, would you?" Such speech act can be interpreted as *request to imagine*. What she is inviting Carol to do, in other words, is to imagine how she would feel if her brother destroyed her tower. The mother knows in advance, of course, that if Carol's perspective-taking exercise is empathically accurate she will arrive at the conclusion not that Larry would neither feel good nor be indifferent about it, but that he would feel bad about it. Additionally, the mother supposes that Carol will evaluate Larry's feelings negatively; she will think that it is bad for Larry to feel bad. Most importantly, however, Carol will view Larry's feelings *normatively*—that is, she will take the prospect of Larry's feeling hurt as a *reason* not to destroy his tower.

As this example illustrates, such educational interactions such as requesting to engage in some relevant exercise of the imagination, involve a complex set of suppositions about the emotional reaction patterns of both the actual and prospective transgressed and the actual or prospective transgressor. These suppositions, although understood on all sides, are rarely if ever spelled out, partly because children might not be able to understand them even if they were but also because an explicit analytic understanding of the technique is neither here nor there from the point of view of its operation.[4] On the other hand, it might be due to this complexity that such requests very often—maybe even most often—do not work and that pedagogies of autonomy are by their very nature apparently limited in their effectiveness. That said, the effectiveness or success of the intervention might just be the wrong place to look for the value of such educational interventions. More important than the success or failure of a discrete educational interaction, perhaps, is rather the way the child is *addressed* within the framework of a pedagogy of autonomy: *as if* she were willing and able to understand and then change her intentions. As if, that is, she were autonomous (cf. Reichenbach, 2001). In this case, the fact that the conditions of such counterfactual suppositions are not met does not render such practices incoherent as long as such forms of communication strengthen the *self*-supposition of the child or young person as being (counterfactually) an autonomous agent. If nothing else, it is an important ingredient in self-efficacy (cf. Bandura, 1977).

---

[3] On the distinction between self- and other-focused perspective-taking see §3.4.2.

[4] It is important to point out as an aside that these descriptive claims about the presuppositions of this moral-educational intervention should not be confused with the distinct philosophical or normative question of whether a rational agent in the position of the potential transgressor should or would be motivationally compelled by such considerations. The claim is merely that the intervention *presupposes* this.

6.3   The Sense in which Emotion Education
is (Still) a Taboo Subject

The goal of emotion education would be, among other things perhaps, the intentional shaping or modification of another person's emotions, often via attempts to shape or modify the expression of the emotion, in ways that both respect the normative ideal of the autonomous learner.[5] Many educators, and especially teachers in their public capacity as professionals, seem to regard any such intervention in the emotional lives of children and young people as illegitimate manipulation. Further and most importantly, they seem to hold this belief in the face of what, as I have already hinted, seems to be the incontrovertible fact that the actual practice of emotional education is not just commonplace but is widely regarded as a legitimate facet of education in general and moral education in particular. While there is no doubting that the emotions are no longer a neglected theme in educational research, the idea of educating the emotions remains, in this sense, a taboo subject.

A taboo subject is one that is simply not discussed because it in some respect goes against cultural and societal norms. Because a subject is taboo, however, does not imply that the activity to which it refers—for instance, extra- or premarital sex, masturbation, or the consumption of pornographic material—does not go on. Quite the contrary. What it means for an activity to be taboo is that it is not openly *acknowledged* as one that is practised. That some subjects are taboo is perhaps understandable, especially those activities which might be seen as damaging interpersonal relations or held in some respect to threaten the social structure. What stands out in the case of the education of the emotions is that it seems instead to be a glaring case of practical educational irrationality: judging in all earnestness some educational activity to be illegitimate but doing it anyway. If the education of the emotions is not just possible, desirable, and necessary, but in fact common educational practice what could explain the moratorium on it in open discussion?

Contemporary philosophical discussions of the emotions almost invariably account for the general lack of philosophical interest that the emotions have drawn in terms of the propensity in western intellectual culture, largely thanks to the Stoic legacy detectable in Descartes (cf. de Sousa, 2001; Nussbaum, 1994, 2001; Garber, 1992), to take the "passions", as just one among other categories of emotions, as typical of the genre (cf. Ben Ze'ev, 2000; Oakley, 1992; de Sousa, 1987). I reviewed two further compatible conceptions of the role of emotions in ethical experience in §4.2: "moral" emotions and emotional dispositions as constitutive elements of character. Superficially, the fact that emotions occur spontaneously suggests that emotions are just not the kinds of entities that can be educated; one could no more

---

[5] Or which is are consistent with Peters' (1972/1998) rough and ready but nevertheless quite serviceable description of education as being concerned with the promotion of knowledge and understanding which I regard, for present purposes, as delineating the ethical bounds of educational methods in much the same terms.

educate the emotions than one could educate a headache. If an emotion is held first and foremost as being an irrational affective response whose principal role in moral life is to interfere with sound moral judgement—as, for instance, when anger leads to a morally inappropriate response to some perceived transgression—then far from being the object of cultivation or education, people should learn strategies for detecting and avoiding or otherwise countering such emotions (cf. Barrett, 1994 who defends a version of this view of emotion education).

The conceptual error lying behind this received idea was already identified in Alexius Meinong's *Psychological-ethical investigations in the theory of value* (1894/1968). As Reisenzein et al. (2003) note, Meinong's approach anticipates all the principal elements of contemporary emotional theory. His main insight was that there are no emotions—or, in his term, "feelings"—without cognition. First, he saw that *something* has to be *in some way* cognitively represented to become the object of a feeling; there can be no feeling without an object. This feature of emotions is now recognized by all contemporary theories of emotion and is referred to in philosophical discussions as the "intentionality" of emotions (cf. de Sousa, 1987; Ben Ze'ev, 2000). Second, and relatedly, Meinong presented an early articulation of the idea of the "rationality" of the emotions (cf. de Sousa, 1987; Ben Ze'ev, 2000; Oakley, 1992) by claiming that cognitions to a large degree differentiate emotions and that different emotions are a function of different cognitions. This cognitive view of the emotion's central contribution to overcoming the notion that emotions are characteristically passionate is by reinterpreting the phenomenon of irrational emotions as emotions based on an unacceptable appraisal (cf. de Sousa, 1987; Peters, 1972/1998; van Dam & Steutel, 1996). The idea is reflected in the way people ordinarily talk about emotions. It not only makes sense but it is perfectly common to try to convince someone that he should not, for instance, be afraid of Koko the dog by trying to expose the grounds of the fear as inadequate by, in this case perhaps, pointing out that the dog is well trained, sitting calmly at the side of its owner, and has never acted aggressively in the past. In short, the fact that emotions can be *ir*rational, based on false or irrelevant beliefs, does not entail that emotions are *a*rational, based on no beliefs at all.

Other possible explanations for the taboo around the education of the emotions are better considered ethical or normative rather than definitional. One such reason is certainly that the notion rests uneasily with the principles of political liberalism. From a normative perspective that values negative individual freedom—that is, the right to pursue one's own private conception of the good life without others interfering—as a primary human good one would tend to view attempts to form the emotions as overstepping limits set by the harm principle; educators, like legislators, have the right and even obligation to sanction behaviour that unfairly harms others' interests but they also have an obligation not to try to impose limits on what people can think, say, or feel. The atmosphere of moral scepticism largely fed by, again, normative concerns related to the imperative to respect value pluralism seems to play a role as well. Experiencing a moral emotion presupposes a substantive value commitment that is often integral to an agent's identity, the type of attachment Taylor (1989) refers to as "strong evaluation". It would seem to follow, then, that the education of the moral emotions would be not just the imposition of the teacher's value priorities and interpretations on children, evaluations which by their very nature are uncertain and fallible. So doing could also be seen as having the further and clandestine effect of playing an apparently illegitimate role in determining who those children *become*.

The liberal concerns about the right to freedom of emotion and feeling and the concerns about indoctrination rooted in moral scepticism are further reinforced by a certain attractive psychological view of the person which has a normative dimension as well: the modern ideal of authenticity. The ideals of authenticity of the individual and the autonomy of the individual, both expressed first by Jean-Jacques Rousseau, can be regarded as the two major reference points around which modern articulations of individual freedom are played out (Menke 1993, 1996; Taylor 1991). One is the autonomy of the Enlightenment that exhorts the use of one's *own* mind. The other, the authenticity of Romanticism, counsels, "Listen to your inner voice" and "Follow your feelings". Not just the right but also the psychological need and, under certain interpretations, even *obligation* to be in contact with one's own feelings has had a great impact on the emancipation of the individual, in a sense liberating it from the barriers and conformity of social life. Therefore, being in touch with one's "inner self"—whatever that might turn out to be—has become something of a modern psychological imperative: in the "depths of the soul" one expects to find the truth of the feelings. In psychological humanist hands this has led to a sort of sanctification of emotions which renders the notion of educating the emotions inevitably a form of manipulation or violation of the natural right to a world of personal feelings and of the untouchable "inner nucleus" of the authentic self (cf. Rogers & Freiberg, 1994).

It might seem appropriate in the context of contemporary moral education to try to locate the point where emotions intersect with morality in the hypothesis that understanding a moral rule cannot be a mere cognitive affair. But from antiquity down to the present day the conclusion has seemed inevitable that how one responds affectively to situations is of ethical significance for people and thus that people, especially as children, have to learn to feel the right thing. According to Aristotle (4th century B.C.E./1955), it is because of our desires we do what is bad and because of pain we neglect to do what is good. Therefore, he thought, one important aim of education is to habituate the young to feel pleasure and pain in the right situations. An *éducation sentimentale* would have to have the impudence to teach the *situational specific* and *adaptive emotional reaction patterns*. In this view, learning routines of emotional reactions—habits of the heart as Bellah et al. (1985) aptly put it—is indeed a necessary aim of moral education. And precisely because the moral education of the emotions is a necessary aim of moral education it undoubtedly goes on today much as it has in the past. It is, for reasons speculated upon above, just not the subject of much discussion.

6.4   A Praxiological Analysis of Moral Emotion Education

I would now, stepping out on something of a limb, like to posit that there is an identifiable set of everyday practices of emotional education which directly target the formation of moral-affective dispositions and responses, that these can be analysed into three general categories of pedagogical interventions or "encounters", and that ordinary observation of interactions between young people and educators will confirm these claim. The first consists in requests to *imagine* other's emotional reactions. The second comprises requests to *imitate* normative emotional reactions and the third to *reappraise* the features of a situation that are relevant to an emotional response. This analysis is labelled a praxiological analysis of moral emotion education because it claims to identify perennial and informal moral emotion education strategies—strategies, that is, which are already in common use or "practised"—rather than addressing some perceived need for moral emotion education and constructively proposing new strategies. In this respect, the analysis aims only to cast in a new light familiar socialization interactions. Otherwise, to paraphrase Wittgenstein, it leaves things as they are.

6.4.1 *Imagination*

The first category comprises requests to exercise the *imagination*, namely to engage in moral role-taking. Parents typically ask: 'How would *you* feel, if your brother did the same thing (e.g., steal or damage a favourite toy) to you?' Of course, this is not a question but rather a request, invitation, or exhortation to imagine how the potential victims or beneficiaries of one's action would or do feel (cf. Spiecker, 1988b). The ability to role-take and imagine the impact of one's actions on others may be a precondition of the possibility of moral agency as such. Consider a person who is incapable of imagining the impact of his or her actions on another person's interests. The possibility of success of the injunction to role-take as an educational device necessitates: (1) *oneself* having typical emotional reactions in specific morally meaningful situations; (2) *understanding* emotional reactions *of others* and *self;* and (3) an ability to *imagine* and predict the typical emotional reactions that particular and possibly unique moral situations evoke. Interpreted more broadly than being simply a request to imagine how one would feel in the position of another, the ability to engage in social perspective-taking, as it is sometimes called (cf. Gibbs, 2003), has long been considered an essential to the possibility of adopting what Baier (1965) famously labelled the "moral point of view", the point of view from which moral questions can be judged impartially. Bentham's felicific calculus, G.H. Mead's notion of ideal role-taking, Rawls' veil of ignorance, and Habermas' combined principles of (U) and (D) can all be understood as formalized philosophical expressions of how imaginative decentering is inseparable from approaching practical problems from the moral point of view (cf. Habermas, 1993b). In this sense, not just moral education but to a large degree also political education necessitates the cultivation of the imaginative faculty (cf. Nussbaum, 1995, 2001 and the discussion of this point in Maxwell, 2006).

   Requests to role-take or "imagine" are surely the most recognizable pedagogical strategy associated with this general conception of the education of the moral emotions. The example of the use of a request to perspective-take as a moral emotion education technique analysed in §6.2, it will be evident, fits squarely under the rubric of a request to imagine and need not be further pursued. It is crucial to observe, however, that imagination specifically targets what were identified in §4.2 as the set of "moral emotions", be they "nice" or "nasty" ones (de Sousa, 2001): those emotions which can be reasonably considered to be favourable to a moral outlook and moral behaviour—sympathy and compassion seem to be the paradigmatic examples—and those like malice, rage, callousness, and hatred, for example, which seem correspondingly unfavourable.

Apart from direct requests to imagine in order to intervene to prevent some harm or to point out, for educational purposes, after the fact the reasons why an act is sanction-worthy, other recurrent suggestions for how to cultivate compassionate empathy involve the use of literature and the arts as occasions to both develop the imagination and put it to use in what could be called a decentration exercise: practise considering others' perspectives and the demands that an appreciation of those perspectives make through vicarious identification (see, e.g., Nussbaum, 2001; Noddings, 1998; Greene, 1995). Noddings' care ethics, not unlike Rousseau, focuses mainly on the contribution of the broader social context on the emergence and development of the moral emotional disposition. Whereas Rousseau (1762/1967) pursues a well-known non-interventionist strategy, promoting informal and unconstrained peer interaction as a means of protecting children's propensity for natural sympathy and justice from the corrupting influences of adults, care ethics recommends the active provision of a rich palette of opportunities to engage in caring relationships. It suggests further that educators can strengthen a commitment to caring among children by explicitly framing school relationships and activities (notoriously, even doing math) as involving a significant caring dimension. This way, they are encouraged to interpret human activity generally as caring activity and themselves as carers, a correct interpretation according to Noddings (cf. Noddings, 1984, 1992).

It is true that care ethics is more faithfully represented as an intellectual descendent of Chodorow's (1978) and Gilligan's (1982) feminist psychoanalytic theory than moral sense theory. Nevertheless, as a contemporary conception of moral education it is the most recognizably aligned with the "imagination" and the educational enhancement and support of the natural emergence of the moral emotions. Noddings, care ethics' undisputed leading proponent, considers caring to be ontologically basic to human experience and has argued for years that the educational worth of any aim, activity, policy, and set of institutional arrangements should be assessed in terms of its potential to preserve and enhance caring relationships (cf. esp. 1992). From this perspective, moral education is distinguishable from other aspects of education only as an analytic category that promotes the "ethical ideal" of caring understood at the highest level of abstraction (cf. esp. 1984, ch. 8).

6.4.2 Imitation

The second distinguishable everyday practice of moral emotion education encompasses requests to *imitate* or *dissimulate*. The demand here is to adjust one's emotional expression in order that they accord with normative expectations. This can be achieved either by altering the intensity of an emotional response (e.g., pretending to feel sadder than one spontaneously feels) or by trying to feel an emotion that one does not spontaneously feel (e.g., shame when one is held to have done something thought to be sanction-worthy). These correspond with the observation that, despite the spontaneity or passivity of emotional reactions they can nevertheless be controlled and managed, a fact which seems to entail the possibility of emotional habituation. Educators might easily deceive themselves and others by using nice and politically correct terms like "cultivation" and "stimulation" to describe attempts to educate the emotions, but real-life educational attempts most often have an *imperative* character. This takes the characteristic form of a more or less stern command issued to a child to have an appropriate emotional reaction. The familiar orders and statements, "Shame on you!", "Try to have fun!", "Don't be angry!", "Try to like him again!", "Quit sulking!", "Calm down!", "Please, be nice!", and "Pull yourself together!" are all injunctions to make one feel what one does not at present feel. Whether or not one agrees with such substantive claims about the kinds of emotional reactions that are appropriate in a given situation is neither here nor there. The claim here is that such reactions are widely and probably universally viewed as the appropriate object of moral evaluation. Even though the content of such evaluations will naturally vary to some degree from cultural community to cultural community, the basic phenomenon of evaluating emotional responses is almost certainly a constant.

Requests to modulate one's emotional reactions so as to achieve the normatively required measure and proportion of emotional response which a situation calls for are not merely demands for an outward show of conformity; nor do they simply promulgate normative standards of affective responding. Imitation as a sentimental-education strategy also seems to suppose that *putting on* an emotional reaction, if done frequently and consistency and under proper tutelage, can over time habituate spontaneous genuine appropriate affective responding (cf. Steutel & Spiecker, 2004). Pretending not to be afraid—"pulling oneself together", in the vernacular—in the face of, say, fear of getting on an airplane can in some cases be the first step towards overcoming fear of flying. So too can a pattern of envy towards others' successes be transformed into a pattern of feeling happy for others by the habitual *dissimulation* of envy and the *display* of gladness.

Unlike requests to imagine which, as we have just observed, attempt to generate or enhance a specific set of emotions that are regarded as conducive to a moral outlook, requests to imitate do not target any specific emotions but can intervene wherever an emotional response deviates from a circumstantially prescribed norm. Still, some emotions seem categorically normatively inappropriate and hence a coherent object only of requests to pretend *not* to experience them. These emotions would cover, surely, all the "nasty" emotions but might encompass such emotions as pride, *Schadenfreude*, and maudlin.

The general regulative strategy operative in requests to imitate has been discussed under the heading of "bootstrapping" (cf. Kristjánsson, 2005; de Sousa, 1987). Bootstrapping, attempts to make oneself experience an emotion, occurs in three distinct cases. First, there are cases where there is a complete absence of the appropriate emotion. Here one must bootstrap oneself into putting on or displaying it. Second, there are cases where some emotional reaction occurs but it is the wrong one. In these cases, one must dissimulate the inappropriate emotion and act out the correct one. A third identifiable instance of bootstrapping occurs in cases where one indeed experiences the right emotion but not at the desired *intensity* as, for instance, when one feigns being very impressed by a three-year-old nephew's "drawing" or, conversely, tempers one's urge to laugh seeing, say, someone absent-mindedly bump into a lamppost.

When it is a question of acting out some emotion, one can do little else than draw on one's skills in the thespian arts. A variety of different emotion-regulation strategies, however, are available to assist the bootstrapping process in cases where existing emotional reactions need to be altered, tempered, or increased. It is certainly safe to say that these techniques are not specifically suggested in requests to imitate but are generally discovered and exercised more or less spontaneously.

One is attentional deployment (cf. Kristjánsson, 2005; Gross, 1998), where one directs one's attention away from the source of the emotion (e.g., when one tries to think of something other than whatever is making one laugh when one should be serious or sad when one should be cheerful) or, possibly, when one dwells on relevant emotion-evoking features of some situation in order to intensify an emotion that is only weakly felt (e.g., trying to think about how sad the family must feel at a funeral, how one would feel in their place, attending to the sad expressions on their faces, etc.).

Another is situation selection and modification (cf. Kristjánsson, 2005; Ben Ze'ev, 2000; Gross, 1998). Typically, this technique is employed in situations where one attempts to avoid an emotional reaction one knows in advance will be provoked by a given set of circumstances (e.g., avoiding becoming irritable by avoiding watching excerpts from the speeches of idiotic politicians on the news; Ben Ze'ev, 2000) which are not of direct relevance to the present discussion.[6] There are nevertheless circumstances where situation selection and modification can be used against inappropriate spontaneous emotions. Many teachers, for example, have at least once been witness to the amusing spectacle of a (usually teen- or tween-age female) student running out of the classroom in a desperate last-ditch attempt to control a bad case of the giggles.

A third and final relevant emotional-regulation strategy is so-called response modulation. Rather than being a single identifiable technique, however, response modulation embraces a whole variety of techniques discussed widely in the psychological literature as a means to control the actions emotions risk motivating: hitting someone or saying something nasty out of anger and the like (cf. Kristjánsson, 2005;

---

[6]The assumption that feelings can be avoided by avoiding the situations that cause the feelings seems to underlie the legal measure known as "restraining orders" where men found guilty of domestic violence are legally barred from entering the proximity of their former victims and diagnosed paedophiles may not go near schools.

Gross, 1998). Kristjánsson (2005) is quite right to point out that since such techniques as counting to ten, taking three deep breaths, and so on[7] are directed at checking behaviours and not the behaviour-motivating emotion they might be more aptly considered "behaviour-" rather than "emotion-regulation" techniques (p. 677). That said, one would have to admit as well, it seems, that while such exercises do not aim to eliminate dangerous or unpleasant emotions altogether they are thought to *diffuse* the emotion and in this sense they do target the emotion.

Because requests to imitate are best understood as a strategy aimed at cultivating emotional dispositions that are in part constitutive of acting well and appropriately—as opposed to just choosing the right action and carrying it out with a good intention—imitation seems intimately linked with the Aristotelian tradition in ethics and clearly corresponds with the conception of the relevance of emotions in moral life described in §4.2 as "Aristotelian": the notion that emotions in part constitute ideals of moral character. Within this tradition, however, long-standing divergences exist over the interrelated meta-ethical questions of the justification of the virtues and why being virtuous is worthy of choice. Is the ideal of a virtuous character highly culturally specific and comprehensible only against a background of traditions and practices (as in, e.g., MacIntyre, 1981; Taylor, 1989; Walzer, 1983)? Or is it a universal ideal of human excellence that expresses what it means to do well or flourish as a human being qua human being (cf. Anscombe, 1958; McKinnon, 2005)? Or some combination of the two? (e.g., Carr, 1996).

Imitation seems to find its natural contemporary home in character education (see, e.g., Lickona, 1992 and Kilpatrick, 1992). Although character education exists in many forms and permutations which more or less reflect the variety of positions available within virtue theory itself, proponents of character education rally around the belief that the formation of moral dispositions is a vital part of moral education and ascribe to a comprehensive definition of character which views character as comprising dispositions of thought, action, and feeling (cf. McLaughlin & Halstead, 1999 and Carr & Steutel, 1999). Steutel and Spiecker (2004, p. 532) have instructively summarized the unifying set of beliefs and suppositions about the education and cultivation of proper affective disposition underlying this contested Aristotelian tradition in moral education. First, sentimental education is *necessary* in the sense that a failure to recognize the need for it is a sign of a fundamental misunderstanding of the very purpose of moral education—namely, to promote moral excellences, excellences which are invariably (but not entirely) defined in terms of particular dispositions to morally appropriate affective response. Second, it is *significant* in the sense that sentimental education should be viewed as being central to the moral education of children. Finally, sentimental education is educationally *basic* in the sense that the *mise en place* of the right kinds of affective dispositions is ancillary to the furthering of non-moral excellences that are essential to the education enterprise more broadly construed—virtues of the will and intellectual virtues.

---

[7] Other examples can be found in the teaching material comprising the popular Second-Step anti-violence program.

6.4.3   Reappraisal

Requests for *reappraisal* focus on emotions as involved in moral perception and moral motivation. What one is asked to reappraise, typically, is whether one's emotional response to a situation is based on an acceptable, justified, or correct reading of a situation, with the suggestion that it is not. As such, reappraisals highlight the rationality of emotions; the appropriateness of an emotional response is subject to assessment in terms of publicly accessible standards of judgement and that practical wisdom involves attentiveness to the propositional beliefs underlying emotional responses. For instance, anger towards a person who, accidentally and without negligence, caused some injury, in jealousy misinterpreting and overestimating threats to a cherished relationship and, through sympathy, offering to help a person based on a false belief that the person is in need of help are all errors of judgement susceptible to correction by reappraisal. Requests to reappraise demand the deployment of so-called cognitive strategies of emotional regulation, attempts to modify one's emotional responses by reconsidering the beliefs that underlie them.[8]

The judgement-distorting propensity or "passionateness" of the emotions was discussed at length in §4.2 and here again we see a clear affinity between this particular informal moral education strategy and a recurrent conception of the emotions' moral significance. Whereas imagination is concerned with the attitudes and feelings connected with a moral outlook, and imitation is concerned with habituation into a more or less pre-given ideal of moral character and conduct, reappraisal is concerned with justification of emotions in relation to public standards of rationality and as a dimension of moral perception and moral motivation.

The Kantian/Piagetan/Kohlbergian structural-cognitive tradition of moral development research and moral education largely reflects these preoccupations. The theoretical base of Kohlberg's theory of moral development, for instance, is primarily an account the reasoning patterns leading up to those typical of morally mature agents (cf., e.g., Kohlberg, 1978). Most importantly for present purposes, from this "moral point of view", embodied in the highest stages, an agent is able to abstract himself from his own interests, traditions, and spontaneous emotional responses and, by submitting them to rational scrutiny, assess their legitimacy as moral action incentives. That said, it is also undoubtedly true that Aristotle held that a central role of the virtue of *phronesis*, practical wisdom, is the moderation of unruly emotions by way of reappraisal. The point in associating reappraisal with Kant and imitation with Aristotle is not meant to deny this. Indeed, the richness of Kant's and Aristotle's ethics is such that we have no hesitation in postulating that one will find in both their work an acknowledgement of all three ways in which emotions have moral significance which we have identified—although differences will be apparent in the fine-grained interpretation of their significance. The claim is merely that

---

[8]On this and other "cognitive" strategies of emotional regulation see Kristjánsson (2005, p. 687) and Ben Ze'ev (2000, pp. 229–233).

Kant's ethics seems to have a greater natural affinity with reappraisal, and Aristotle's with imitation, mainly because of the centrality that each thinker seems to assign to the respective role of these strategies in the achievement of their respective moral ideals. Though the issues here are of a degree of complexity which resists simple formulation, Kant is wary of more or less mindless habituation because it is difficult to square with his ideal of rational autonomy. For his part, Aristotle, and on this point he contrasts sharply with Kant, generally regards the conformity of actions to one's moral obligations *willingly* and, in some cases, frankly *enjoying* it as a requirement of virtue. Habituation plays a crucial role in the achievement of this ideal because in many cases—the typical example is facing the enemy courageously in battle—the only way of getting there is by desensitizing oneself (or, depending on the case, sensitizing oneself) by way of repeated experiences where one tries to perform the virtuous act virtuously (cf. Aristotle, 4th century B.C.E./1955, 1103a14ff.).

6.5   Conclusion

Leaving the substantive and invariably ethically precarious question of which emotions should be encouraged in which particular circumstances entirely aside, it seems clear that requests to *reappraise* the judgements providing the cognitive basis of an affective reaction to a situation, requests to *imitate* or to act *as if* one feels otherwise than one feels spontaneously in a set of circumstances in order to meet normative expectations, and, finally, requests to *imagine* what it would be like to stand in the shoes of the other, can be regarded as not just three necessary and legitimate means of education of emotions understood as part of the moral education process, but processes with which every educator—indeed every*one*—even now is intimately familiar (see Table 6.1).

   In closing, a caveat: the three emotion education strategies or imagination, imitation, and reappraisal should be understood as analytic categories which are not always (and possibly never) wholly distinguishable in practice. One can imagine situations in which all three are appealed to as, for instance, in a case where a parent says to her sulking child moments before visiting a family friend the child dislikes, "When we go inside, try to put a brave face on it (request to imitate). You know he's really not a bad person at all (request to reappraise). And in any case, having you sitting there pouting just makes for an uncomfortable experience for everyone (request to consider others' perspectives)". Most importantly, however, we should not fail to observe that these educational strategies do not appear in any sense to be forms of manipulation or indoctrination. Manipulation and indoctrination are corrupt forms of emotional education because they operate without appealing to the child's assumed faculty of autonomous judgement. Emotional manipulating in particular seems by definition to involve the use of a variety of techniques to get a person to experience a desired emotion without the person being aware that he is being manipulated. The requests to imitate, to reappraise, or to imagine are by contrast transparent to judgement because they state explicitly that the student or child is indeed strongly expected or urged to change his or her evaluations and emotional reactions. It remains up to the child to choose whether to try to behave according to these expectations. In this sense "education of the moral emotions" is not inconsistent with the autonomy principle of modern moral pedagogy and in this sense the mainspring of education of the moral emotions, like education more generally, is to challenge interpretations and beliefs, and to stimulate reflection.

Finally, the analysis of practices of moral emotion education in this chapter also suggests close conceptual affinities between different conceptions of the role of affect in moral life and certain identifiably recurrent conceptions of moral education and their respective associated accounts of moral reflection. If this analysis, true to its intention, is not just an exercise in eclecticism but reflects genuine conceptual relationships between the various ideas discussed, two conclusions seem forthcoming. First, perhaps too obvious to state, well-rounded moral-affective formation would be concerned with: (1) the emergence and enhancement of moral emotions like concern for others, sympathy, and compassion; (2) guidance in the moderation of emotional responses in conformity with an ideal of moral character or practical wisdom; and (3) the development of the faculty of moral judgement and its capacity for the regulative constraint of emotionally grounded desiderative tendencies. Second, and more broadly, it seems to suggest not only *that* part of what distinguishes recurrent conceptions of moral education from one another is the disagreements about the role of affect in moral life. It also helps clarify more specifically *what* those disagreements are about: namely, which of the three roles of affect in moral life that we have discussed should be accorded pride of place in the most defensible account of moral maturity.

Table 6.1 Educating moral emotions: A praxiological analysis

	Characteristic request	Targeted emotions	Regulative strategies	Conception of emotions	Moral educational affinity
Imagination	To consider another's perspectives	"Moral emotions"	Perspective-taking	Naturalist	Care ethics
Imitation	To display a normatively required emotional response	Emotions deviating from circumstantially prescribed norms	Bootstrapping; attentional deployment; situation selection and modification; response modulation	Aristotelian	Character education
Reappraisal	To reconsider the acceptability of an emotional response's cognitive grounds	"Passions"; emotions based on false beliefs	Rational scrutiny	Rationalist	Cognitive developmentalism

Chapter 7
Compassionate Empathy in Professional and Practical Ethics Education

This terminal chapter revisits the conclusions of this work's four substantive studies on the disambiguation of the term "empathy", on compassionate empathy's conceptual and empirical profile, on the question of its moral value, and finally on the place of empathic responding in the process of moral deliberation in order to interpret their significance for practical and professional ethics education. The discussion is loosely framed in terms of the three areas of moral emotion education referred to in Chapter 6 as "imagination", "imitation", and "reappraisal".

7.1   Imagination and the Fallacy of the Golden Rule

John Dewey, in *Art as experience* (1934), advanced this intriguing notion: "the imagination is the great instrument of the good" (p. 344). Dewey was talking about what aesthetic experience and moral experience have in common: evaluation. But more than that, what Dewey seemed to be getting at was that modern intellectual culture has got in wrong in its assumption that the experience of evaluation is one-off, subjective, and personal. Rather, evaluation is something intersubjective and richly so. It is social and shared. Conceiving, perceiving, valuing, observing, speaking, and the other operations that mediate that shared experience, Dewey suggests, are accessible to a person only through the exercise of the imagination.[1]

There is another far more pedestrian sense in which imagination may be considered as an instrument of the good and that is as a route to compassionate empathy and beneficence. In one sense, this is obviously (and perhaps self-evidently) true. Reasoning about a moral problem involves the coordination of different perspectives. Very simply, the coordination of others' perspectives requires that one know what their perspectives are and there is only one way to achieve such insight: by

---

[1] See Rethorst (1997) for a discussion of this quote and the question of the relationship between art, imagination, and moral education.

perspective-taking.[2] In another sense, the claim that imagination is an instrument of the good is almost certainly false. The possession of insight into another person's perspective, and in particular the knowledge that he faces some form of undeserved suffering or that other important interests are otherwise unfairly threatened, does not in and of itself issue in feelings of solidarity or sympathy. To turn the idea around, the (false) belief in question is that it is a *lack* of "imagination" that prevents people from understanding and perceiving moral problems and caring about addressing them. For ease of reference, let us call this idea the fallacy of the Golden Rule; loosely speaking the Golden Rule, treat others as you would be treated yourself, is only compelling as a guide for decision-making on the assumption that one *already* takes another's interests as one's own. We have seen in these pages two considerations, one conceptual and the other empirical, which suggest that the fallacy of the Golden Rule is indeed a fallacy.

Chapter 3 saw that, in general terms, compassionate empathy may be satisfyingly characterized as a state of involvement in another person's suffering as something to be relieved or avoided (cf. esp. §3.3). The perception of suffering as being in need of *alleviation* is definitive since it sets compassionate empathy apart from other possible ways of being involved in another's suffering. In *Schadenfreude*, for instance, one takes pleasure in another's suffering and a clinician might view a person's suffering principally as a technical problem or as a matter of intellectual curiosity. "Punch and Judy" shows and similar sadistic entertainments take suffering as cause for amusement. Furthermore, even aversive or unpleasant feelings, directly connected with the perception of another's actual or prospective suffering, are not in and of themselves the solidarity-evoking emotion of compassionate empathy. For example, inarticulate horror at the sight of a wretched, half-naked itinerant lying unconscious and baking in the midday sun is not empathic distress but what Batson (cf., Batson & Coke, 1981, Batson, 1991) calls "personal distress". Compassionate empathy is, again, a state of solidarity and other-directed concern where such aversive feelings are experienced subjectively as feeling *for* or *with* a suffering person.[3] In short, there is no conceptual necessity linking the perception of undeserved suffering with concern and not all distressing feelings based on the belief that another person is suffering can be characterized as concern for that person.

Contrary to the folk psychology view assumed by the Golden Rule, then, compassionate empathy has utterly distinct cognitive and affective dimensions. Triangulating empirical evidence for this notion was considered in Chapter 5. The moral psychology

---

[2] In this instance, I am using "perspective-taking" as the faculty of other-directed insight as it tends to be used in social psychology. It was seen in §3.4 that perspective-taking so broadly conceived may be highly imaginative or be mediated by simpler associative cognitive operations and conditioning.

[3] Admittedly, compassionate empathy and personal distress are not invariably distinct phenomena. It is possible and indeed probably not uncommon for personal distress to become empathic distress as when feelings of repulsion at a person's aversive state turn to thoughts for her well-being. In this way, she becomes the object of those feelings and concurrently the object of genuine compassionate empathy. This point is discussed in §3.2.1.

and characteristic patterns of moral functioning associated with the abnormal psychological diagnostic category of psychopathy indicate that psychopaths—those diagnosed with a nosologically controversial psychological disorder characterized by shallow emotional responding and an apparent absence of such "moral emotions" as guilt, remorse, and other-directed concern but not cognitive impairment—are nevertheless fully able to perceive, comprehend, and assess moral problems with no more or less difficulty than those who test in the normal range of emotionality (cf. §5.4). Significantly, in the psychopath we have a paradigmatic case of a person who has excellent perspective-taking abilities yet who is utterly unconcerned with others. In fact, far from being motivated by insight into others' present or perspective woes to "treat others as he would be treated" it is well documented that psychopaths, on the contrary, use their characteristically advanced social perspicacity to manipulate others in pursuit of what they seem to regard as their own narrow self-interest.

An explanation of the enduring appeal of the fallacy of the Golden Rule is not far to seek. A basic empathic disposition, a disposition to care about others' weal and woe, is perfectly normal and commonplace. Hoffman's (2000) pioneering research on empathic development shows that the main achievements of "empathic development", as he calls it, occur prior to adolescence (see pp. 63–77). It is the arrival of tertiary cognitive abilities in late childhood and adolescence, which then begin to work in conjunction with an already established disposition to respond with concern to others' distress, that enables the kind of abstract and complex empathizing characteristic of deliberation over practical moral problems (see Hoffman, 2000, p. 85; and Gibbs, 2003, pp. 88–89). Hoffman's theory, that is, traces a developmental process which occurs and then plateaus at the dawn of a human individual's life; it allows much less room for development across the lifespan than does Kohlberg's theory of cognitive moral development. Abnormality and stagnation in empathic development, sometimes cited to as aetiological factors in Antisocial Personality Disorder (ASPD) and psychopathy (cf. §5.4), are traced either to grossly inadequate socialization or to some physiological anomaly, congenital or advenient. From this perspective, the reinforcement of children's empathic dispositions through such basic parenting techniques as "induction" (cf. §4.5) is a worthy early educational objective, but by late adolescence and early adulthood any comprehensive deficit in students' affective faculties is probably beyond the reach of a standard educational regime (cf. Gibbs, 2003).

This is why Hoffman (2000) says that, where children have been provided with adequate empathy socialization, empathizing is "a reliable human response" (p. 61). In essence, the many modes of empathic arousal perform the adaptive function of making *not* empathizing with a suffering human being a near impossibility. This occurs in several interrelated ways. First, it makes observers susceptible to a wide variety of cues, enabling them to respond empathically to whatever distress cues happen to be available in a set of circumstances. A personal narrative would trigger language-mediated association, distressed looks or sounds trigger conditioning, a recognizably distressing observed situation cognitive networking, and so on (p. 59). Second, the primitive reactive modes enable human beings with weak or undeveloped cognitive abilities to respond empathically. Most notably, conditioning, mimicry, and direct association make empathic responding possible among very young children and provide them with a stock of basic empathic experiences that may later be drawn on once the more advanced modes come on line cognitively (p. 59). Third, the reactive processes, operating as they do "instantly, automatically, and outside of conscious awareness" (p. 61) impede what Hoffman calls "empathic avoidance" (p. 61); even if one attempts to avoid exposure to the stimuli that trigger automatic empathy (e.g., by closing one's eyes or focusing one's attention on something else) compassionate empathy might be triggered by some other cue in the situation. Fourth, the introspective processes, especially language-mediated association and perspective-taking, in addition to expanding the number of avenues of empathic stimulation, also broaden the possible range of objects of compassionate empathy to include not just people who are not present but also people in situations that are entirely *imaginary*—characters in fiction of course but also in the hypothetical situations typical in moral deliberation (Hoffman, 2000, pp. 61, 91). In sum, given the fact that typically both the primitive and more cognitively advanced arousal mechanisms come into operation and are mutually supporting in any particular experience of compassionate empathy (see pp. 59–60), in Hoffman's assessment, the multifacetedness of the empathic arousal modes virtually compels a caring response to a person in distress (p. 61).[4]

Hoffman was careful not to depict human beings as "saintly empathic-distress-leads-to-helping machines" (p. 33) and I would not either. Such a portrayal flies in the face of the most superficial experience with the past and present of human association: *l'homme est un loup pour l'homme*. Later, we will go back to the question of at least the cognitive factors, errors of judgement essentially, that are frequently responsible for failures to appropriately empathize. But some of the intuitive implausibility of the claim that an empathic disposition is developmentally normal diminishes when one appreciates two things: first, the intractability of empathic bias and selective empathic attention (cf. §4.4.1); and, second, that the motivations for human behaviour are varied, complex, mutually conflicting, and little understood. Compassionate empathy is only one motivation among many.[5] Seen in this light, the crucial question from the point of view of moral education and moral development is less, "What accounts for individual differences in empathic sensitivity?" than "What accounts for individual differences in the prioritization, *as action incentives*, of concern for others over other values and motivations?".[6]

---

[4] These "reactive" and "introspective" processes implicated in experiences of compassionate empathy were described and compared in detail in §3.4.

[5] For one discussion of this point see Hoffman (2000, pp. 33–35).

[6] As research theme in empirical moral psychology, this problem is studied under the heading of moral motivation and has today coalesced into an agenda investigating the interconnected constructs of moral identity, moral personality, the moral self, and moral exemplarity (cf. esp. Lapsley & Narváez, 2004).

Let us frame these points in terms of the moral emotion educational intervention of "request to imagine" introduced in Chapter 6 and state outright the educational implications of the fact that compassionate empathy constitutes a union of other-directed insight and a psychologically distinct orientation of concerned involvement in the well-being of the object of the imaginative process. Encouraging vicarious introspection as a means of intentionally provoking compassionate empathic involvement with another in a state of adversity only works—and plenty of empirical evidence supports the belief that it does work (cf. §3.4.2)—because people are on the whole already disposed towards concern for others. A triviality this may seem; questioning about education for compassionate empathic responding, however, frequently begins with precisely the opposite assumption, namely that it addresses, either in the context of a perceived socio-moral crisis or as an item on the roster of humanistic upbringing, one dimension of "becoming human" or a "fully functioning person" (cf., Rogers & Freiberg, 1994; Greene, 1995; Noddings, 1998; and Verducci, 1999, 2000). These studies of compassionate empathy have shown this gambit to be developmentally imprecise. There are, however, other treatments of the problem of educating for compassionate empathy which take as foundational from precisely the opposite assumption and the assumption that parallels this work's findings: that people are, on the whole, highly susceptible to empathic distress. Nussbaum (2001) and Warnock (1996) argue, for their parts that it is just wrong to think of children and young people as lacking other-directed sensitivity. The most decisive educational question in their minds is thus not how children *become* caring towards others but how they *broaden out* their natural propensity for compassion towards those whom they know and with whom they identify and come to be appropriately affected by issues that are unfamiliar to them and to respond to the needs of strangers as well.

Of more practical consequence to the use of requests to imagine the context of professional and practical ethics education, perhaps, is the distinction between other-directed and self-directed perspective-taking. Recall from §3.4.2 the presentations of Stotland's (1969) and Batson et al.'s (1997) research which showed that it is not only possible for a person to willingly adopt one viewpoint of empathic engagement or the other but, most importantly, that the two perspectives stimulate empathic engagement of rather different qualities. Self-focused perspective-taking, imagining how one would feel *oneself* in another's aversive situation, and other-focused perspective-taking, imagining how another feels *himself or herself* in an aversive situation, stimulate comparative levels of measurable empathic responding. However, self-focused perspective-taking is associated with a tendency towards to empathic *dis*engagement, a process of "empathic drift" (Hoffman, 2000) where concern for another triggers concern for oneself and, in this way, shifts from being compassionate empathic involvement to a potentially disturbing and distracting state of personal worrying. We already know that the request to imagine is an effective means of stimulating empathic involvement. Without failing to appreciate the multiplicity of forms that the request to imagine might take in the context of professional and practical ethics instruction (case studies, reading, and reflecting on literary fiction or film, as well, but probably rarely, as a direct injunction to imagine), at least from the instrumental perspective of maximizing compassionate empathic involvement in practical problems, the request to imagine should specifically encourage other-focused perspective-taking and discourage self-focused perspective-taking.

7.2   Imitation and the Use of Literature and Narrative as a Route to Compassionate Empathizing

But what is the educational point of encouraging affective engagement with moral problems? One compelling answer-canvassed briefly in Chapter 1 (§1.2) and revisited in the consideration of compassionate empathizing as an ethical achievement (§4.3) and as foundational to moral perception (§5.3) -was that a moral problem when seen through the lens of concern for others, as a demand, that is, to judiciously negotiate and address competing claims to well-being, comes to seem more pressing and urgent. But beyond casting features of a moral problem in a *different* light, affective engagement also *brings* to light features of a moral problem that one may not otherwise have remarked. Sherman (1990) has expressed the point thus. When the emotions are implicated in moral assessment, she says,

> Not only do we notice, but we notice with a certain intensity or impact that would be absent if emotions weren't engaged. We focus in a way we wouldn't otherwise. And once focussed, we bring to bear further considerations that are relevant; we make inferences that would otherwise not have arisen or be thought of in a compelling way. Sensitivity thus becomes more than a purely perceptual or cognitive matter. (p. 150)

But Sherman stops short of stating the clincher: insofar as such engagement is not sentimental or mawkish—that is, "passionate" to use the term introduced in §4.2 to characterize emotions in their capacity to interfere with and distort normative judgement—but intelligent, judicious, and rational, with "sensitivity", as she calls it, comes a heightened normative awareness, a greater appreciation of relevant considerations, and it triggers (putatively valid) inferences in connection with the moral issue at hand. This is why affective engagement with a moral problem can be seen as a route to viewing it more *truthfully* and the epistemological leverage that affective engagement supplies—and I intend "epistemological" in the most expansive sense—is *the* argument and justification for deliberately attempting to, borrowing the label Scholz and Groarke (1996) pick for their second *Seven principles for better practical ethics*, "engage ethics students in non-intellectual ways" (p. 364). In one sense, this educational concern touches on the dimension of moral emotion education referred to above as "imitation". Imitation, and in particular the moral emotion education intervention that consists in a request to imitate, presented in Chapter 6, supposes what could be loosely referred to as affective obligations—that is, prescriptions to feel a certain way towards a certain object in a certain circumstance and, perhaps, backed by reasons to want to feel. This section looks at one way that requests to imitate are made in professional and applied ethics: through the study of literature and narrative.

Literature and *a fortiori* narrative may be put to use in practical ethics education in different ways and for different purposes. Case-based ethics teaching, for example, proceeds by analysing moral problems that are always presented in narrative form. The stories studied may even on occasion tug at the heart strings. Emotional arousal, however, is anything but their point (cf. §1.5). Using literature and narrative to elicit a certain type of affective response intentionally, by contrast, is well established in practical ethics if somewhat experimental insofar as it does not constitute a standard pedagogical approach to the field of study (cf. §1.5). Scholz and Groarke (1996), for example, report the successful deployment of Brantenberg's anti-utopian novel *Egalia's daughters* (1977/1985) in order to "develop the moral imagination and facilitate the ability of women and men to understand injustice based on gender" (p. 347). In human rights education, personal commitment to social progress, understood specifically in terms of the advancement of human rights, is commonly promoted using a pedagogical procedure whereby articles of the Universal Declaration of Human Rights (or a connate document) are presented and then given a human face in the form of cases, hypothetical or historical, and ranging in their moral content from the unfortunate to the execrable, of human rights abuse and neglect (cf. Starkey, 1991; Reardon, 1995; and Andreopoulos & Claude, 1997). To borrow Britzman's (2003) compelling expression, the "difficult knowledge" of human immorality conveyed in such cases and by way of narrative tends to be regarded as crucial to the construction of the meaning of discrete human rights as a demand for the protection and promotion of specific forms of fundamental human well-being.

On the face of it, these and parallel pedagogical uses of narrative to stimulate compassionate empathic involvement may seem to have more to do with the moral emotion education strategy of imagination than with imitation. After all, the request to imagine is the request to vicariously dwell in the perspective of a person facing adversity and this precisely for the sake of eliciting emotions meant to serve moral ends (cf. §§ 4.2 and 6.4.1). This characterization, it is true, fits the use of literature in professional and practical ethics education just invoked to a tee.

Finding issues raised in this work that fall neatly under the heading of imitation is confounded by the very emotion on which it focuses: compassionate empathy. Imagination, it will be recalled from §6.4.1, has as its proper object the special and restricted set of moral emotions. Arguably, compassionate empathy is the most unalloyed of all the emotions that might reasonably be considered to fit into this class (cf. §4.3). This does not imply, of course, that compassionate empathy is not the coherent object of a request to imitate. On the contrary, whereas the objects of imagination are finite, the objects of imitation are in principle limited only by the human capacity to experience emotions that deviate from circumstantially prescribed norms—which must surely mean that, in effect, they have no object limits at all. Requests to feel compassionate empathy may, then, take the form of a direct injunction but this, one suspects, is rare. The belief that imaginative involvement in another's adversity has a way of issuing in feelings of solidarity is pervasive and, as was argued in §7.1, well founded. This state of affairs predicts a preference for imagination over imitation as the educational route to appropriate compassionate empathizing. Moreover, it is a preference that is strengthened all the more in the present cultural context, described in §6.3, which tends to regard emotional experiences as private and inviolable. Even if the intent in both cases is for all intents and purposes identical, telling someone to perspective-take in hopes of evoking sympathy is not the same thing as telling someone to sympathize. The request to imagine is a way of avoiding the indelicacy of demanding the right emotional reaction but, crucially, it is a way that is available *uniquely* in the case of compassionate empathy and other moral emotions.

By attending to the aspect of the educational use of literature as education for compassionate empathizing which consists in a demand to *experience* compassionate empathy towards particular human beings in particular circumstances—rather than to the aspect which consists in a demand to *vicariously dwell* in another person's experience—one can, perhaps, come to better appreciate how it might also constitute a form of imitation. Educators can easily deceive themselves into thinking they can be disculpated from making an "indoctrinatory" demand for specific and substantive moral responses by using literature in this way. To suppose that students do not realize that they are the subject of just such a request is naïve. To deny that that is precisely the intent is disingenuous. Of course, how individual students respond to narrative is unpredictable; in *éducation sentimentale*, as elsewhere, there can be no algorithm. Doubtless, little is understood about how, whether, and under what conditions people learn moral ideas from encounters with the suffering of others. But when an instructor hands a student such a text and presents it as an *aid* to ethical insight or as an *expression* of ethical understanding the message is clear: that they are intended to sympathize, that they are thought to have good reason to sympathize, that, in sum, they have now become the subject of a request to imitate.

As a foil, then, for investigating this didactic use of literature and narrative in professional and practical ethics, Martha Nussbaum's work on literature as a means of educating for compassionate citizenry is apposite. From the perspective of the present chapter's intention to tease out some educational meaning from these studies' claims about the moral psychology of compassionate empathy, seeing how her treatment of empathizing through literature gets it right, provides an important angle on the problem of educating for compassionate empathic responding in practical ethics education. But seeing where it goes wrong is equally instructive. A proper appreciation of the multifacetedness of empathic responding, I want to argue, exposes literature's limitations as a curricular tool for fostering moral insight via affective engagement.

In *Upheavals of thought* (2001), Nussbaum's argument for using literature in higher education as a route to compassionate empathizing extends and brings together previous work on literature and political education in *Poetic justice* (1995) and her own particular eudaimonistic conception of social obligation as developed, for instance, in *Women and human development* (2000) (cf. also Nussbaum, 1992). Her aim in regard to the latter promises nothing short of a monumental advance for political theory. In essence she wishes to propose an alternative to minimalist and largely negative conceptions of citizenship obligations favoured by liberalism and long on the defensive in face of persistent critical pressure to come clean about its own clandestine substantive ethical suppositions (cf. esp. Sandel, 1982). Her more substantive alternative outlines basic social entitlements grounded in a conception of fundamental preconditions of a flourishing human life. She formulates these entitlements in terms of a set of ten "central human capabilities". The list includes such familiar items as life and bodily health and integrity but also identifies various sorts of possibilities of attachment to other human beings, concern for the natural world, and even "play", or the ability to "laugh [...] and enjoy recreational activities" (Nussbaum, 2001, pp. 416–417).

To arrive at a precise formulation of the role, Nussbaum thinks, compassion plays in the promotion and protection of these ten capabilities requires some extrapolation. It draws on her carefully delineated cognitive view of compassion, which she calls variously "appropriate compassion" and "rational compassion". In general terms, her characterization of compassion, sketched in §4.3, parallels that of Blum (1980a, 1980b) and others (e.g., Nagel, 1970; Wispé, 1986) in picturing compassion as an ethical achievement that consists in viewing the suffering of others as something to be relieved. In two different formulations, Nussbaum characterizes compassion as "valuing another person as part of one's own circle of concern" (2001, p. 336) and as a state of "concern to make the lot of the suffering as good, other things being equal, as it can be—because that person is an object of one's concern" (2001, p. 342). Compassion, on her account, depends further on "empathy and the judgement of similar possibilities" (pp. 425–426), where empathy is the "imaginative exercise of putting oneself in that person's place" (p. 342), or what is commonly known as perspective-taking. For its part, the judgement of similar possibilities is cognisance that the state of suffering is something that could happen to anyone, and especially to oneself (cf. Blum, 1980b; Nussbaum, 2001, p. 342). Having a cognitive core in fallible beliefs, compassion is susceptible to misdirection and inappropriateness. In particular, Nussbaum says, when compassion goes awry it can usually be accounted for in terms of one of three judgements typically connected with compassion. The first is the judgement of "seriousness" or mistaking trivial suffering for serious suffering (p. 415). The second is "non-desert" or the belief that people who are suffering deserve it (p. 419), an idea with obvious parallels to the well-documented just-world hypothesis (cf. Rubin & Peplau, 1975). Finally, she identifies the question of "extended concern", the difficult and controversial issue of the degree of concern people owe to others especially in virtue of the special relationships—as family members, neighbours, co-citizens, co-workers, etc.—that pertain between them (p. 420).[7] Compassion is an important ingredient of good citizenship, for Nussbaum, because compassion towards one's co-citizens is an important ingredient in (if not a precondition of) appreciating the fact that a *lack* of the basic human capacities she identifies constitutes a "tragic predicament" (2001, p. 418) or "catastrophe" for an individual in the sense of seriously hampering

---

[7] "The three judgements" are Nussbaum's analogues to the "judgements of compassionate empathy" presented in §3.1.

the possibility of doing well *qua* human being (cf. 2001, p. 453). In other words, compassion plays, first, a *moral-perceptive* role in helping citizens see that there are such basic human goods. But it also seems to play a second *moral-motivational* role of enabling one to appreciate that we owe each other the provision and protection of the conditions of human flourishing. It is these realizations, or something like them, that compassion towards one's co-citizens helps to bring to light in Nussbaum's view. The education of compassion for citizenship implies the cultivation of appropriate judgements, but also support of extension of concern through the strengthening of the "psychological mechanisms" of empathy and the judgement of similar possibilities (pp. 425–426). And it is in its potential for this that the study of literature holds educational pride of place.

The focal point of Nussbaum's pedagogical proposal is the "extension of concern" and it is hard to deny that this is well founded. Her working assumption, consistent with both common sense and contemporary knowledge in empirical psychology (cf. esp. Hoffman's review in 2000, pp. 206–213), is, again, *not* that education for rational compassion is needed as a bulwark against a generalized state of apathy, anomie, or a pandemic of exaggerated self-concern. The danger, instead, is that citizens will fail to extend their natural propensity for compassion towards their kith and kin—those whom they know personally and those with whom they otherwise identify—to the strangers with whom they also share the broader social world. Basically normally functioning people, the assumed subjects of standard education (cf. Reichenbach & Oser, 1995, p. 192), in other words, need no special assistance to recognize and be motivated by the demands that their fellows' needs place on them. The pressing educational question is rather how to encourage similar appreciation for the needs of strangers as well.

Nussbaum's specific curricular prescription consists partly in the promotion of empathizing conceived of as a so-called soft skill but also and unmistakeably in didacticism. First, studying literature develops "empathy": the faculty of what Kohut (1959) called other-directed vicarious introspection and what is usually referred to as perspective-taking, the ability to arrive at a comprehension of another person's experience by imagining oneself in another person's situation. Reading stories in general (cf. 2001, pp. 426–429) and novels in particular, Nussbaum claims, "exercises the muscles of the imagination, making people capable of inhabiting for a time the world of a different person, and seeing the meaning of events in that world from the outsider's viewpoint" (2001, p. 431). The second, more didactic orientation of the approach, begins, she says, by asking what groups student–citizens "are likely to understand easily and what groups might need more mental exercise before empathy can take hold" (p. 430). The answer to this question provides the educator with a criterion for selecting novels which encourage the creation of "bonds of identification and sympathy" (1995, p. 7) with the groups with whom pupils are less likely to empathize. She argues convincingly that the artistic form of the novel, especially in its realist social mode—as exemplified by such classics of the liberal literary canon as Charles Dickens' *Hard times*, Ralph Ellison's *Invisible man*, John Steinbeck's *The grapes of wrath*, and Richard Wright's *Native son*—is uniquely significant as a platform for compassionate imagining.

To give a sense of the kind of empathic engagement that novels encourage, Nussbaum explains how a reader of *Hard times* might respond to Dickens' account of the lives of factory workers in nineteenth-century England. The reader, she says, would see that, while the lives of factory workers in his or her own society are less harsh than in the past, in some equally important respects they are very much the same, in particular in respect of "certain very general norms of human flourishing" and a corresponding evaluation of "what is serious damage to a life and what is not" (1995, p. 7). As she summarizes the idea in *Poetic justice* (1995), social realist novels:

> [...] present persistent forms of human need and desire realized in specific social situations. These situations frequently, indeed usually, differ a good deal from the reader's own. Novels, recognizing this, in general construct and speak to an implicit reader who shares with the characters certain hopes, fears and general human concerns, and who for that reason is able to form bonds of identification and sympathy with them, but who is also situated elsewhere and needs to be informed about the concrete situation of the characters. In this way, the very structure of the interaction between the text and its imagined reader invites the reader to see how the mutable features of society and circumstances bear on the realization of shared hopes and desires. (p. 7)

In this way, Nussbaum claims, reading the right books and through the connected exercise of the imagination enables the reader in one sense to become a participant in the protagonists' social struggles. This constitutes the provision of a form of moral perception or insight that the dry didactic learning of "facts about classes, races, nationalities, sexual orientations"—that is, the usual substance of political, social, and economic history (2001, p. 432)—does not so readily afford.

This, in brief, is the "vital political function" (p. 433) that literature plays in Nussbaum's assessment: first, it cultivates the imaginative or empathic abilities central to political life and supports the extension of concern. The bonds of sympathy and identification that reading judiciously selected social realist novels helps to create between otherwise estranged and compassionately detached citizens give substance to the very idea of the obligations of citizenship as Nussbaum conceives them: that our views about human freedom, functioning, and flourishing, ideas that so readily and spontaneously generate demands on us in the case of our kith and kin, make similar demands on us in the case of all citizens (2001, pp. 432–433). No mere recital of facts and statistics can achieve this. Only literature, Nussbaum claims, is up to the task.

Now I think we can appreciate without undue extrapolation that the language of Nussbaum's proposal—that of "capacities", "tragic predicaments", and the "extension of concern"—is consistent with the general portrait of compassionate empathizing that has emerged in these pages and, further, that its structure is readily transferable, *mutatis mutandis*, to the familiar didactic function assigned to literature in professional and practical ethics education and sketched at the beginning of this section. I am willing to go along with Nussbaum that there is no substitute for narrative as a means of communicating the kinds of human experiences as a way to get inside another person's social perspective. And I am willing to accept that reading novels is good for the development of imaginative powers—at any rate, good for the development of the kind of imaginative powers that are needed to appreciate novels.

But I suspect that it takes the influence of a very strong bias towards bookishness to be insensitive to this decisive fact: the world of narrative expression is rich, time is short, and people's abilities and interests are highly variable. What is the particular allure of literature? Why not, say, watch movies, plays, or listen to music instead?

Nussbaum actually has good theoretical reasons to assign to the novel, for the purposes of education for compassionate empathizing, such an elevated stature in the hierarchy of narrative forms. Attending to these grounds is instructive because it reveals how it is that Nussbaum's account succumbs to the bit of folk psychology I called the "perspective-taking/compassionate empathy hypothesis"—that is, that the principal psychological mechanism which mediates experiences of compassion is other-directed vicarious introspection (see §3.4).

Nussbaum, indeed, does not deny that other forms of narrative such as histories, biographies, and films and expressive media such as music, dance, theatre, and poems and even "economic treatises" (1995, p. 4) make a contribution to compassionate citizenry (cf., e.g., 1995, pp. 4–7; 2001, pp. 428, 431–432) but there is no doubting, however, that the realist social novel holds an incomparable pride of place in her schema. The reason for this is plain: none of these other forms of expression have as much potential to develop the ability to perspective-take, or imagine oneself in another person's position. She calls this ability "empathy", as we saw, and considers empathizing in this sense to be part and parcel of experiencing compassion towards another human being. Indeed, Nussbaum remarks that even when literature lacks explicitly political content, it still serves a "vital political function" because it cultivates empathy, this imaginative ability she considers central to political life (p. 433). What makes the realist social novel so attractive for Nussbaum is that it is here, in the *realist social* novel, that the form of the novel, with its rich capacity to draw the reader into the lives and world of its character, converges with narratives of struggles for social justice, making for a powerful educational cocktail indeed (cf. also 1995, especially Ch. 2 and related comments in Nussbaum, 1992). One can see already that this assumption turns on the uncritical acceptance of the perspective-taking/compassion hypothesis. To put the point counterfactually, if compassion did not suppose a process of perspective-taking with a person *qua* object of compassion, as she assumes, the grounds for her prioritization of literature over other narrative expressive forms would be lost. The properly directed stimulation of imaginative development is the royal road to compassionate citizenship only if compassion actually has rich imaginative content.

The limitations of restricting educational attempts to elicit feelings of solidarity and identification through exclusively language-mediated narrative means are apparent. It fails to draw on the full range of psychological mechanisms connected with empathic arousal. In particular, it neglects the potential contribution the reactive mechanisms have to make in compassion-eliciting experiences.[8]

---

[8] Owing to this, Nussbaum treats childhood primarily as a period of latency where the principal achievement is the development of the imagination viewed as a "soft skill" in preparation for fully fledged compassion which comes only at a later stage (2001, cf. pp. 426–428). This underestimates children's capacity for compassion and identification for reasons already elaborated upon.

The multidimensionality of compassionate arousal and, again, its reactive dimension in particular (see §§6.3 and 3.4) would suggest that if one was forced to identify *one single* medium of communication that is of outstanding value in its potential to foster the appreciation of certain groups' historico-social situations as "tragic predicaments" à la Nussbaum we might have a more promising candidate in the realist social *film*—films such as *Philadelphia*, *Schindler's list*, *Norma Rae*, and *Dead man walking*—not the realist social novel. That said, the length of novels and the opportunities for character development and rich identification and the opportunity for imaginative development they provide should not be underestimated. The truth of the matter, surely, is that in most groups of human beings a variety of abilities and dispositions are represented. To put the point in terms used in Gardner's (1983) not uncontroversial theory of multiple intelligences, for those with strong linguistic-verbal intelligence, one can reasonably suppose that the most effective avenue to appropriate compassion is the realist social novel. For interpersonally intelligent people, it is likely to be things like service learning and other face to face experiences. For visually spatially oriented minds, it might be the visual and plastic arts, theatre, or the synaesthetic experience of a contemporary feature film. Among those with musical-rhythmic intelligence, much could be said in favour of listening to and even performing music. Finally, and though it might be difficult for the literary-minded to appreciate, the logical or mathematically minded might be most deeply moved by the facts and statistics that populate the pages of textbooks on sociology and economic development. In short, the fact that a broad palette of psychological processes is genetically involved in experiences of compassion, coupled with the fact that human beings, even within the same age and developmental ranges, have widely differing psychological capacities for compassion, speaks in favour of using a rich variety of approaches to the promotion of a compassionate citizenry and strongly against any one-sided diets.

In conclusion, when viewed from one perspective the multifacetedness of empathic responding—the fact, in other words, that any given experience of compassionate empathy is mediated by a range of identifiable psychological processes of varying degrees of cognitive sophistication—goes some distance towards explaining empathic bias, in particular the here and now bias or the tendency to identify with others who share experiences of suffering that are meaningful to the empathizer. However, when viewed from another perspective, however, the multifacetedness of empathic responding can be regarded not as a *cause* of unbalanced compassionate empathy but rather as an educational *resource* in the promotion of appropriate compassion. To put the point bluntly, in light compassionate empathy's psychological multifacetedness, the imperative of promoting rational compassion would seem to call for a more varied curricular response than the near-exclusive use of language-mediated communication that is traditional in higher education.[9]

---

[9] This section draws heavily on Maxwell (2006) where a more elaborated version of this critique of Nussbaum's curricular proposal is presented.

7.3   Emotions as Appraisal, Judgement as Reappraisal, and Final Appraisal

In a lesser-known paper, Peters (1972/1998) argues that it is only because emotions are rational or, as he put it, because "emotions are basically forms of cognition" (p. 180) that they are or could become coherent objects of educational attention. His claim about the possibility of emotion education turns on what he means by "education". Peters' convictions on the question of the signification of "education" shift in his writings. In earlier work, "education" opposed pragmatically minded "industrial psychology" (cf. Kohlberg & Mayer, 1972) or "human capital" (cf. Walker, 2006) strategies for defining educational aims. From this perspective, curriculum should be vocationally oriented and market-driven and, accordingly, the fundamental notion of "education as preparation for life" is interpreted narrowly, in terms of the skills and knowledge thought to confer to its recipients competitive social and economic advantages. Drawing on a careful analysis of the way "education" is used in ordinary language, Peters argued that this familiar educational ideology amounts to an abuse of language. Employing means which appeal to the basic human capacity of rational and independent thought, "education" transmits knowledge and understanding which is not instrumentally but rather intrinsically worthwhile to those who acquire it (cf. Peters, 1966; cf. White, 2001, pp. 119–120). "Education", he concluded, "suggests the intentional bringing about of a desirable state of mind in a morally unobjectionable manner" (Peters, 1966) and by "desirable state of mind" he meant the acquisition of the "different view" that comes with an "understanding of the world and one's place in it" (Peters, 1964, p. 47). Here in his paper on emotion education, Peters' (1972/1998) ideas about the meaning of "education" seem to cut a wider swathe. "Education" appears now merely as "involving a family of experiences through which knowledge and understanding develop" (p. 179) and an important distinction between activities which contextualize educational processes and the process of education itself is brought to the definitional foreground. Providing conditions favourable to learning, like maintaining a clean and attractive classroom, teaching with a sense of humour, and aiming at the achievement of performance-optimizing levels of stress around evaluations, Peters suggests (op. cit., p. 171), are certainly ethical and undoubtedly ancillary to education but they are not strictly proper to education as such. What remains in the definition, most importantly, is the idea that the very possibility of education utterly depends on the existence of public standards of assessment and that appealing to such standards in the process of building up of understanding and knowledge is the keystone of pedagogical ethics. Emotions involve appraisals and appraisals are evaluative beliefs about the world. These beliefs, in turn, are susceptible to assessment in terms of publicly accessible standards. This is what makes emotions educable or, in Peters' (1972/1998) more cautious phrase, allows from some "scope for educating the emotions" (p. 180).

  In the context of moral emotion education, this distinction between educability and scope for educability is especially significant but let us first attend to the fact that what Peters has in mind by "educating the emotions" is coterminous with the moral-education intervention referred to earlier as "requests to reappraise": assessing the adequacy and relevance of the beliefs which form the cognitive core of an emotional response. Requests to reappraise seem to suppose that emotions are perceptive in that they draw a person's attention to morally salient features of a situation (cf. §6.4.3). More obviously, they also assume that emotions propose action incentives, that they are motivations. It may not be, say, that one feels hard done by *because* one first perceives having been treated unfairly as much as it is that the feeling of being hard done by is *itself* perceptive of unfair treatment. In this case, the feelings also somehow have a hand in letting one know that one has been treated unfairly. In this way, emotions do—or seem to—"reveal value", as Stocker (1996) had it. Most relevant for present purposes, however, is the fact that the request to reappraise supposes that an emotional reaction can simply be wrong: to pursue the example further, one may feel hard done by and one may honestly believe that one has been the victim of mistreatment. But the feeling has a certain inalienable rationale even where the belief to which it is connected is entirely fallacious. Recall that Callahan (1980) thought that professional and practical ethics pedagogy should prioritize over every other educational aim attempts to achieve imaginative and affective involvement with moral problems not because they merely "encourage" or "promote" rich, truthful, and engaging insight into moral problems. Such moral imaginative involvement in moral problems actually irreducibly *constitutes* a form of moral insight for which there is no substitute (cf. §1.2). Callahan, however, was fully alive too to the fact that even if affective responses to a moral problem are always rational—that is, "rational" taken as the contrary of arational, based on no reasons at all—this does not entail that they may not sometimes be irrational—that is, wrapped up with an erroneous belief set. This was what Callahan meant when he said, "imagination and analysis need each other" (1980, p. 65): with the pedagogical imperative to stimulate the moral imagination comes a concomitant imperative to submit spontaneous emotional responses to the regulative constraint of reflective judgement (cf. Callahan, 1980, p. 65 and §1.2 above) that is, to request to reappraise.

Peters (1972/1998) states firmly that the rational scrutiny of spontaneous affective responses is a process which has a claim to being a genuine (and perhaps *the only* genuine) emotion-educating process, in his terms. Observe, however, that there is a subtle but important tension built into this very idea. So construed, emotion education, by focusing necessarily on the cognitive dimension of emotional experience, the dimension susceptible to scrutiny by reference to public standards of assessment, has a weak identity as *éducation sentimentale*. Concisely stated, it attempts at emotional formation not directly but through forms of rational reflection. Now this prima facie banal observation is not meant as a critique of Peters' conception of emotion education; I believe, in fact, that any suggestion to disqualify reappraisal as a variety of emotion education on such grounds would amount to conceptual hair-splitting. Its importance for the purposes of this chapter, which (to repeat) is to consider the implications of the foregoing studies for contemporary practices of professional and practical ethics education, is that it explains and justifies my intentional avoidance of any direct commentary on the theme of the pedagogy of reappraisal. The education paths in the field of the epistemological relation between beliefs and the world and the basics of valid inference are extensive and well trodden; my intention has not been to speak to concerns that are proper to critical thinking. Three issues which are, however, consistent with these studies' remit and that relate to the cognitive dimension of compassionate empathic responding beg commentary and they will be treated in this chapter's and this work's terminal subsections respectively. First, there is the issue of education for moral sensitivity and whether it constitutes a form of moral emotion education. Second, it is observed that the necessary particularity of compassionate empathic responding implies the necessary particularity of education for rational compassionate empathizing. Third, I claim that the close moral-psychological connection between active concern for others and the ability to grasp the notion of moral bindingness (or normativity) that has been recorded in these pages suggests one way to refresh the standard theoretical content that is now a typical feature of practical and professional ethics.

7.3.1 "Moral Sensitivity": A Misnomer?

Situational moral perception, or "moral sensitivity" as it is sometimes called (cf. Rest, 1986), draws on capacities of empathic response. This claim featured in §1.2 as one of the reasons in favour of bringing empathic development into the fold of top aims in professional and practical ethics education. Moral sensitivity, largely owing to the influence of Rest's four-component model of morality (cf. Rest, 1983, 1984, 1986) is an established, if variously interpreted, construct in research in moral education and moral psychology.[10] According to Rest's (1983, 1984, 1986) account, if moral judgement is the capacity which facilitates the identification of morally right or preferable action choices on the basis of considered reflection (component 2), if moral motivation is synonymous with moral integrity or moral responsibility, the prioritization of moral values over other values and action incentives (component 3), and if moral character corresponds to questions surrounding the determination to pursue moral goals and overcome impediments to the execution of moral acts (component 4), the moral sensitivity component embraces the perception of situations as presenting a moral problem and imagining and predicting the effects of action alternatives on the welfare of potentially affected parties (component 1). Among the outcomes of the scientific investigation of moral sensitivity

---

[10] In the early 1980s, James Rest developed the four-component model of morality in order to combine various theoretical perspectives on moral functioning into a single coherent framework (cf. Rest, 1983). Rest perceived that the theories of moral functioning vying for dominance during that period—the cognitive-developmental approach, the psychoanalytic approach, the empathy-based approach, and the socialization approach—made unwarranted claims to comprehensiveness. In his alternative view, each theory was better conceived as highlighting just one of several aspects of moral functioning. These aspects became the basic constructs of his multi-component model. Much as Rest intended it (cf. 1986), the four-component model continues to have taxonomic importance, loosely delineating four branches of moral psychology as a field of empirical research and four corresponding areas of moral educational intervention. You and Bebeau (2005) have recently reviewed the empirical research on the construct of moral sensitivity.

has been, in addition to no less than 20 psychological measures of moral sensitivity at You and Bebeau's (2005) count, a modest body of empirical evidence on the effect of ethics teaching on capacities of moral sensitivity. The result should bring comfort to educators concerned that most professional and practical ethics teaching is not fit for purpose as a device for the development of skills in situational moral perception. You and Bebeau (2005) cite the results of six studies as grounds that moral sensitivity "can be taught and improved through instruction" (p. 11). Methodologically, each study used comparative scores on standard psychological tests of moral sensitivity between an experiment group and a control group and, in all cases except one, the independent variable was participation in what appear from You and Bebeau's (2005) description to be a rather standard subject area-specific ethics course (cf. Ofsthun, 1986; Liebowitz, 1990; Clarkeburn, 2002; Myyry & Helkama, 2002; Sirin et al., 2003).[11] And all these studies observed a modest improvement in situational moral perception abilities.

Professional and practical ethics education, then, would appear to address moral sensitivity in spite of itself.

But is situational moral perception a predominantly *affective* capacity and would the educational promotion of capacities of situational moral perception constitute a form of *éducation sentimentale*? Rest (1986), for one, seemed to think it was. He implies that Hoffman's (1978, 1981, 2000) account of empathic development lends credence to the assumption that moral sensitivity is a centrally affective process in that it presupposes a basic aversive affective response ("distress") to others' actual or prospective distress. Indeed, the term "moral sensitivity" itself is loaded in favour of this interpretation; the very words connote the rallying of affective insight. Scholars in both psychology and ethics who work with the construct have rarely, however, scrutinized this claim, tending instead to apparently assume that moral sensitivity depends on affective capacities of response (e.g., Morton, et al., 2006, p. 390; cf. Rest, 1986; Bebeau, 1994; Pizarro, 2000; Sherman, 1990, p. 150; cf. Murdoch, 1970; Blum, 1980, 1991; Vetlesen, 1996; Callahan, 1980; Combs, 1998) or to diplomatically avoid taking a stand on the question (e.g., Volker, 1984; Hébert et al., 1990, 1992; Herman, 1996; Akabayashi, 2004).

The discussion in §5.4 on the role of affect in moral judgement calls into serious doubt the suggestion that the education of situational moral perception is unambiguously a form of moral emotion education. There, it was reasoned that if the process of moral sensitivity does draw significantly on affective capacities of response, that would predict that *impairment* of moral sensitivity should be characteristic of psychopathy, a diagnostic category in abnormal psychology associated with intact cognitive accompanied affective inertness.

Drawing on evidence concerning the moral functioning of psychopaths it was argued that moral sensitivity does not appear to be a predominantly affective moral

---

[11] The unique exception was the study by Ofsthun (1986) which investigated the impact of a novel pedagogical model specifically designed for the purposes of enhancing moral sensitivity and connected processes.

faculty. For psychopaths are indeed morally sensitive in the relevant situational-moral perceptive sense. They have no apparent endemic trouble in "picking out morally salient features of a situation". From this conjecture follows an important and perhaps counterintuitive educational truth. There is no doubt, of course, that setting out in practical and professional ethics education to support the development of capacities of situational moral perception is to target some important aspect of moral functioning. But if one believes that in educationally addressing situational moral perception one is *thereby* addressing the hitherto educationally "neglected" affective dimensions of moral functioning, one seems simply to be mistaken.[12]

7.3.2 Empathic Décalage

The overview in §§3.4 and 4.4, respectively, of the psychological processes which underlie experiences of compassionate empathy and forms of empathic bias was illuminating for at least three reasons. First, a theory of these processes helps to account two widely recognized features of compassionate empathic responding: (1) that compassionate empathic responses are partial to those who are in one's immediate spatial and temporal proximity (i.e., the here and now bias) and with whom one identifies; and, (2) that, among people whose conscience and capacities for advanced situational moral insight are present and generally strong and intact, compassionate empathizing is on the whole a highly reliable and predictable response (cf. also the discussion in §7.1). Second, the fact that compassionate empathizing seems to be mediated by a range of psychological processes calls into serious question the persistent moral-psychological folk belief that one may *only* come to empathize by way of an imaginative process of perspective-taking, through "changing places in fancy with the sufferer" in Smith's (1790/1976) evocative phrase. Third, and most importantly from the present perspective, the fact that experiences of compassionate empathy are associative and conditioned, as we saw, predicts that compassionate empathic responding will display a high degree of individual-specificity given their dependence on conditioning, personal associations with surface cues, or the narrative structure of the situation, and so on. A range of discrete ways that such predispositions could run against the imperative of balanced or rational compassion are well documented, all of which may be considered for our purposes forms of developmental "décalage".

"Décalage", a term borrowed from classical cognitive development theory, refers to inconsistencies in the level of differentiation of cognitive operations across a range of physical or social activities (cf. Reimer, 1989). Viewed from a pedagogical standpoint, the educational problem décalage identifies is akin to the educational

---

[12] The finding that moral sensitivity is not dependent on affective capacities of response should not be taken to imply the reductivist thesis that moral sensitivity is therefore "nothing but" a form of moral judgement. Moral sensitivity's status as an analytically distinct component of moral functioning depends in no way on it being predominantly affective.

problem of "transference", or how and whether skills and competencies gained in formally structured or more or less dry didactic contexts (like getting good at Sudoku puzzles or becoming vicariously involved in the life of a character in a novel) improves performance when it comes to other activities which draw on some of the same abilities (like remembering to tie ones shoes or becoming vicariously involved in the lives of actual human beings). In moral development theory, "décalage" describes, for instance, the well-documented phenomenon where adolescent boys show a degree of competence and sophistication in thinking about moral questions related to areas such as law or property which is not available to them in regards to the domain of sexuality (cf. Gilligan et al., 1971).[13]

That addressing compassionate empathic *décalage* must be a central preoccupation of education for compassionate empathy in professional and practical ethics education is, I think, a fairly direct implication of the position arrived at in §7.1 about the reliability of compassionate empathic responding. Worries about wholesale or comprehensive empathic torpidity get education for appropriate compassionate empathic responding off on the wrong foot; it is a starting point that reflects a profound mis-appreciation of empathic responding. It is a fundamental and necessary social capacity. There is, then, the possibly banal claim that psychologically normal adults do not need to be taught basic responsiveness to others' needs. And there is the even more obvious fact that many human beings who would clearly count as normal from the point of view of social functioning are capable of monstrous systematic departures from the ideal of appropriate empathic responding. I posit that the second phenomenon is not so difficult to square with the first when seen as the manifestation of what are almost certainly heavily socially informed varieties of empathic décalage. If empathy is not teachable to adults, what they more plausibly can learn in higher education is the appropriate extension of naturally occurring empathic capacities in three identifiable ways corresponding to three identifiable forms of empathic décalage. First, there are cases where a person has an exaggerated sensitivity or, alternatively, is perceptually very weak faced with harms connected with one or another issue of recurrent moral concern, issues such as punishment, property, law, freedom, and the roles and concerns of authority and affection, life, fairness, truth, to borrow from Kohlberg's (1978, p. 39) rough and ready list of the "ten universal moral values or issues of concern". One may, for

---

[13] This phenomenon is sometimes referred to as "moral segmentation" (cf. Rest, 1979). Both moral segmentation and décalage are theoretical postulates which are supposed to account for empirical data on moral judgement which speaks against Kohlberg's Piagetan hypothesis that the stages of moral judgement are "structured wholes" (cf. Colby & Kohlberg, 1987). The long and short of it is that according to classical stage theory an individual should consider any cognitive problem from the perspective of his or her current stage of development but data on moral judgement almost always seems to record a stage preference "spread" over not two but *three* stages; if subjects showed preference for two stages, these data could presumably be accounted for by the hypothesis that they are in transition from one stage to another. Some authors speak of décalage and moral segmentation as two distinct constructs (cf., e.g., Beck et al., 1999) but for our purposes it is sufficient to treat them as interchangeably referring to the assumption that people commonly use different stage principles or, in more common parlance, moral standards in different situations.

instance, be keenly attuned to unfairness or injustice but be quite callous towards, say, the kind of suffering caused by disappointment in fair competition or towards physical or psychological discomfort or pain (cf. Blum, 1991, p. 716). Second, an individual's moral sensitivity may be inconsistent across what Nunner-Winkler (1994) refers to as "moral objects" and what Taylor (cf. 1989) discusses under the heading of "moral ontology": who is considered to be the appropriate recipient of moral attention. Again, basically normal moral agents would recognize some moral objects but they might lack appropriate unity by being more or less (or in extreme cases only) sensitive to the suffering of one or another category of moral being, if you will. Typical categories of this sort would be, of course, people of a certain identifiable ethnicity or social class, adults or children but could also be manifest in greater moral sensitivity towards animals or nature as a whole against people (cf. Blum, 1991, p. 716). Third, just as the same moral agent can display strong *moral reasoning* competencies in some theme area (e.g., bioethics or the environment) but weak in others (e.g., sexuality) so too might one expect there to be variations in *moral sensitivity* across different moral theme areas. One who, say, is numb at the prospect of committing egregious harms to others in the course of their business or financial dealings may well be affronted by, say, the prospect of stem cell research or assisted suicide. These forms of empathic décalage may overlap and such overlaps may be worth exploring but even this admittedly unrefined account has significant heuristic value. Again, it eases the tension between the psychological normality of intact capacities of empathic response to suffering with the fact of selective human callousness, but it also maps out the specific areas where one can begin to educationally address forms of empathic décalage (i.e., vis-à-vis recurrent moral issues, categories of moral being, and moral theme areas). Finally it shows how addressing compassionate empathy in practical ethics education is not singular and monolithic but as particularist as empathic responding is itself. In Blum's words, cultivating compassionate empathy "will involve nurturing or developing some distinct sensitivities and will involve different tasks and processes for different persons with respect to different objects of sympathy or empathy" (1991, p. 717).

Compassionate-empathic décalage as a challenge of ethics teaching in higher education takes us right back, of course, to a concern that lies at the heart of Nussbaum's justification of literary study as a form of education for compassionate citizenry in particular and, in general, the use of literature in professional and practical ethics education as a "request to imitate" as we had it in §7.2, to evoke a sense of solidarity and compassion with certain people or groups in certain aversive circumstances. A tragic predicament for one—a woman, a disabled, social excluded or vulnerable person, a migrant, perhaps an animal as a sentient being—is a tragic predicament for all. It is clear that, for that purpose, the right books to read are the ones that assist in overcoming ontological décalage—or, in Nussbaum's language, "extending concern"—by encouraging identification with social groups or other categories of moral identity with whom students are liable to *resist* identifying. This feature of Nussbaum's proposal underscores, again, the strong and necessary particularism of education for appropriate compassionate empathic responding; there can be guidelines but no recipes. What is certain, though, is that in order for an educator to be in a position to choose educational material appropriate for the purposes of countering empathic décalage he must know his students well and have an accurate reading of their states of empathic segmentation.

When considering the source of empathic décalage, informal socialization and, in particular, the influence of families, friends, the media, and the like naturally come first to mind. But empathic segmentation can occur as a result of socialization within the context of academic and especially professional formation in higher education itself. Although interventions designed to target such dispositions could at best cover up the symptoms but, as it were, not cure the disease itself, it is not difficult to imagine how specific pedagogical initiatives could be devised to counter precisely this influence. There is no doubt that such a process of, if you will, demoralization occurs to varying degrees in programmes of professional preparation other than in medicine but here the phenomenon seems more pronounced; while its causes are still poorly understood, the phenomenon itself is well documented and so it will serve as our example.

The results of empirical research into the moral development of medical students paints an unsettling picture: when compared with their peers in other programmes of study, medical students tend to start their studies with atypically high "moral ideals" and then gradually to lose them, and frequently lose them quite dramatically, as they progress through their studies (cf., e.g., Feudtner et al., 1994; Coulehan & Williams, 2001). Comparative stagnation of cognitive moral development is also endemic to this group (cf. reviews in Self & Baldwin, 1994; and in Rest et al., 1999). The so-called hidden curriculum, the personality profile of candidates attracted to medical studies, and the competitive, hierarchical, and stressful context of professional medical training are consistently conjectured as contributing factors (cf., e.g., Boon & Turner, 2004; Coulehan & Williams, 2001; Kelly & Verghese, 1997; Hafferty & Franks, 1994).

From the present perspective, however, the most important observed tendency among medical students is that over the course of their studies they seem to become more *dis*passionateness and less *com*passionate towards patients. Recorded among medical students is increasing cynicism about their helping role and fiduciary responsibility, and the use of embarrassingly pejorative terms to describe patients; some commentators regard these attitudes and behaviours as symptomatic of the socialization of medical students into a medical culture which dehumanizes patients (cf., e.g., Hafferty & Franks, 1994; Mizrahi, 1986; Liederman & Grisso, 1985).[14] Whatever one may think of the focus of medical training to instruct in the curing of disease rather than the healing of the person and especially its effects in terms of medical socialization—a controversial issue even among medical educators themselves—few could fail to appreciate that the kind of continual confrontation with suffering, disease, and death that is typical in the first years of clinical work is enough to traumatize any young person. Indeed, Kelly and Verghese (1997) speculate, not

---

[14] The phenomenon of patient dehumanization in medical culture was brought to widespread public attention by Shem's novel, *The house of God* (1986) and Konner's anecdotal non-fictional work, *Becoming a doctor* (1987).

implausibly, that weak empathizing and patient dehumanization on the part of medical students might very well be saddening attempts at psychological self-defence.

Irrespective of its causes, one can well imagine a medical educator familiar with the research on this phenomenon to view his or her students as being at risk of developing precisely a form of empathic décalage consisting of inappropriate weak empathizing with patients as a group and, especially considering the centrality of empathy and compassion to medical role morality,[15] resolve to use curricular time to address it. Barnbaum (2001) has developed a pedagogical tool that such an educator might seriously consider adopting. Her proposal was not explicitly intended with the dehumanization phenomenon in mind but one can see immediately its applicability. Very briefly, Barnbaum's strategy tries to provide support for identification with patients and teach pathology at the same time by using what she calls "lottery assignments". At the beginning of the semester, each student is randomly assigned a disease that they "get". Throughout the semester, the students are invited to place themselves vicariously in the patient's position by preparing and presenting periodic reports on the disease's progress from birth to death. An explicit requirement of the learning activity is to report on the effects of the disease on the personal and private aspects of the sufferer's life. In our terms, this multistage learning activity is, if you will, a protracted request to imagine: to engage in other- rather than self-focused perspective-taking, the more empathically evocative of the two primary sub-forms of perspective-taking (cf. §§6.3 and 3.4.2).

7.3.3 Consideration for Others and Teaching the Theory of Moral Judgement

Courses in practical ethics traditionally begin with a unit which overviews "approaches to ethics".[16] Until only about a decade ago, this duty required the presentation of only deontologism and consequentialism but it has, in response to significant recent developments in normative ethics, been latterly extended to virtue ethics. The educational utility of this exercise depends to some degree on the kind of course that is to follow. In academic courses, courses which proceed by studying a selection of philosophical essays which develop and defend a policy position vis-à-vis one or another morally controversial practice (self-regarding suicide, capital punishment, vivisection, and so on), the theoretical introduction can provide an analytical framework in reference to which the argumentative essays' justificatory appeals may be categorized and comprehended on an abstract level. In case-based courses, the theory of moral reasoning may operate as a set of guidelines describing

---

[15] See the discussion of this point in §1.2.

[16] Extensive critical discussions of the three general theories of normative ethics can be found in Baron et al. (1997).

basically correct if possibly incompatible procedures which may be used to generate a justified position vis-à-vis the particular moral problem a case presents.[17]

Owing to the fact that contemporary practical ethics' pedigree lies in realist conceptions of moral philosophy rather than moral psychology (cf. §1.1), the theory of cognitive moral development is rarely treated in such theoretical introductions. The inclusion of such a unit, say, on Kohlberg's theory is, of course, not inconceivable and possibly justified.[18] My intention in raising this possibility, however, is not to recommend its ascension to the cannon of theoretical ideas about moral reasoning traditionally introduced in courses in practical ethics as much as it is to draw attention to some empirical research that speaks to the general significance of moral theory in the context of professional and practical ethics education. Research into the effects of the direct teaching of Kohlberg's theory on cognitive-moral development modestly supports the tradition of a theoretical introduction in practical ethics. In an ageing but still widely cited meta-analysis of moral education intervention studies using the Defining Issues Test (DIT), Schläfli et al. (1985) found that study participants who were *not* asked to learn about Kohlberg's theory typically made about half the gain in terms of a positive effect on moral reasoning as did those to whom the theory was taught. The gains recorded were modest but it is nevertheless an interesting result; from it I take nothing more than, again, that there might indeed be a kernel of wisdom in the habit of including some relevant aspects of moral theory as part of the content of practical ethics courses.

This inference, however, seems open to two objections. First, and against the evidence that learning about Kohlberg's theory improves DIT scores itself, *obviously*, one might claim, far from being indicative of any structural-cognitive changes, the teacher has simply "taught to the test". In effect, by introducing the students to Kohlberg's theory she just gave the students the right answers to the DIT. This objection loses much of its force, however, when one considers that it has become part of the standard explanation for why higher stages of moral development are not just different but "better" than lower stages to point out that while it is easy for anyone to identify considerations that represent stages of moral judgement lower than one's own stage—that is to say, to "fake down"—efforts to "fake up" almost invariably fail (cf. Rest et al. 1969; McGeorge, 1975; and Rest, 1994). But, one could object further, even if we accept that registered increases in post-test scores in these cases is not the result of clever manipulation on the part of the test subjects but a true indication of development; what is true of the theory of cognitive developmentalism might not be true of the theory of normative ethics. Consequentialism and deontologism are typically categorized as post-conventional or Level III modes of moral thinking (Rest et al., 1997). According to the Blatt effect, people are generally unable to recognize the strategic advantage of modes of reasoning beyond one stage above their own (cf. discussions in Schrader, 1993; and Reimer, 1989) and so the theoretical

---

[17] The standard pedagogical approaches to teaching practical ethics and the theory-based/case-based teaching distinction is discussed in more detail in §1.5.

[18] See Schrader (1993) for an example of a model of ethics education for professionals in education based on Kohlberg's theory of cognitive moral development.

discussion of these approaches would be all but incomprehensible to every student except those who would score on the upper conventional range of Level II. To the rest it would be of little educational value from the point of view of cognitive moral development. Lucky thing for teachers of practical ethics in higher education, then, that demographically speaking the achievement of stage 4 happens not to be atypical of their constituency (cf. Rest & Narváez, 1994).[19]

Undaunted by these objections, I thus repeat that the results recorded in Schläfli et al. (1985) provide some modest confirmation of what I think most instructors suspect: that the standard theoretical introduction to practical ethics courses not only improves general philosophical culture, it also contributes in a meaningful way to the development of practical wisdom. These considerations suggest to me that, *mutatis mutandis*, a similar benefit may be derived from a theoretical introduction to consideration for others as an aspect of moral experience. But what kind of benefit should one expect from insight into the apparent fact that morality is a product of a human tendency towards consideration for others in this sense?

In light of the foregoing discussion of the role of compassionate empathy in moral judgement, it seems to me that one should emphatically not expect direct measurable preference for higher quality moral reasons or consistent spontaneous generation thereof in the manner of Kohlberg's theory of cognitive moral development.[20] Nor, presumably, should one expect greater competency in generating convincing arguments in favour of one action alternative or another in the face of a moral problem. Moral maturity, in this sense, seems to suppose at most the *cognitive mastery* of various and in all likelihood incommensurable categories of harm (e.g., pain, embarrassment, tragedy, humiliation, injustice, death, destitution, disappointment, etc.) and well-being (e.g., dignity, happiness, fairness, flourishing, care, respect, life, freedom) but it does not seem to imply *caring about* avoiding them or promoting them among human beings (cf. discussion of Herman, 1996 and in §§6.3 and 5.4). What one can realistically hope that such insight would provide is greater lucidity about the normativity of moral judgements—that is, the reason why moral

---

[19] It is worth noting that the notion that learning about the theory of cognitive developmentalism is favourable to cognitive moral development, by contrast, is not open to this objection but one should not lose sight of the fact that those exposed to the theory probably benefit not from learning about the theory *as a whole* but from the explication of the stages of moral reasoning one step above their own and, connectedly, the inadequacies of their own current level of moral development and those levels below it. To my knowledge, the hypothesis that the traditional introductory unit on approaches to normative ethics in practical ethics courses is beneficial to the development of moral reasoning competencies has never been the subject of empirical investigation.

[20] There seems to be a state of theoretical stalemate over whether the correct conceptualization of "being in" a particular stage of moral development is best characterized as a "preference" for or "consistent acceptability-rating" of certain types of justificatory reasons corresponding to Kohlberg's basic 6-stage schema. The Defining Issues Test, a standard psychological measure in North America supposes "stage-preference" whereas Lind's upstart Moral Judgement Test, widely used in Europe, is constructed on the "stage-consistency" approach (cf. Rest et al., 1997; Lind, 2002). The admittedly awkward formulation attempts to recognize both approaches without taking a position on the question.

reasons *should* be motivationally compelling or what it actually *means* to act in accordance with a moral reason.

A common tendency can perhaps be detected, as clear as it is apparently misguided, to view the problem of moral motivation as a problem of self-mastery or self-control. A choice to act in accordance with one's best moral judgement, in other words, is widely thought to be *controlled by* rather than *imbued with* reason. This gives the false impression that the decision to act in a way that one has come to regard, possibly after a period of rational reflection, as morally best is an internal matter or an entirely personal affair. However, when faced with the choice, in a particular set of circumstances, of acting either the way one regards as being morally best or according to one or another countervailing hypothetical motivation like material interest, fear of social sanction, or the promotion of a particular social ethos, a person who conceives of what is at stake in a moral problem as being human weal and woe at least has a clear-sighted comprehension what the choice is *between*: that is to say, and to adopt Vetlesen's (1994) formulation, the decision is over whether or not to support the social institution of morality and its constitutional aim of protecting individuals in their natural vulnerability (cf., e.g., pp. 312–315). From this perspective, the problem of moral motivation appears as an *inter-* but not as an *intra*-subjective problem—that is, an evaluative question of the quality of one's relations with one's co-subjects. It is a (probably untestable) empirical question and remains to be seen whether people who *interpret* moral problems as problems of how to best further well-being and avoid harm—as opposed, say, to interpreting moral problems as turning on the ethical–existential question of "What kind of person am I?" (Walker & Henning, 2004; and various texts in Lapsley & Narváez, 2004; cf. also n. 6 above) or the practical–rational problem of determining whether the moral reasons relevant to a particular problem are sufficiently compelling to be will-determining in the face of countervailing hypothetical reasons (Habermas, 1993b)—tend towards greater consistency between moral judgement and moral motivation. The moral psychology of consideration for others, or empathy, seem to suggest that they just might: there is an internal conceptual connection between consideration for others and motivation in that empathy just is an emotion characterized as a regard for others present or perspective suffering as something to be alleviated or avoided (cf. Blum, 1980b). Moreover, 30 years of research in social psychology on empathy and pro-social and helping behaviour bears the connection out (see discussions in §§2.2.2. and 3.3). If bothering about morality is of a piece with something like responding to the recognition of others' vulnerability with concern for their weal and woe, to this extent, moral wisdom necessarily draws on insight into others' perspectives, assessing their demands, and taking those demands seriously. Some of the blame for the fact that this is almost never brought to the attention of students of professional and practical ethics can be laid at the door of the persistently dualistic thinking about reason and emotion in popular ethical culture and a symptom of this dualism in practical ethics education is the tendency for students, not infrequently following the example of their instructors, to view approaching a moral problem with sublime disinterestedness as a sign of intellectual sophistication rather than philistine insensitivity. If a compassionate empathic disposition is the backdrop for the operations of moral perception, moral reasoning, and moral integrity, making this apparent fact of moral life explicit may well be the most important and least considered thing that teachers of practical ethics can do to advance the cause of appropriate compassionate empathizing in professional and practical ethics education.

References

Adelman, P.K., & Zajonc, R. (1989). Facial efference and the experience of emotion. Annual review of psychology, 40, 249–280.

Aderman, D., Brehm, S.S., & Katz, L.B. (1974). Empathic observation of an innocent victim: The just world revisited. Journal of personality and social psychology, 29, 342–347.

Afronreed, J. (1968). Conduct and conscience: The socialization of internalised control over behavior. New York: Academic Press.

Akabayashi, A., Slingsby, B.T., Kai, I., Nishimura, T., & Yamagishi, A. (2004). The development of a brief and objective method for evaluating moral sensitivity and reasoning in medical students. BMC medical ethics, 5 (1).

Alcoff, L., & Potter, E. (eds.). (1993). Epistemologies. New York: Routledge.

Allison, H. (1990). Kant's theory of freedom. Cambridge.: Cambridge University Press.

American Association of Medical Colleges Core Curriculum Working Group (2000). Graduate medical education core curriculum. Washington DC: Association of American Medical Colleges.

Andreopoulos, G.J., & Claude, R.P. (eds.). (1997). Human rights education for the twenty-first century. Philadelphia: University of Pennsylvania Press.

Annis, D.B. (1992). Teaching ethics in higher education. Metaphilosophy, 234 (1 & 2), 187–202.

Anscombe, G.E.M. (1958). Modern moral philosophy. Philosophy, 33, 1–19.

Arendt, H. (1961/1994). Eichmann in Jerusalem: A report on the banality of evil. New York: Penguin.

Aristotle. (4th century B.C.E./1955). Nicomachean ethics, 2nd ed., J.A.K. Thomson (trans.). London: Penguin.

Aristotle. (1991). On rhetoric, G.A. Kennedy (trans.). Oxford: Oxford University Press.

Arnold, M.B. (1960). Emotion and personality. New York: Columbia University Press.

Arsenio, W.F. & Lemerise, E.A. (2004). Aggression and moral development: Integrating social information processing and moral domain models. Child Development, 75, 987–1002.

Ashcroft, R. (2001). How does empathy develop? Lancet, 357 (9250), 331.

Atkinson, R.L., Atkinson, R.C., & Hilgard, E. (1983). Introduction to psychology, New York: Harcourt Brace and Jovanovich.

Averill, J.R. (1973). Personal control over aversive stimuli and its relationship to stress, Psychological bulletin, 80, 286–303.

Baier, K. (1965). The moral point of view. New York: Random House.

Bandura, A. (1977). Self-efficacy: Toward a unifying theory of behavioral change. Psychological review, 84 (2), 191–215.

Barnbaum, D.R. (2001). Teaching empathy in medical ethics. Teaching philosophy, 24 (1), 63–75.

Baron, M. (1984). The alleged moral repugnance of acting from duty. Journal of philosophy, 81, 197–219.

Baron-Cohen, S. (1989). The autistic child's theory of mind: a case of specific developmental delay. Journal of Child Psychology and Psychiatry, 30, 285–297.

Baron, M. (1991). Impartiality and friendship. Ethics, 101, 836–857.

Baron, M. (1997). Kantian ethics. In M. Baron, P. Pettit, & M. Slote (eds.), Three methods of ethics (pp. 3–91). Oxford: Blackwell.

Baron, M., Pettit, P., & Slote, M. (1997). Three methods of ethics. Oxford: Blackwell.

Barrett, R. (1994). On emotion as a lapse from rationality, Journal of moral education, 23 (2), 135–143.

Batson, C.D. (1991). The altruism question: Toward a social-psychological answer. Hillsdale. NJ: Erlbaum.

Batson, C.D., & Coke, J.S. (1981). Empathy: A source of altruistic behavior? In J. P. Rushton & R. M. Sorrento (eds.), Altruism and helping behavior: Social, personality, and developmental perspectives (pp. 167–211). Hillsdale: Erlbaum.

Batson, C.D., & Shaw, L.L. (1991). Evidence for altruism: Toward a pluralism of prosocial motives. Psychological inquiry, 2, 107–122.

Batson, C.D., & Weeks, J.L. (1996). Mood effects of unsuccessful helping: Another test of the empathy-altruism hypothesis. Personality and social psychology bulletin, 11, 148–157.

Batson, C.D., Early, S., & Salvarani, G. (1997). Perspective taking: Imagining how another feels versus imagining how you would feel. Personality and social psychology bulletin, 23 (7), 751–758.

Batson, C.D., Klein, T.R., Highburger, L., & Shaw, L. (1995). Immorality from empathy-induced altruism. Journal of personality and social psychology, 68, 1042–1054.

Batson, C.D., Shaw, L.L., & Oleson, K.C. (1992). Differentiating affect, mood and emotion: Toward functionally based conceptual distinctions. In M.S. Clarke (ed.), Review of personality and social psychology, Vol. 13 (pp. 294–326). Newbury Park: Sage.

Batson, C.D., Sympson, S.C., & Hindman, J.L. (1996). "I've been there, too": Effect on empathy of prior experience with a need. Personality and social psychology bulletin, 22, 474–482.

Batson, C.D., Turk, C.L., Shaw, L.L., & Klein, T.R. (1995). Information function of empathic emotion: Learning that we value the other's welfare. Journal of personality and social psychology, 68 (2), 300–313.

Beauchamp, T.L., & Childress, J.F. (2001). Principles of biomedical ethics, 5th ed. New York: Oxford University Press.

Bebeau, M. (1994). Influencing the moral dimensions of dental practice. In J. Rest & D. Narváez (eds.), Moral development and the professions (pp. 121–146). Mahwah, NJ: Erlbaum.

Bebeau, M.J., Rest, J.R., & Yamoor, C.M. (1985). Measuring dental students' ethical sensitivity. Journal of Dental Education, 48(4), 225–235.

Bebeau, M. (2002). The Defining Issues Test and the four component model: Contributions to professional education. Journal of moral education, 31(3), 121–295.

Beck, K., Heinrichs, K., Minnameier, G., & ParcheKawik, K.. (1999). Homogeneity of moral judgement? Apprentices solving business conflicts. Journal of moral education, 28 (4), 429–443.

Bellah, R., Madsen, R., Sullivan, W.M., Swidler, A., & Tipton, S.M. (1985). Habits of the heart: Individualism and commitment in American life. Berkeley, CA: University of California Press.

Benbassat, J., & Baumal, R. (2004). What is empathy and how can it be promoted during clinical clerkships? Academic medicine, 78 (9), 832–839.

Benner, D. (1979). Lässt sich das Technologieproblem durch eine Ersatztechnologie lösen? eine Auseinandersetzung mit N. Luhmann und K.-E. Schorrs Thesen zum Technologiedefizit der Erziehung [Can the technology problem be solved by a technology of replacement? A debate with N. Luhmann and K-E. Schorr on the technological deficit of education]. Zeitschrift für Pädagogik [Journal of pedagogy], 25 (3), 367–375.

Ben Ze'ev, A. (2000). The subtlety of emotions. Cambridge, MA: MIT Press.

Ben Ze'ev, A. (2001). Are envy, anger, and resentment moral emotions? Philosophical explorations, 5 (2), 148–154.

Bevis, O., & Watson, J. (1989). Toward a caring curriculum. New York: National League for Nursing.

Blackburn, P. (1988). On moral judgement and personality disorders. British journal of psychiatry, 153, 505–512.

Blair, R.J.R. & Cipolotti, L. (2001). Impaired social response reversal: a case of 'acquired sociopathy'. Brain, 123, 1122–1141.

Blair, R.J.R., Jones, L., Clark, F., & Smith, M. (1995). Is the psychopath 'morally insane'? Personality individual differences, 19, 741–752.

Blair, R.J.R. (1996). Brief report: morality in the autistic child. Journal of Autism and Developmental Disorders, 26, 571–579.

Blair, J., Mitchell, D., & Blair, K. (2005). The psychopath. Oxford: Blackwell.

Blasi, A. (1980). Bridging moral cognition and moral action: A critical review of the literature. Psychological bulletin, 88, 1–45.

Blasi, A. (1999). Emotions and moral motivation. Journal for the theory of social behaviour, 29 (1), 1–19.

Blum, L. (1980a). Friendship, altruism and morality. London: Routledge & Kegan Paul.

Blum, L. (1980b). Compassion. In A.O. Rorty (ed.), Explaining emotions (pp. 506–517). Berkeley, CA: University of California Press.

Blum, L. (1991). Moral perception and particularity. Ethics, 101 (3), 701–725.

Blustein, J. (1991). Care and commitment. Oxford: Oxford University Press.

Boon, K., & Turner, J. (2004). Ethical and professional conduct of medical students: Review of current assessment measures and controversies. Journal of medical ethics, 30, 221–226.

Bowie, N.E. (2003). The role of ethics in professional education. In R. Curren (ed.), Companion to the philosophy of education (pp. 617–628). Oxford: Blackwell.

Boyd, D.R. (1990). The study of moral development: A bridge over the is–ought gap. In T. Wren (ed.), The moral domain: Essays in the ongoing discussion between philosophy and psychology (pp. 129–150). Cambridge, MA: MIT Press.

Brantenberg, G. (1977/1985). Egalia's Daughters. Seattle, WA: Seal Press.

Bricker, D.C. (1993). Character and moral reasoning: An Aristotelian perspective. In K.A. Strike & P.L. Ternasky (eds.), Ethics for professionals in education (pp. 13–26). New York: Teachers College Press.

Brink, D. (2001). Impartiality and associative duties. Utilitas, 19 (3), 152–172.

Britzman, D. (2003). Lost subjects, contested objects: Toward a psychoanalytic inquiry of learning. AlbanyNY: State University of New York Press.

Burkhardt, M.A., & Nathaniel, A.K. (2001). Ethics and issues in contemporary nursing, 2nd ed. Louisville, KY: Delmar.

Callahan, D. (1980). Goals in the teaching of ethics. In D. Callan & S. Bok (eds.), Hastings Center report on ethics teaching in higher education (pp. 61–80). New York: Plenum Press.

Callan, E. (1995). Common schools for common education. Canadian journal of education, 20, 251–271.

Campbell, R.L. (2005). Today, moral identity; tomorrow, self-esteem? Applied developmental psychology, 26, 235–240.

Carr, D. (1991). Educating the virtues. New York: Routledge.

Carr, D. (1996). After Kohlberg: Some implications of an ethics of virtue for the theory of moral education and development. Studies in philosophy and education, 15, 353–370.

Carr, D. (2000). Professionalism and ethics in education. London: Routledge.

Carr, D. (2001). Making sense of education. London: Routledge.

Carr, D. (2002). Moral education and the perils of developmentalism. Journal of moral education, 31 (1), 5–19.

Carr, D., & Steutel, J. (1999). The virtue approach to moral education: pointers, problems, and prospects. In D. Carr & J. Steutel (eds.), Virtue ethics and moral education (pp. 241–255). London: Routledge.

Chodorow, N. (1978). The reproduction of mothering: Psychoanalysis and the sociology of gender. Berkeley, CA: University of California Press.

Clarkeburn, H. (2002). A test for ethical sensitivity in science. Journal of moral education, 31 (4), 439–453.

Cleckley, H. (1950). The mask of sanity, 2nd ed. St Louis, MO: C.V. Mosby.

Code, L. (1991). What can she know: Feminist theory and the construction of knowledge. Ithaca, NY: Cornell University Press.

Code, L. (1994). "I know just how you feel": Empathy and the problem of epistemic authority. In E.S. Moore & M.A. Milligan (eds.), The empathic practitioner. New Brunswick, Canada: Rutgers University Press.

Cohen, D. (ed.). (1999). Educating minds and hearts: Social and emotional learning and the passage into adolescence. New York: Teacher's College Press.

Colby, A., & Damon, W. (1992). Some do care: Contemporary lives of moral commitment. New York: The Free Press.

Colby, A., & Kohlberg, L. (1987). The measure of moral judgement. 2 vols. Cambridge: Cambridge University Press.

Colby, A., Kohlberg, L., Speicher, B., Hewer, A., Candee, D., Gibbs, J., Power, C. (1987). The measurement of moral judgement, Vol. 1: Theoretical foundation and research validation, Vol. 2. Standard issue scoring manual. Cambridge: Cambridge University Press.

Coombs, J.R. (1998). Educational ethics: Are we on the right track?. Education theory, 48 (4), 555–570.

Cosmides, L. & Tooby, J. (1989). Evolutionary psychology and the generation of culture, Part II. Case study: A computational theory of social exchange. Ethology and sociobiology, 10, 51–97.

Costin, S.E., & Jones, C.J. (1992). Friendship as a facilitator of emotional responsiveness and prosocial interventions among young children. Developmental psychology, 28, 941–947.

Cottingham, J. (1983). Ethics and impartiality. Philosophical studies, 43, 83–99.

Coulehan, J., & Williams, P.C. (2001). Vanquishing virtue: The impact of medical education. Academic medicine, 76, 598–605.

Coulehan, J., & Williams, P. (2003). Conflicting professional values in medicine. Cambridge quarterly of healthcare ethics, 12 (1), 7–20.

Crick, N.R. & Dodge, K.A. (1996). Social information-processing mechanisms in reactive and proactive aggression. Child Development, 67, 993–1002.

Crisp, R. (ed.). (1998). How should one live? Essays on the virtues. Oxford: Oxford University Press.

Crisp, R., & Slote, M. (eds.). (1997). Virtue ethics. Oxford: Oxford University Press.

Dadds, M.R., Perry, Y., Hawes, D.J., Merz, S., Riddell, A.C., Haines, D.J., Solak, E., & Abeygunawardane, A.I. (2006). Attention to the eyes and fear-recognition deficits in child psychopathy. British journal of psychiatry, 189, 280–281.

Damasio, A.R. (1994). Descartes' error. New York: Putnam Group.

D'Silva, K., Dugan, C., & McCarthy, L. (2004). Does treatment really make psychopaths worse? A review of the evidence. Journal of Personality Disorders, 18, 163–77.

Darley, J.M., & Latane, B. (1968). Bystander intervention in emergencies: Diffusion of responsibility. Journal of personality and social psychology, 8, 377–383.

Darwall, S. (1995). The British moralists and the internal 'ought': 1640–1740. New York: Cambridge University Press.

Darwall, S. (ed.). (2002). Virtue ethics. Oxford: Blackwell.

Darwall, S., Gibbard, A., & Railton, P. (1992). Toward Fin de siècle ethics: Some trends. Philosophical review, 101 (1), 115–190.

Darwall, S.L., Gibbard, A., & Railton, P. (eds.). (1997). Moral discourse and practice: Some philosophical approaches. New York: Oxford University Press.

Davis, M.H. (1983). Measuring individual differences in empathy: Evidence for a multidimensional approach. Journal of personality and social psychology, 44 (1), 113–126.

Davis, M.H. (1994). Empathy: A social psychological approach. Madison, WI: Brown & Benchmark.

Davis, M.H., Conkin, L., Smith, A., & Luce, C. (1996). The effect of perspective taking on the cogntive representation of persons: A merging self and other. Journal of personality and social psychology, 70, 713–726.

de Sousa, R. (1987). The Rationality of emotion. Cambridge, MA: MIT Press.

de Sousa, R. (2001). Moral emotions. Ethical theory and moral practice, 4, 109–126.

Deigh, J. (1989). Morality and personal relations. In G. Graham & H. LaFollette (eds.), Person to person. Philadelphia, PA: Temple University Press.

Deigh, J. (1995). Empathy and universalizability. Ethics, 105 (3), 743–763.

Descartes, R. (1649/1984). The passions of the soul. In J. Cottingham, R. Stoothoff, D. Murdoch, & A. Kenny (trans. and eds.), The philosophical writings of Descartes, Vol. 1. Cambridge: Cambridge University Press.

Dewey, J. (1916/1944). Democracy and education. New York: The Free Press.

Dewey, J. (1934). Art as experience. New York: Minton Balch.

Dodge, K.A. & Coie, J.D. (1987). Social-information-processing factors in reactive and proactive aggression in children's peer groups. Journal of Personality and Social Psychology, 53, 1146–1158.

Dolan, M. & Fullam, R. (2004). Theory of mind and mentalizing ability in antisocial personality disorders with and without psychopathy. Psychological medicine, 34, 1093–1102.

Dolan, M. & Fullam, R. (2006). Face affect recognition deficits in personality-disordered offenders: Association with psychopathy. Psychological medicine, 36, 1563–1570.

Doris, J.M., & Stich, S.P. (2003). As a matter of fact: Empirical perspectives on ethics. In F. Jackson & M. Smith (eds.), The Oxford companion to contemporary philosophy (pp. 114–152). Oxford: Oxford University Press.

Dunlop, F. (1984). The education of feeling and emotion. London: George Allen & Unwin.

Dunn, J. (1995). Intersubjectivity in psychoanalysis: A critical review. International journal of psychoanalysis, 76, 723–738.

Edelstein, W., & Fauser, P. (2001). Demokratie lernen und leben: Materialen zur Bildungsplanung und zur Forschungsförderung. Bonn: Bund-Länder-Kommission für Bildungsplanung und zur Forschungsförderung.

Eisenberg, N., & Miller, P. (1987a). The relation of empathy to prosocial and related behaviours. Psychological bulletin, 101, 91–119.

Eisenberg, N., & Miller, P. (1987b). Empathy, sympathy and altruism: Empirical and conceptual links. In N. Eisenberg & J. Strayer (eds.), Empathy and its development (pp. 292–316). Cambridge: Cambridge University Press.

Eisenberg, N., & Strayer, J. (1987). Critical issues in the study of empathy. In N. Eisenberg & J. Strayer (eds.), Empathy and its development (pp. 3–13). Cambridge: Cambridge University Press.

Eisenberg, N., Murphy, B.C., & Shepard, S. (1997). The development of empathic accuracy. In W. Ickes (ed.), Empathic accuracy (pp. 73–116). New York: Guilford.

Eisenberg, N., Shea, C.L., Carlo, G., & Knight, G.P. (1991). Empathy-related responding and cognition: A "chicken and the egg" dilemma. In W.M. Kurtines & J.L. Gewirtz (eds.), Handbook of moral behavior and development, Vol. 2: Research (pp. 63–88). Hillsdale, NJ: Earlbaum.

Elliott, C., & Gillett, G. (1992). Moral sanity and practical reason. Philosophical psychology, 5 (1), 53–67.

Epictetus (1st century C.E./1925). Discourses: Books 1 and 2. In W.A. Oldfathter (trans.). Cambridge: Harvard University Press.

Epictetus (1st century C.E./1925). Discourses: Books 3 and 4. In W.A. Oldfathter (trans.). Cambridge: Harvard University Press.

Escalona, S.K. (1945). Feeling disturbances in very young children. American journal of orthopsychiatry, 15, 76–80.

Ferrell, O.C., Fraedrich, J., & Ferrell, L. (2004). Business ethics: Ethical decision making and cases, 6th ed. Boston, MA: Houghton Mifflin College.

Feshbach, N.D., & Roe, K. (1968). Empathy in six- and seven-year olds. Child development, 39, 133–145.

Feudtner, C., Christakis, D.A., & Christakis, N.A. (1994). Do clinical clerks suffer ethical ero-sion? Students' perception of their ethical environment and personal development. Academic medicine, 69, 670–679.

Fishbein, D. (ed.). (2000). The science, treatment, and prevention of antisocial behaviors. Kingston, NJ: Civic Research Institute.

Flanagan, O. (1991). Varieties of moral personality: Ethics and psychological realism. Cambridge: Harvard University Press.

Flanagan, O. (1996). Ethics naturalized. In L. May, M. Friedman, & A. Clark (eds.), Mind and morals. Cambridge, MA: MIT Press.

Flanagan, O., & Jackson, K. (1987). Justice, care and gender: The Kohlberg-Gilligan debate revis-ited. Ethics, 97, 622–637.

Flavell, J.H. (1992). Perspectives on perspective taking. In H. Beilin & P. Pufall (eds.), Piaget's theory: Prospects and possibilities (pp. 107–139). Hillsdale, NJ: Erlbaum.

Foot, P. (1972). Morality as a system of hypothetical imperatives. Reprinted in Virtues and vices. Los Angeles, CA: University of California Press.

Foot, P. (2001). Natural goodness. Oxford: Clarendon Press.

Fraenkel, J.R. (1978). The Kohlberg bandwagon: Some reservations. In P. Scharf (ed.), Readings in moral education (pp. 250–262). Oak Grove, MO: Winston Press.

Frankena, W. (1973). Ethics, 2nd ed. Englewood Cliffs, NJ: Prentice-Hall.

Frankfurt, H. (1971). Freedom of the will and the concept of a person. Journal of philosophy, 67 (1), 5–20.

Freud, S. (1953–1975). The standard edition of the complete psychological works of Sigmund Freud. In J. Strachey (ed.), Vols. 1–24. London: Hogarth Press.

Freud, S. (1986). The ego and the id. In A. Freud (ed.). The essentials of psychoanalysis. London: Penguin.

Gaertner, S.L. & Dovidio, J.F. (1977). The subtlety of white racism, arousal, and helping behavior. Journal of personality and social psychology, 35, 3691–707.

Garber, D. (1992). Descartes' metaphysical physics. Chicago, IL: Chicago University Press.

Gardner, H. (1983). Frames of mind. New York: Basic Books.

Geach, P.T. (1956). Good and evil. Analysis, 17, 23–42.

Gibbard, A. (1990). Wise choices, apt feelings: A theory of normative judgement. Oxford: Oxford University Press.

Gibbs, J.C. (1991). Toward an integration of Kohlberg's and Hoffman's moral development theo-ries. Human development, 34, 88–104.

Gibbs, J.C. (2003). Moral development and reality: Beyond the theories of Kohlberg and Hoffman. Thousand Oaks, CA: Sage.

Gilligan, C. (1982). In a different voice: Psychological theory and women's development. Cambridge: Harvard University Press.

Gilligan, C., Kohlberg, L., Lerner, J., & Belenky, M. (1971). Moral reasoning about sexual dilem-mas: Technical report of the commission on obscenity and pornography, Vol. 1, no. 52560010. Washington, DC: GPO.

Glannon, W. (1997). Psychopathy and responsibility. Journal of applied philosophy, 14, 263–275.

Glass, S.J. & Newman, J.P. (2006). Recognition of Facial Affect in Psychopathic Offenders. Journal of Abnormal Psychology, 115, 815–2.

Godwin, W. (1926). Enquiry concerning political justice, Vol. 1. R.A. Prestion (ed.). New York: Knopf.

Goldman, A. (1980). Moral foundations of professional ethics. Totowa, NJ: Rowman & Littlefield.

Goleman, D. (1995). Emotional intelligence. New York: Bantam.

Gordon, R. (1986). Folk psychology as simulation. Mind and language, 1, 158–171.

Gordon, R. (1987). The structure of emotions. Cambridge: Cambridge University Press.

Gordon, R. (1995). Simulation without introspection or inference from me to you. In M. Davies & T. Stone (eds.), Mental simulation: Evaluations and applications. Oxford: Blackwell.

Gordon, R. (1996). Sympathy, simulation, and the impartial spectator. In L. May, M. Friedman, & A. Clark (eds.), Mind and morals: Essays on ethics and cognitive science. Cambridge, MA: MIT Press.

Greene, M. (1995). Releasing the imagination: Essays on education, the arts, and social change. San Francisco, CA: Jossey-Bass.

Gross, J.J. (1998). The emerging field of emotional regulation: An integrative review. Review of general psychology, 2, 271–299.

Gunther, D.F., & Diekema, D.S. (2006). Attenuating growth in children with profound developmental disability. Archives of pediatrics and adolescent medicine, 160, 1013–1017.

Gutek, G.L. (1995). A history of the western educational experience, 2nd ed. Prospect Heights, IL: Waveland.

Habermas, J. (1984, 1987). Theory of communicative action, 2 vols. T. McCarthy (trans.). Boston, MA: Beacon Press.

Habermas, J. (1990a). Discourse ethics: Notes on a program of philosophical justification. In C. Lenhardt & S.W. Nicholsen (trans.), Moral consciousness and communicative action. Cambridge, MA: MIT Press.

Habermas, J. (1990b). Moral consciousness and communicative action. C. Lenhardt & S.W. Nicholsen (trans.). Cambridge, MA: MIT Press.

Habermas, J. (1993a). Lawrence Kohlberg and Neo-Aristotelianism. In C. Cronin (trans.), J. Habermas (ed.), Justification and application: Remarks on discourse ethics (pp. 113–132). Cambridge: MIT Press.

Habermas, J. (1993b). Morality and the ethical life: Does Hegel's critique of Kant apply to discourse ethics? In R. Beiner and W. Booth (eds.), Kant and political philosophy: The contemporary legacy (pp. 320–336). New Haven, CT: Yale University Press.

Hafferty, F.W., Franks, R. (1994). The hidden curriculum, ethics teaching and the structure of medical education. Academic medicine, 69 (11), 861–871.

Hardwig, J. (1997). In search of an ethics of personal relationships. In J. Steward (ed.), Bridges not walls. Washington, DC: Washington University Press.

Hare, R.D. (1983). Diagnosis of antisocial personality disorder in two prison populations. American journal of psychiatry, 140, 887–890.

Hare, R.D. (1991). The Hare psychopathy checklist-revised. Toronto: Multi-Health Systems.

Hare, R.D. (1999). Without conscience: The disturbing world of the psychopaths among us. New York: The Guilford Press.

Hare, R.D., Clark, D., Grann, M., & Thornton, D. (2000). Psychopathy and the predictive validity of the PCL-R: an international perspective. Behavioral Sciences and the Law, 18, 623–645.

Hare, R.D., Hart, S.D., & Hartrup, T.J. (1991). Psychopathy and the DSM–IV criteria for Antisocial Personality Disorder. Journal of abnormal psychology, 100, 391–398.

Heller, A. (1979). A theory of feelings. Assen, The Netherlands: Van Gorcum.

Hardimon, M. (1994). Role obligations. The journal of philosophy, 91, 333–363.

Hatfield, E., Cacioppo, J.T., & Rapson, R.L. (1992). Emotional contagion. In M.S. Clark (ed.), Review of personality and social psychology, Vol. 14: Emotional and social behavior (pp. 151–177). Newbury Park, CA: Sage.

Hayden, P.T. (2003). Ethical lawyering: Legal and professional responsibilities in the practice of law. St. Paul, MN: West.

Hébert, P.C., Meslin, E.M., Dunn, E.V., Byrne, N., & Reid, S.R. (1990). Evaluating ethical sensitivity in medical students: Using vignettes as an instrument. Journal of medical ethics, 16, 141–145.

Hébert, P.C., Meslin, E.M., & Dunn, E.V. (1992). Measuring the ethical sensitivity of medical students: A study at the University of Toronto. Journal of medical ethics, 18, 142–147.

Heller, A. (1979). A theory of feelings. Assen, The Netherlands: Van Gorcum.

Henning, J. (1991). The physiology of moral maturity. Journal of moral education, 20 (1), 127–137.

Herman, B. (1984). Rules, motives and helping actions. Philosophical studies, 45, 369–377.

Herman, B. (1985). The practice of moral judgment. The Journal of Philosophy, 82(8): 414–436.

Herman, B. (1996). The practice of moral judgement. Cambridge: Harvard University Press.

Hicks, B.M., & Patrick, C.J. (2006). Psychopathy and negative emotionality: Analyses of suppressor effects reveal distinct relations with emotional distress, fearfulness, and anger-hostility. Journal of Abnormal Psychology, 115, 276–287.

Higgins, E.T. (1981). Role taking and social judgement: Alternative developmental perspectives and processes. In J.H. Flavell & L. Ross (eds.), Social cognitive development: Frontiers and possible futures (pp. 119–153). Cambridge: Cambridge University Press.

Hilfiker, D. (2001). From the victim's point of view. Journal of medical humanities, 22 (4), 255–263.

Hill, T. (2000). Respect, pluralism and justice: Kantian perspectives. Oxford: Oxford University Press.

Hill, T. (2002). Human welfare and moral worth (pp. 277–309). Oxford: Clarendon.

Hoffman, M.L. (1978). Empathy, its development and prosocial implications. In C.B. Keasey (ed.). Nebraska symposium on motivation, 25, 169–218.

Hoffman, M.L. (1981). Is altruism part of human nature?. Journal of personality and social psychology, 40 (1), 121–137.

Hoffman, M. (1991). Empathy, social cognition, and moral action. In: W.M. Kurtines & J.L. Gerwirtz (eds.), Handbook of moral behavior and development, Vol. 1 (pp. 275–301). Hillsdale, NJ: Erlbaum.

Hoffman, M.L. (1994). Empathy, role taking, guilt and development of altruisitc motives. In B. Puka (ed.), Reaching out: Caring, altruism, and prosocial behavior (pp. 196–218). New York: Garland.

Hoffman, M.L. (2000). Empathy and moral development: Implications for caring and justice. Cambridge: Cambridge University Press.

Houston, D.A. (1990). Empathy and the self: Cognitive and emotional influences on the evaluation of negative affect in others. Journal of personality and social psychology, 59, 859–871.

Hughes, W. (2000). Critical thinking. Toronto: Broadview Press.

Hügli, A. (1999). Philosophie und Pädagogik [Philosophy and pedagogy]. Darmstadt: Wissenschaftliche Buchgesellschaft.

Hume, D. (1751/1957). Inquiry concerning the principles of morals. New York: Prentice Hall.

Humphrey, G. (1922). The conditioned reflex and the elementary social reaction. Journal of abnormal and social psychology, 17, 113–117.

Hursthouse, R. (1999). On virtue ethics. Oxford: Clarendon Press.

Hutcheson, F. (1729/2003). Inquiry into the origins of our ideas of beauty and virtue. Whitefish, MT: Kessinger.

Ickes, W. (ed.). (1997). Empathic accuracy. New York: Guilford.

Ishikawa, S., Raine, A., Lencz, T., Bihrle, S., & Lacasse, L. (2001). Autonomic stress reactivity and executive functions in successful and unsuccessful criminal psychopaths from the community. Journal of Abnormal Psychology, 110, 423–432.

Jaggar, A. (1996). Love and knowledge: Emotion in feminist epistemology. In Garry and Pearsall (eds.), Women knowledge and reality, 2nd ed. (pp. 166–190). New York: Routledge.

James, W. (1884). "What is an emotion?". Mind, 19, 188–204.

Jeske, D. (1998). Families, friends, and special obligations. Canadian journal of philosophy, 28, 527–556.

Jeske, D. (2002). Special obligations. In E.N. Zalta (ed.), The Stanford encyclopedia of philosophy. Accessed on 1 March 2007 at http://plato.stanford.edu/entries/special-obligations/.

Joas, H. (1985). G.H. Mead: A contemporary examination of his thought. Cambridge, MA: MIT Press.

Jonsen, A.R., & Toulmin, S. (1988). The abuse of casuistry: A history of moral reasoning. Berkeley, CA: University of California Press.

Kant, I. (1785/1987). Fundamental principle of the metaphysics of morals. T.K. Abbott (trans.). Buffalo, NY: Prometheus.

Kant, I. (1789/1974). Anthropology from a pragmatic point of view. M. Gregor (trans.). The Hague: Nijhoff.

Kant, I. (1797/1996). The metaphysics of morals. M. Gregor (ed. and trans.). Cambridge: Cambridge University Press.

Kant, I. (1803/1992). On education. A. Churton (trans.). Bristol, UK: Thoemmes.

Karniol, R. (1982). Settings, scripts and self-schemata: A cognitive analysis of the development of prosocial behavior. In N. Eisenberg (ed.), The development of prosocial behavior (pp. 251–278). New York: Academic.

Karniol, R. (1995). Development and individual differences in predicting others' thoughts and feelings: Applying the transformation rule model. In N. Eisenberg (ed.), Review of personality and social psychology, Vol. 15: Social development (pp. 27–48). Thousand Oaks, CA: Sage.

Katz, I., Glass, D.C., & Cohen, S. (1973). Ambivalence, guilt, and the scapegoating of minority-group victims. Journal of experimental psychology, 9, 423–436.

Keefer, M.W. (2006). A critical comparison of classical and domain theory: Some implications for character education. Journal of Moral Education, 35(3): 369–386.

Kekes, J. (1981). Morality and impartiality. American philosophical quarterly, 18, 295–303.

Kelly, B., & Varghese, F. (1997). The emotional hazards of medical practice. In M.R. Sanders, C. Mitchell, & G.J.A. Byrne (eds.), Medical consultation skills (pp. 472–488). Australia: Addison-Wesley.

Kilpatrick, W. (1992). Why Johnny can't tell right from wrong. New York: Simon & Schuster.

Klein, R. (1971). Some factors influencing empathy in six- and seven-year-old children varying in ethic background (Doctoral dissertation, University of California, Los Angeles, 1970). Dissertation abstracts international, 31, 3960A.

Kohlberg, L. (1969). Stage and sequence: The cognitive-developmental approach to socialization. In D.A. Goslin (ed.), Handbook of socialization theory and research (pp. 347–480). Chicago, IL: Rand McNally.

Kohlberg, L. (1978). The cognitive-developmental approach to moral education. In P. Scharf (ed.), Readings in moral education (pp. 36–51). Minneapolis, MN: Winston Press.

Kohlberg, L. (1981). Essays on moral development, Vol. 1: The philosophy of moral development. Moral stages and the idea of justice. San Francisco, CA: Harper & Row.

Kohlberg, L. (1984). Essays on moral development, Vol. 2: The psychology of moral development. The nature and validity of moral stages. San Francisco, CA: Harper & Row.

Kohlberg, L., & Mayer, R. (1972). Development as the aim of education. Harvard educational review, 42, 449–496.

Kohlberg, L., Boyd, D.R., & Levine, C. (1990). The return of stage 6: Its principle and point of view. In T.E. Wren (ed.), The moral domain: Essays in the ongoing debate between philosophy and the social sciences (pp. 151–181). Cambridge, MA: MIT Press.

Kohn, A. (1997). The trouble with character education. In A. Molnar (ed.), The construction of children's character, Part II (pp. 154–162). Chicago, IL: University of Chicago Press.

Kohut, H. (1959). Introspection, empathy and psychoanalysis. Journal of the American psychoanalytic association, 7, 459–483.

Kohut, H. (1971). The analysis of the self. New York: International Universities Press.

Kohut, H. (1977). The restoration of the self. New York: International Universities Press.

Kohut, H. (1980). Reflections. In A. Goldberg (ed.), Advances in self psychology (pp. 473–554). New York: International Universities Press.

Kohut, H. (1984). How does analysis cure? A. Goldberg & P. Stepansky (eds.). Chicago, IL: University of Chicago Press.

Konner, M. (1987). Becoming a doctor. New York: Viking.

Korsgaard, C. (1996). The origin of value and the scope of obligation. In O. O'Neill (ed.), The sources of normativity (pp. 131–166). Cambridge: Cambridge University Press.

Korsgaard, C. (1999). Self-constitution in the ethics of Kant and Plato. Journal of ethics, 3, 1–29.

Krebs, D.L. (1975). Empathy and altruism. Journal of personality and social psychology, 32, 1124–1146.

Kristjánsson, K. (2003). Fortunes-of-others emotions and justice. Journal of philosophical research, 28, 107–130.

Kristjánsson, K. (2005). Can we teach justified anger?. Journal of philosophy of education, 39 (4), 671–689.

Kymlicka, W. (1999). Education for citizenship. In J.M. Halstead & T. McLaughlin, Education in morality (pp. 79–103). London & New York: Routledge.

Lang, J.A. (1994). Is empathy always "nice"? In E.S. More & M.A. Milligan (eds.), The empathic practitioner (pp. 99–112). New Brunswick, NJ: Rutgers University Press.

Lanzetta, J.T., & Orr, S.P. (1986). Excitatory strength of expressive faces: Effects of happy and fear expressions and context in the extinction of a conditioned fear response. Journal of personality and social psychology, 50, 190–194.

Lao-Tzu. (6th century B.C.E./1961). Tao teh ching. T. Cleary (trans.). Boston, MA: Shambahala.

Lapsley, D., & Narváez, D. (eds.). (2004). Moral development, self, and identity. Mahwah, NJ: Erlbaum.

Lapsley, D., & Narváez, D. (2005). Moral psychology at a crossroads. In D. Lapsley & F.C. Power (eds.), Character psychology and character education (pp. 18–35). Notre Dame, IN: University of Notre Dame Press.

Lapsley, D., & Power, F.C. (eds.). (2005). Character psychology and character education (pp. 36–66). Notre Dame, IN: University of Notre Dame Press.

Lazarus, R.S. (1966). Psychological stress and the coping process. New York: McGraw-Hill.

Lazarus, R.S., & Launier, R. (1978). Stress-related transactions between person and environment. In: L.A. Pervin & M. Lewis (eds.), Perspectives in interactional psychology (pp. 287–327). New York: Plenum.

Larmore, C. (1987). Patterns of moral complexity. Cambridge: Cambridge University Press.

Lempert, W. (1989). Moralisches Denken, Handeln und Lernen in der betrieblichen Arbeit [Moral thought, action and in the work place]. In G. Lind & G. Pollitt-Gerlach (eds.), Moral in 'unmoralischer' Zeit. Zu einer partnerschaftlichen Ethik in Erziehung und Gesellschaft [Morality in "immoral" times. Towards a partnership ethics in education and society] (pp. 153–169). Heidelberg, Germany: Asanger.

Lenman, J. (2006). Moral naturalism. In E.N. Zalta (ed.), Stanford encyclopedia of philosophy. Accessed on 29 Nov. 2006 at http://plato.stanford.edu/entries/naturalism-moral/.

Lickona, T. (1992). Educating for character: How our schools can teach respect and responsibility. New York: Bantam.

Liebowitz, S. (1990). Measuring change in sensitivity to ethical issues in computer use. Unpublished doctoral dissertation. Boston College, Boston, Massachusetts.

Liederman, D.B., & Grisso, J. (1985). The gomer phenomenon. Journal of health and social behaviour, 26, 222–232.

Lilienfeld, S.O. (1998). Methodological advances and developments in the assessment of psychopathy. Behaviour research and therapy, 36, 99–125.

Lind, G. (2000). Ist moral lehrbar?. Berlin: Logos Verlag.

Lind, G. (2002). The meaning and measurement of moral judgement competence revisited: Dual-aspect model. In D. Fasko & W. Willis (eds.), Contemporary philosophical and psychological perspectives on moral development and education. Cresskill, NJ: Hampton Press.

Link, N.F., Sherer, S.E., & Byrne, P.N. (1977). Moral judgement and moral conduct in psychopathy. Canadian psychiatric association journal, 22 (7), 341–346.

Lipps, T. (1903/1960). Empathy, inner imitation and sense-feelings. In M. Rader (ed.), A modern book of aesthetics: An anthology, 3rd ed. (pp. 371–378). New York: Holt, Reinhart & Winston.

Lipps, T. (1906). Das wissen von fremden Ichen. Psychologische Untersuchung, 1, 694–722.

Locke, J. (1690/1991). Two treatises of government. P. Niddich (ed.). Oxford: Clarendon Press.

Longino, H. (1990). Science as social knowledge: Values and objectivity in scientific inquiry. Princeton, NJ: Princeton University Press.

Lose, C.A. (1997). Level of moral reasoning and psychopathy within a group of federal inmates. Dissertation abstracts international: Section B: The sciences and engineering, 57 (7-B), 4716.

Luhmann, N., & Schorr, K.E. (1894/1982). Das Technologiedefizit der Erziehung und die Pädagogik [The technological deficit of education and pedagogy]. In N. Luhmann & K.-E.

Schorr (eds.), Zwischen Technologie und Selbstreferenz [Between technology and self-reference] (pp. 11–40). Frankfurt am Main, Germany: Suhrkamp.

Luban, D. (2003). Professional ethics. In R.G. Frey & C.H. Wellman (eds.), A companion to applied ethics (pp. 583–596). Oxford: Blackwell.

Lykken, D. (1995). The antisocial personalities. Hillsdale, NJ: Erlbaum.

MacIntyre, A. (1981). After virtue. Notre Dame, IN: University of Notre Dame Press.

MacIntyre, A. (1983). The magic in the pronoun "my". Ethics, 94, 113–125.

Mappes, T.A. (2000). Biomedical ethics, 3rd ed. New York: McGraw-Hill.

Mathias, M.B. (1999). The role of sympathy in Kant's philosophy of moral education. Philosophy of education society yearbook. Accessed on 28 Jan. 2004 at http://www.ed.uiuc.edu/EPS/PES-yearbook/1999/verducci_body.asp.

Maxwell, B. (2006). Naturalized compassion: A critique of Nussbaum on literature in education for compassionate citizenry. Journal of moral education, 35 (3), 335–352.

Maxwell, B., & Reichenbach, R. (2005). Imagination, re-appraisal and imitation: The education of the moral emotions. Journal of moral education, 34 (3), 291–307.

Maxwell, B., & Reichenbach, R. (2007). Educating moral emotions: A praxiological analysis. Studies in philosophy and education, 26 (2), 147–163.

McCord, W. & McCord, J. (1964). The psychopath. Princeton: Van Nostrand.

McFall, L. (1987). Integrity. Ethics, 98, 17–20.

McGeorge, C. (1975). The susceptibility to faking of the Defining Issues Test of moral development. Developmental psychology, 44, 116–122.

McGinn, C. (1992). Moral literacy. Indianapolis: Hackett.

McKinnon, C. (2005). Character possession and human flourishing. In K.D. Lapsley & F.C. Power (eds.), Character psychology and character education (pp. 36–66). Notre Dame, IN: University of Notre Dame Press.

McLaughlin, T., & Halstead, M. (1999). Education in character and virtue. In M. Halstead & T. McLaughlin (eds.), Education in morality (pp. 132–163). London: Routledge.

McNeel, P. (1994). College teaching and student moral development. In J.R. Rest & D. Narvaez (eds.), Moral development in the professions: Psychology and applied ethics (pp. 27–49). Hillsdale, NJ: Erlbaum.

Mead, G.H. (1934). Mind, self and society. Chicago, IL: University of Chicago Press.

Meindl, J.R., & Lerner, M.J. (1984). Exacerbation of extreme responses to an out-group. Journal of personality and social psychology, 47, 71–84.

Meinong, A. (1894/1968). Psychologisch-ethische Untersuchungen zur Werttheorie [Psychological-ethical investigations into value theory]. In J.A. Barth (eds.), Gesamtausgabe [Complete works], Vol. 3. Graz, Austria: Graz, Akademische Druck- u. Verlagsanstalt.

Menke, C. (1993). Liberalismus im Konflikt [Liberalism in conflict]. In M. Brumlik & H. Brunkhorst (eds.), Gemeinschaft und Gerechtigkeit [Community and justice] (pp. 218–243). Frankfurt am Main, Germany: Fischer.

Menke, C. (1996). Tragödie im Sittlichen: Gerechtigkeit und Freiheit nach Hegel [Tragedy of morals: Justice and freedom after Hegel]. Frankfurt am Main, Germany: Suhrkamp.

Mercer, P. (1972). Sympathy and ethics. Oxford: Oxford University Press.

Milo, R.D. (1984). Immorality. Princeton, NJ: Princeton University Press.

Milo, R.D. (1998). Virtue, knowledge, and wickedness. In E.F. Paul, F.D. Miller, & J. Paul (eds.), Virtue and vice (pp. 196–215). Cambridge: Cambridge University Press.

Mizrahi, T. (1986). Getting rid of patients: Contradictions in the socialization of physicians. New Brunswick, Canada: Rutgers University Press.

Moore, G.E. (1903). Principia ethica. Cambridge: Cambridge University Press.

More, E.S., & Milligan, M.A. (eds.). (1994). The empathic practitioner: Empathy, gender and medicine. New Brunswick, Canada: Rutgers University Press.

Morton, K.R., Worthley, J.S., Testerman, J.K., & Mahoney, M.L. (2006). Defining features of moral sensitivity: Pathways to moral reasoning in medical students. Journal of moral education, 35 (3), 387–406.

Murdoch, I. (1970). The sovereignty of good. London: Routledge and Kegan Paul.

Murphy, J. (1972). Moral death: A Kantian essay on psychopathy. Ethics, 82, 284–298.

Murphy, P.E. (1999). Character and virtue ethics in international marketing. Journal of business ethics, 18, 107–124.

Myyry, L., & Helkama, K. (2002). The role of value priorities and professional ethics training in moral sensitivity. Journal of moral education, 31 (2), 35–50.

Nagel, T. (1970). The possibility of altruism. Oxford: Clarendon Press.

Nagel, T. (1986). The view from nowhere. New York: Oxford University Press.

Narváez, D., & Lapsley, D.K. (2005). The psychological foundations of everyday morality and moral experience. In D.K. Lapsley and F.C. Power (eds.), Character psychology and character education (pp. 140–165). Notre Dame, IN: University of Notre Dame Press.

Narváez, D., Bock, T., & Endicott, L. (2003). Who should I become? Citizenship, goodness, human flourishing, and ethical expertise. In W. Veugelers & F. Oser (eds.), Teaching in moral and democratic education (pp. 43–63). Bern, Switzerland: Peter Lang.

Nelson, K. (1982). Social cognition in a script framework. In J.H. Flavel & L. Ross (eds.), Social cognitive development: Frontiers and possible futures (pp. 97–118). Cambridge: Cambridge University Press.

Neumann, C.S., Vitacco, M.J., Hare, R.D., & Wupperman, P. (2005). Reconstruing the 'reconstruction' of psychopathy: a comment on Cooke, Michie, Hart, and Clark. Journal of personality disorders, 19, 624–640.

Nichols, S. (2002). How psychopaths threaten moral rationalism: Is it rational to be amoral? Monist, 85, 285–304.

Nichols, S. (2004). Sentimental rules. New York: Oxford University Press.

Nietzsche, F. (1954). The antichrist. In W. Kaufman (ed. and trans.), The portable Nietzesche (pp. 565–656). London: Penguin.

Nietzsche, F. (1999). On the genealogy of morals. Oxford: Oxford University Press.

Noddings, N. (1984). Caring: A feminine approach to ethics & moral education. Berkeley, CA: University of California Press.

Noddings, N. (1992). The challenge to care in schools. New York: Teacher's College Press.

Noddings, N. (1998). Thinking, feeling, and moral imagination. In P.A. French & H.K. Wettstein (eds.), Midwest studies in philosophy, XXII (pp. 134–145). Notre Dame, IN: University of Notre Dame Press.

Nucci, L. (2001). Education in the moral domain. Cambridge: Cambridge University Press.

Nunner-Winkler, G. (1993). The growth of moral motivation. In G. Noam & T. Wren (eds.), The moral self. Cambridge, MA: MIT Press.

Nunner-Winkler, G. (1994). Moral development. In T. Husen and T.N. Postlethwaite (eds.), The international encyclopedia of education, 2nd ed. (pp. 3914–3920). Oxford: Elsevier.

Nunner-Winkler, G. (1998). The development of moral understanding and moral motivation. International journal of educational research, 27 (7), 587–603.

Nussbaum, M. (1992). Human functioning and social justice: In defence of Aristotelian essentialism. Political theory, 20 (2), 202–246.

Nussbaum, M. (1994). The therapy of desire: Theory and practice in Hellenistic ethics. Princeton, NJ: Princeton University Press.

Nussbaum, M. (1995). Poetic justice. Boston, MA: Beacon Press.

Nussbaum, M. (2001). Upheavals of thought: The intelligence of the emotions. Cambridge: Cambridge University Press.

Oakley, J. (1992). Morality and the emotions. London: Routledge and Kegan Paul.

Ofsthun, H.A. (1986). Developing professional responsibilities in counseling psychology students: A teaching model evaluation study. Unpublished doctoral dissertation, University of Minnesota, Minneapolis.

Ogden, T. (1996). Reconsidering three aspects of psychoanalytic technique. International journal of psychoanalysis, 77, 883–899.

O'Kane, A., Fawcett, D., & Blackburn, R. (1996). Psychopathy and moral reasoning: Comparison of two classifications. Personality and individual differences, 20 (4), 505–514.

Olinck, S. (1984). A critique of empathy and sympathy. In J. Lichtenberg, M. Bornstein, & D. Silver (eds.), Empathy (pp. 137–166). Hillsdale, NJ: Erlbaum.

O'Neill, O. (1996). Towards justice and virtue: A constructive account of practical reasoning. Cambridge: Cambridge University Press.

Oser, F., & Althof, W. (1992). Moralische selbstbestimmung. Stuttgart, Germany: Klett-Cotta.

Penner, L.A., Fritzsche, B.A., Craiger, J.P., & Freifeld, T. (1995). Measuring the prosocial personality. In J.N. Butcher & C.D. Spielberger (eds.), Advances in personality assessment, Vol. 10. Hillsdale, NJ: Erlbaum.

Peters, R.S. (1964). Education as initiation. London: Harrap.

Peters, R.S. (1966). Ethics and education. London: George Allen Unwin.

Peters, R.S. (1972/1998). The education of the emotions. In P.H. Hirst & P. White (eds.), Philosophy of education, major themes in the analytic tradition, Vol. 2 (pp. 179–194). London: Routledge.

Peters, R.S. (1973). Aims of education—a conceptual inquiry. In R.S. Peters (ed.), The philosophy of education (pp. 11–29). Oxford: Oxford University Press.

Peters, R.S. (1978). The place of Kohlberg's theory in moral education. Journal of moral education, 7, 147–157.

Peters, R.S. (1981). Moral development and moral education. London: George Allen Unwin.

Piaget, J. (1932). The moral judgement of the child. New York: Harcourt.

Piaget, J. (1955). The language and thought of the child. New York: Meridian.

Piaget, J. (1981). Intelligence and affectivity: Their relationship during child development. T. Brown & C. Kaegi (trans. and eds.). Palo Alto, CA: Annual Reviews Monographs.

Pizzaro, D. (2000). Nothing more than feelings? The role of emotions in moral judgement. Journal for the theory of social behavior, 30 (4), 354–375.

Power, F.C., Higgins, A., & Kohlberg, L. (1989). Lawrence Kohlberg's approach to moral education. New York: Columbia University Press.

Raphael, D.D. (1976). Introduction. In A. Smith (eds.), Theory of moral sentiments. Oxford: Clarendon Press.

Rawls, J. (1971). A theory of justice. Cambridge: Harvard University Press.

Reardon, B.A. (1995). Educating for human dignity. Philadelphia, PA: University of Pennsylvania Press.

Reichenbach, R. (2001). Demokratisches Selbst und dilettantisches Subjekt. Demokratische Bildung und Erziehung in der Spätmoderne [The democratic self and the dilettante subject: Teaching and education in late modernity]. Münster, Germany: Waxmann.

Reichenbach, R., & Maxwell, B. (2007). Moralerziehung als Erziehung der Gefühle [Moral education as the education of the emotions]. Vierteljahresschrift für Wissenschaftliche Pädagogik [Systematic Pedagogy Quarterly], 83 (1), 11–25.

Reichenbach, R., & Oser, F. (1995). On noble motives and pedagogical kitsch. Teaching and teacher education, 11 (2), 189–193.

Reik, T. (1948/1983). Listening with the third ear: The inner experience of a psychoanalyst. New York: Farrar, Straus & Giroux.

Reimer, J. (1989). From moral discussion to democratic governance. In F.C. Power, A. Higgins, & L. Kohlberg (eds.), Lawrence Kohlberg's approach to moral education (pp. 7–32). New York: Columbia University Press.

Reisenzein, R., Meyer, W.-U., & Schützwohl, A. (2003). Einführung in die Emotions-psychologie [Introduction to the psychology of the emotions] (Vol. 3). Bern, Switzerland: Huber.

Rest, J.R. (1979). Development in judging moral issues. Minneapolis, MN: University of Minnesota Press.

Rest, J.R. (1983). Morality. In P.H. Mussen (ed.), J.H. Flavell & E.M. Markman (vol. eds.), Handbook of child psychology, 4th ed., Vol. IV (pp. 556–629). New York: Wiley.

Rest, J.R. (1984). The major components of morality. In W.M. Kurtines & J.L. Gewirtz (eds.), Morality, moral behavior, and moral development (pp. 24–38). New York: Wiley.

Rest, J.R. (1986). An overview of the psychology of morality. In J. Rest (ed.), Moral development: Advances in research and theory (pp. 1–27). New York: Praeger.

Rest, J.R. (1994). Background: Theory and research. In J. Rest & D. Narváez (eds.), Moral development and the professions: Psychology and applied ethics (pp. 1–26). Hillsdale, NJ: Erlbaum.

Rest, J.R. & Narváez, D. (eds.). (1994). Moral development and the professions: Psychology and applied ethics. Hillsdale, NJ: Erlbaum.

Rest, J.R., Edwards, L., & Thomas, S. (1997). Designing and validating a measure of moral judgement: Stage preference and stage consistency approaches. Journal of educational psychology, 89 (1), 2–28.

Rest, J.R., Narvaez, D., Bebeau, J.J., & Thoma, S.J. (1999). Postconventional moral thinking: A neo-Kohlbergian approach. Mahwah, NJ: Erlbaum.

Rest, J.R., Turiel, E., & Kohlberg, L. (1969). Relations between level of moral judgement and preference and comprehension of the moral judgement of others. Journal of personality, 37, 225–252.

Rethorst, J. (1997). Art and imagination: Implications of cognitive science for moral education. Philosophy of education society yearbook. Accessed on 23 April 2007 at http://www.ed.uiuc.edu/EPS/PES-yearbook/97_docs/rethorst.html.

Rice, M.E. (1997). Violent offender research and implications for the criminal justice system American Psychologist, 52, 414–423.

Rice, M.E., Harris, G.T., & Cormier, C.A. (1992). An evaluation of a maximum security therapeutic community for psychopaths and other mentally disordered offenders. Law and Human Behavior, 16, 399–412.

Richell, R.A., Mitchell, D.G.V., Newman, C., Leonard, A., Baron-Cohen, S., & Blair, R.J.R. (2003). Theory of mind and psychopathy: can psychopathic individuals read the 'language of the eyes'? Neuropsychologia, 41, 523–526.

Rogers, C.R. (1951). Client-centered therapy. Boston, MA: Houghton Mifflin.

Rogers, C.R. (1959). A theory of therapy, personality and interpersonal relationships, as developed in the client-centered framework. In S. Koch (ed.), Psychology: A study of science (pp. 184–256). New York: McGraw-Hill.

Rogers, C.R. (1961). On becoming a person. Boston, MA: Houghton Mifflin.

Rogers, C.R. (1975). Empathic: An unappreciated way of being. The counseling psychologist, 2, 2–10.

Rogers, C.R. (1977). Carl Rogers on personal power. New York: Delacorte Press.

Rogers, C.R., & Freiberg, H.J. (1994). Freedom to learn. New York: Macmillan.

Ross, W.D. (1930). The right and the good. Oxford: Clarendon Press.

Rousseau, J.-J. (1762/1967). The social contract. L.G. Crocker (ed.). New York: Washington Square Press.

Rubin, Z., & Peplau, L.A. (1975). Who believes in a just world? Journal of social issues, 31 (3), 65–89.

Russell, B. (1929/1970). Marriage and morals. New York: Liveright.

Samenow, S. (2004). Inside the criminal mind. New York: Random House.

Sandel, M.J. (1982). Liberalism and the limits of justice. Cambridge: Cambridge University Press.

Sandin, R.T. (1989). Values and collegiate study. Atlanta, GA: Mercer University Press.

Schantz, C.V. (1975). The development of social cognition. In E.M. Hetherington (ed.), Review of child development research, Vol. 5 (pp. 257–323). Chicago, IL: University of Chicago Press.

Scheler, M. (1954). The nature of sympathy. P. Heath (trans.). London: Routledge & Kegan Paul.

Schläfli, A., Rest, J., & Thoma, S.J. (1985). Does moral education improve moral judgement? A meta-analysis of intervention studies using the Defining Issues Test. Review of educational research, 55 (3), 319–352.

Scholz, S. & Groarke, L. (1996). Seven principles for better practical ethics. Teaching philosophy, 19 (4), 337–355.

Schopenhauer, A. (1840/1995). On the basis of morality. E.F.J. Payne (trans.). Oxford: Berhahn.

Schrader, D.E. (1993). Lawrence Kohlberg's approach to the moral education of educational professionals. In K. Strike & P.L. Ternasky (eds.), Ethics for professionals in education (pp. 84–101). New York: Teachers College Press.

Secker, B. (1999). The appearance of Kant's deontology in contemporary Kantianism: Concepts of patient autonomy in bioethics. Journal of medicine and philosophy, 24 (1), 43–66.

Self, D.J., & Baldwin, D.C. (1994). Moral reasoning in medicine. In J.R. Rest & D. Narvaez (eds.), Moral development in the professions: Psychology and applied ethics (pp. 147–162). Hillsdale, NJ: Erlbaum.

Self, D.J., Gopalakrishna, G., Kiser, W.M., & Olivarez, M. (1995). The relationship of empathy to moral reasoning in first-year medical students. Cambridge quarterly of healthcare ethics, 2, 448–453.

Selman, R.L. (1980). The growth of interpersonal understanding. New York: Academic.

Seneca, L.A. (1st century C.E./1969). Letters from a Stoic. Robin Campbell (trans.). London: Penguin.

Shaffer, J.B. (1978). Humanistic psychology. Englewood Cliffs, NJ: Prentice-Hall.

Shaftesbury, A.A.C. (1711/1999). Characteristics of men, manners, opinions, times. L.E. Klein (ed.). Cambridge: Cambridge University Press.

Sharma, R.M. (1992). Empathy: A retrospective on its development in psychotherapy. Australian and New Zealand journal of psychiatry, 26, 377–391.

Shem, S. (1978). The house of God. New York: Dell.

Sherman, N. (1989). The fabric of character. Oxford: Oxford University Press.

Sherman, N. (1990). The place of emotions in Kantian morality. In O. Flanagan & A.O. Rorty (eds.), Identity, character and morality. Cambridge, MA: MIT Press.

Sherman, N. (1998). Empathy and imagination. In P. French & H.K. Wettstein (eds.), Midwest studies in philosophy, Vol. XXII (pp. 82–119). Notre Dame, IN: University of Notre Dame Press.

Sidgwick, H. (1902/1988). Outlines of the history of ethics. Indianapolis: Hackett.

Sidgwick, H. (1907/1981). The methods of ethics. Indianapolis: Hackett.

Singer, P. (1972). Famine, affluence, and morality. Philosophy and public affairs, 1 (1), 229–243.

Singer, P. (1993). Practical ethics, 2nd ed. Cambridge: Cambridge University Press.

Sirin, S.R., Brabeck, M.M., Satiani, A., & Rogers-Serin, L. (2003). Validation of a measure of ethical sensitivity and examination of the effects of previous multicultural and ethics courses on moral sensitivity. Ethics and behavior, 13 (3), 221–235.

Sloan, D. (1980). The teaching of ethics in the undergraduate curriculum, 1876–1976. In D. Callahan & S. Bok (eds.), Ethics teaching in higher education (pp. 1–61). New York: Plenum.

Slote, M. (2003). Sentimentalist virtue and moral judgement. Metaphilosophy, 34, 131–143.

Smetana, J. & Braeges, J. (1990). The development of toddlers' moral and conventional judgments. Merrill-Palmer Quarterly, 36, 329–34.

Smith, A. (1759/1976). Theory of moral sentiments. Oxford: Clarendon Press.

Smith, M. (1994). The moral problem. Oxford: Blackwell.

Snow, N. (2000). Empathy. American philosphical quarterly, 37 (1), 65–78.

Sober, E., & Wilson, D.S. (1998). Unto others: The evolution and psychology of unselfish behavior. Cambridge, MA: Harvard University Press.

Sockett, H. (1993). Professional expertise as virtue. In K.A. Strike & P.L. Ternasky (eds.), Ethics for professionals in education (pp. 62–88). New York: Teachers College Press.

Solomon, R. (1984). The passions: The myth and nature of human emotions. New York: Doubleday.

Spiecker, B. (1988a). Psychopathy: The incapacity to have moral emotions. Journal of moral education, 17, 98–104.

Speicker, B. (1988b). Education and the moral emotions. In B. Speicker & R. Straughan (eds.), Philosophical issues in moral education (pp. 42–63). Milton Keynes, UK: Open University Press.

Sterenly, K., & Griffiths, P. (1999). Sex and death: An introduction to the philosophy of biology. Chicago, IL: Chicago University Press.

Sternberg, R. (1994). In search of the human mind. Fort Worth, TX: Harcourt Brace.

Steutel, J. (1999). The virtues of will-power: Self-control and deliberation. In D. Carr & J. Steutel (eds.), Virtue ethics and moral education. London: Routledge.

Steutel, J., & Spiecker, B. (2004). Cultivating sentimental dispositions through Aristotelian habituation. Journal of philosophy of education, 38 (4), 531–549.

Stocker, M. (with Hegeman, E.). (1996). Valuing emotions. Cambridge: Cambridge University Press.

Stotland, E. (1969). Exploratory investigations of empathy. In L. Berkowitz (ed.), Advances in experiemental and social psychology, Vol. 4 (pp. 271–313). New York: Academic.

Strack, F., Martin, L.L., & Stepper, S. (1988). Inhibiting and facilitating conditions of the human smile: A nonobtrusive test of the facial feedback hypothesis. Journal of personal and social psychology, 54, 768–776.

Strawson, P.F. (1982). Freedom and resentment. In G. Watson (ed.), Free will (pp. 59–80). Oxford: Oxford University Press.

Strike, K.A., & Soltis, J.F. (1998). The ethics of teaching, 3rd ed. New York: Teacher's College Press.

Strike, K.A., & Ternasky, P.L. (1993). Ethics in educational settings. In K.A. Strike & P.L. Ternasky (eds.), Ethics for professionals in education: Perspectives for preparation and practice (pp. 1–9). New York: Teachers College Press.

Tappolet, C. (2000). Emotions et valeurs. Paris: Presses Universitaires de France.

Taylor, C. (1989). Sources of the self. Cambridge: Harvard University Press.

Taylor, C. (1991). The malaise of modernity. Toronto: Anansi.

Taylor, G. (1985). Pride, shame and guilt: Emotions of self-assessment. Oxford: Oxford University Press.

Thomson, J.J. (2001). Goodness and advice. Princeton, NJ: Princeton University Press.

Titchener, E. (1909). Experimental psychology of the thought processes. New York: Macmillan.

Titchener, E. (1915). A beginner's psychology. New York: Macmillan.

Todd, S. (2007). Teachers judging without scripts, or thinking cosmopolitan. Ethics and education, 2 (1), 25–38.

Tong, R. (1997). Feminist perspectives on empathy as an epistemic skill and caring as a moral virtue. Journal of medical humanities, 18 (1), 153–68.

Toumlin, S. (1981). The tyranny of moral principles. Hastings Center report, 11, 31–39.

Trainer, F.E. (1977). A critical analysis of Kohlberg's contribution to the study of moral thought. Journal for the theory of social behaviour, 7, 41–63.

Trevethan, S.D., & Walker, L.J. (1989). Hypothetical versus real-life moral reasoning among psychopathic and delinquent youth. Development and psychopathology, 1 (2), 91–103.

Turiel, E. (1983). The development of social knowledge: Morality and convention. Cambridge: Cambridge University Press.

van Dam, E. & Steutel, J. (1996). On emotional rationality: A response to Barrett. Journal of moral education, 25 (4), 395–400.

Verducci, S. (1999). Empathy and morality. Philosophy of education society yearbook. Accessed on 28 Jan. 2004 at http://www.ed.uiuc.edu/EPS/PES-yearbook/1999/verducci_body.asp.

Verducci, S. (2000). A conceptual history of empathy and a question it raises for moral education. Educational theory, 50 (1), 63–80.

Vetlesen, A.J. (1994). Perception, empathy, and judgement: An inquiry into the preconditions of moral performance. University Park, PA: Pennsylvania State University Press.

Volker, J.M. (1984). Counselling experience, moral judgement, awareness of practice, and moral sensitivity in counselling practice. Unpublished doctoral dissertation, University of Minnesota, Minneapolis.

Walker, L.J., & Hennig, K.H. (2004). Differing conceptions of moral exemplarity: Just, brave, and caring. Journal of personality and social psychology, 86, 629–647.

Walker, M. (2006). Higher education pedagogies. Maidenhead, UK: Open University Press.

Wallace, R.J. (1994). Responsibility and the moral sentiments. Cambridge: Harvard University Press.

Walzer, M. (1983). Spheres of justice. New York: Basic Books.

Warnock, M. (1996). Moral values. In J.M. Halstead & M. Taylor (eds.), Values in education and education in values (pp. 45–53). London: Falmer.

White, J. (1998). The education of the emotions. In P.H. Hirst & P. White (eds.), The philosophy of education, Vol. 2: Education and human being (pp. 195–210). London: Routledge.

White, J. (2001). R.S. Peters. In J. Palmer (ed.), Fifty modern thinkers on education: From Piaget to the modern day (pp. 118–121). London: Routledge.

Weiner, B. (1995). Judgements of responsibility: A foundation for a theory of social conduct. New York: Guilford Press.

Williams, B. (1976). Persons, character and morality. In A.O. Rorty (ed.), The identities of persons. Berkeley, CA: University of California Press.

Williams, B. (1981). Moral luck. Cambridge: Cambridge University Press.

Williams, B. (1985). Ethics and the limits of philosophy. Cambridge: Harvard University Press.

Williams, B. (1993). Shame and necessity. Berkeley, CA: University of California Press.

Williams, B., & Smart, J.J.C. (1973). Utilitarianism, for and against. Cambridge: Cambridge University Press.

Wilson, J. (1974). The study of moral development. In J. Wilson, G. Collier, & P. Tomlinson (eds.), Values and moral development in higher education (pp. 5–19). London: Croom Helm.

Wilson, J. (1991). A new introduction to moral education. Fakenham, UK: Cassell.

Wispé, L. (1986). The distinction between sympathy and empathy: To call forth a concept, a word is needed. Journal of personality and social psychology, 50 (29), 314–321.

Wispé, L. (1987). History of the concept of empathy. In N. Eisenberg & J. Strayer (eds.), Empathy and its development (pp. 17–37). Cambridge: Cambridge University Press.

Wittgenstein, L. (1953/1992). Philosophical investigations. G.E.M. Anscombe (trans.). Oxford: Blackwell.

Wolf, D. (2000). What is self psychology? Self psychology page. Accessed on 15 July 2004 at http://www. selfpsychology.com/whatis.htm.

Wringe, C. (2006). Moral education: Beyond the teaching of right and wrong. Dordrecht, Germany: Springer.

Wynne, E.A. (1986). The great tradition in education: Transmitting moral values. Educational leadership, 43, 4–9.

You, D., & Bebeau, M.J. (2005). Moral sensitivity: A review. Paper presented at the annual meeting of the Association for Moral Education, 3–5 November, Boston, Massachusetts, USA.

Zajonc, R.B. (1968). Attitudinal effects of mere exposure. Journal of personality and psychology monograph supplement, 9 (2, Pt. 2), 1–27.

Index

Printed in the United States
107667LV00003B/289-315/P